D0866734

L O V I N G   G A R B O

Random House  *New York*

LOVING GARBO

The Story of Greta Garbo, Cecil Beaton, and Mercedes de Acosta

HUGO VICKERS

 Published in the United States by Random House, Inc., New York, and simultaneously in Canada by Random House of Canada Limited, Toronto.

Grateful acknowledgment is made to the following for permission to use both published and unpublished material: Pundit Ram Gopal: Excerpts from letters by Pundit Ram Gopal to Mercedes de Acosta. Used by permission. *The Literary Executors of the Late Sir Cecil Beaton:* Excerpts from Cecil Beaton's letters and diaries; excerpts from various published works by Cecil Beaton. Letters and diaries copyright © The Literary Executors of the Late Sir Cecil Beaton. Used by permission. *The Anita Loos Trust:* Letter to Cecil Beaton from Anita Loos. Copyright © The Anita Loos Trust. Used by permission of Ray Pierre Corsini, literary executor.

Library of Congress Cataloging-in-Publication Data
Vickers, Hugo.
Loving Garbo : the story of Greta Garbo, Cecil Beaton, and Mercedes de Acosta / Hugo Vickers.
p. cm.
Includes bibliographical references and index.
ISBN 0-679-41301-4
1. Garbo, Greta, 1905–1990. 2. Beaton, Cecil Walter Hardy, Sir, 1904–1980. 3. Acosta, Mercedes de, 1893–1968. I. Title.
PN2778.G3V53 1994 791.43′028′092—dc20 93-44745

Manufactured in the United States of America on acid-free paper
98765432
First Edition

Book design by J. K. Lambert

TO D.D.G.C.

ACKNOWLEDGMENTS

A considerable quantity of the papers on which this book is based are the Cecil Beaton papers, housed at St. John's College, Cambridge. I did not need to trouble the college during the writing of this book, since I had retained my notes from my 1985 biography of Beaton, and I drew from these.

Cecil Beaton's letters to Garbo probably no longer exist, but the carbon copies he made are in his papers. So are thirty-seven of the fifty letters that Garbo wrote him. A dozen or so are not. These were removed from his house at Broadchalke, probably without his knowledge, though this cannot now be proved. They were sold in New York in 1990, and I purchased three of them myself. I also purchased Hal Burton's letters from Cecil Beaton in 1988.

The majority of papers relating to Cecil Beaton and Greta Garbo remain sealed indefinitely, but as I have frequently pointed out to irritated would-be researchers, there is little more than what originally appeared in his diaries, my biography, or finally in this book. Beaton's letters and diaries are under the copyright of his literary executors. Garbo's are under the copyright of her niece, Mrs. Gray Reisfield, of New York City. Mrs. Reisfield has explained to me her reasons for not giving permission for the direct quotation of these letters, which are therefore paraphrased.

Mercedes de Acosta's papers are in the Rosenbach Museum in Philadelphia. I spent many happy days researching there and am particularly grateful to the former curator at the Rosenbach, Leslie A. Morris, for her help.

I do not propose to rethank all those who helped me over Cecil Beaton in the past. There is a full list in my biography, and anyone specifically quoted is acknowledged in the source notes of this book. But I would like to thank the following for their specific help with my research: Sybille Bedford, Chloë Blackburn, Jennifer Arnold-Wallinger, Patricia Countess Jellicoe, Samuel Adams Green, Verena Vickers, Louise Corrigan, Lady Balniel, Philip Hoare, Roderick Coupe, Wilder Luke Burnap, Charles Higham, the Countess of Avon, Mrs. John Barry Ryan, John Byrne, Barry Paris, Shaun Gunson, John Richardson, Lady Quennell, Jimmy Douglas, David Dibble (Humanities Research Center, University of Texas at Austin), Dr. Nicholas Scheetz (Georgetown University Library, Washington, D.C.), Elizabeth E. Fuller (Rosenbach Museum and Library), Baroness Vaes, Lyndon Mason, Hasan Ezberci (front-office manager, Hotel Pera Palace, Istanbul), the late Commandant Paul-Louis Weiller, the late Miss Dorothy Fellowes-Gordon, James Fergusson, Marianne Hinton, and Patrick O'Connor.

In the early 1980s I enjoyed several conversations with Mrs. Valentina Schlee, Garbo's rival and neighbor, and twice visited her at 450 East Fifty-second Street.

Just as this book was in the process of going to press I enjoyed two long and interesting talks with Pundit Ram Gopal, who is possibly the last person alive who knew Mercedes well. Their friendship lasted thirty years.

I would also like to thank Philippe Garner and Lydia Cresswell-Jones, custodians of the invaluable Beaton archive of photographs at Sotheby's in London.

I am grateful to Tom Maschler at Jonathan Cape for commissioning this project; but it was Sharon DeLano at Random House who brought the book to life in its present form, and I thank her particularly for her advice in reshaping and restructuring the book in a way that has considerably widened its original intention.

Finally, as ever, I am grateful to Gillon Aitken, my agent, for his much-needed protection once again.

CONTENTS

ILLUSTRATIONS

PHOTO INSERT

LOVING GARBO

Garbo in Grand Hotel, *1932.*

CHAPTER 1

FRIENDS AND LOVERS

Hollywood 1932: ". . . so much going on in our set here."

In the fall of 1932, shortly after his return to London from a visit to Hollywood, the twenty-eight-year-old English photographer Cecil Beaton received a letter from a friend, Anita Loos, the author of *Gentlemen Prefer Blondes.* Loos was living in Los Angeles, writing screenplays for MGM.

> Darling Cecil,
> It was wonderful having that grand long letter from you. What a divine vacation you must have had with Peter. It sounds too heavenly.*

*Cecil had traveled with Peter Watson, a rich young Englishman with whom he was unhappily obsessed, to Le Touquet, Paris, Majorca, Nîmes, Arles, Aix-en-

> There has been so much going on in our set here that every time I think of writing I am swamped with the very idea of trying to tell it all. The Garbo-Mercedes business has been too amazing. They had terrific battles, and Garbo left without saying goodbye. Then Mercedes flew to NY to see her and Garbo wouldn't. Mercedes flew back despondent—lost her job with MGM and is in the most awful state. Also says she is broke—can't get a break and it's too terrible. The story is as long as the dictionary—but much more amazing—so will hope you get together with Mercedes one day and hear it from her lips.[1]

Loos related further Hollywood news: of Tallulah Bankhead's career problems; of *Red-Headed Woman,* a comedy scripted by Loos for Jean Harlow, failing to pass the English censors; and of the American playwright Zoë Akins and her husband fighting "like battleships." Loos also had news of Edmund Goulding, another friend of Cecil's and the director of *Grand Hotel,* which had opened that spring to rave reviews, most especially for Garbo, who played the exquisitely desolate *femme fatale* with whom John Barrymore fell in love.

> Eddie Goulding left here on 12 hours notice after giving a party for eight girls which wound up with two of them having to be sent to the hospital. Hearst stepped in and squashed the story being printed except for vague allusions in Winchell's column. Hearst must have been furious about it.* One of the newspapers told the studio people not to worry about the story being printed as it was so filthy it couldn't be. Don't know myself what it was that happened—but that's the gossip about town. Please don't spread it—as Eddie seems to be going over great in London.[2]

Provence, Marseilles, Cassis, Toulon, and Cannes. They had continued via Monte Carlo to Parma and Venice. The trip had been far from idyllic. Cecil was forever jealous of Peter and unable to concentrate or work.

*Edmund Goulding (1891–1959), London-born director of such films as *Love* (1927, with Garbo), *The Broadway Melody* (1929), and several Bette Davis vehicles, including *That Certain Woman* (1937) and *Dark Victory* (1939), had just directed *Blondie of the Follies,* starring Marion Davies, the mistress of William Randolph Hearst. Loos supplied dialogue for the film. Hearst was the producer.

In Hollywood in the thirties, the inner circle knew all that was happening and the general public very little. The "Garbo-Mercedes business" was another of the Hollywood secrets that studio PR people kept under wraps, and Cecil would have been interested in the most recent installment as a matter of course. But Loos's account, coming when it did, must have piqued his interest more than she could have guessed. Cecil had been obsessed with Garbo for some time and had pursued her assiduously when he was in California, hoping to photograph her for *Vogue* or for a book he was preparing. She had avoided him until just before he returned to England. Then one afternoon, at the Gouldings' Spanish-style mansion, where Cecil was staying, they had had a surprisingly intense encounter that went on until dawn. Cecil apparently, and uncharacteristically, kept the news of this meeting to himself.

—

Greta Garbo lived for the most part quietly, away from the world of Hollywood parties and public occasions. She was happiest alone or with a few friends. Throughout her life she was known as a recluse, though sometimes as "a recluse about town." She did occasionally go to small social events, and at one such, given by the Polish-born screenwriter Salka Viertel* in the early months of 1931, she met Mercedes de Acosta, poet, playwright, and scriptwriter, who soon became an intimate friend. From the account left by Mercedes, it would appear that Garbo sought her out, arranging that they should meet and then inviting Mercedes to her house. The first night they were together, according to Mercedes, they sat up late, talking and eating, and then went down to the beach.

> We talked of . . . things, profound and trivial. Then finally, as the moon sank and disappeared and a tiny streak of light fell across

*Salka Viertel (1889–1978) was trained as an actress and played Marthy opposite Garbo in the German-language film version of Eugene O'Neill's play *Anna Christie* (Marie Dressler played Marthy in the English-language version). She and her husband, the Austrian writer and director Berthold Viertel (1885–1953), had come to Hollywood in 1929. She began her screenwriting career with Garbo's *Queen Christina.* Her house in Santa Monica was something of a salon for Europeans living in Hollywood.

> the sky in the east, we were silent. Slowly the dawn came. As the sun rose we walked down the mountain and picked rambler roses . . .[3]

In the summer of 1931, Garbo and Mercedes disappeared to a little house on Silver Lake in the Sierra Nevada owned by the actor Wallace Beery, where they shared a solitary idyll for some time, although not as long as Mercedes later claimed:

> How to describe the next six enchanted weeks? Even recapturing them in memory makes me realize how lucky I am to have had them. Six perfect weeks out of a lifetime. This is indeed much. In all this time there was not a second of disharmony between Greta and me or in nature around us.[4]

Mercedes observed Garbo closely. In an extract she omitted from her autobiography, she described Garbo's legs:

> They were not tan or the sunburned color which is commonly seen, but the skin had taken on a golden hue and a flock of tiny hairs growing on her legs were golden too. Her legs are classical. She has not the typical Follies girl legs or the American man's dream of what a woman's legs should be. They have the shape that can be seen in many Greek statues.[5]

Garbo lived in the Brentwood section of Los Angeles, and Mercedes moved in next door. She had been writing a film script for Pola Negri. When it was rejected, Garbo hit on the idea of Mercedes writing one for her. The project was called *Desperate.* Registered at MGM on January 21, 1932, it was the story of a girl whose mother jumps off a cliff. Thereafter the girl follows Nietzsche's code: "One must learn to live desperately." Mercedes described the heroine as she might have described Garbo herself:

> One feels in her a strange, wild nature, with the conflicting struggles of her mother and father combined—of the old world

> and the new—from an early age this inner battle had raged. One feels in her sadness and gayety, sanity and neuroticism, vitality and listlessness, reticence and restlessness, shyness and daring—all of these mixed in a mad contradiction that spends her own strength and throws her back upon herself—that makes her forever a mystery to the ordinary mortal. In her eyes one already sees the doom that comes from the soul rather than outward events—unmoved eyes, holding in their depths that look of eternity.[6]

For much of *Desperate,* Garbo was to be dressed as a boy in order to escape from the police and others. Irving Thalberg, head of production at MGM, would have none of this. "Do you want to put all America and all the women's clubs against her?" he asked. "You must be out of your mind. . . . We have been building Garbo up for years as a great glamorous actress, and now you come along and try to put her into pants and make a monkey out of her."[7] That was the end of the project.

Garbo then made *Grand Hotel* and *As You Desire Me,* which was released in June 1932. During negotiations over a new contract with MGM, she left Hollywood for New York, hiding out at the St. Moritz Hotel on Central Park South before sailing for her native Sweden. Mercedes was left behind in the condition described by Anita Loos in her letter to Cecil Beaton. But since Mercedes was soon being swamped with flowers by Marlene Dietrich, who had embarked on a determined campaign to seduce her, she may not have been suffering as much as Loos thought.

Mercedes: "Who of us is only one sex?"

Mercedes de Acosta is now a forgotten figure, but in her day she was well known in literary and film circles. She was born on March 1, 1893, the youngest of eight children of Ricardo de Acosta, and was brought up in a strict Spanish Catholic household in New York in the years before World War I. She had dark hair and brown eyes and was about five feet four inches tall. She claimed Spanish (Castilian) descent, but it is generally accepted that the family came from Cuba. Mercedes wrote novels, plays, and film scripts, and her poetry was published, although nobody reads it now.

One of Mercedes's sisters was Rita Lydig, a striking beauty who was painted by Sargent and Boldini. "As fantastic as any character in romantic literature, Mrs. Rita de Acosta Lydig graced the opening cycles of the twentieth century with a perfectionism that would have been rare in any period since the Renaissance,"[8] Cecil Beaton wrote in *The Glass of Fashion,* his idiosyncratic survey of twentieth-century style.

New York in the days of Mercedes's childhood had a charm that is hard to imagine now. Italian organ-grinders still roamed the streets with monkeys tethered on chains. Horse-drawn coaches rattled along the avenues, with footmen as postilions. Through her sister Rita, Mercedes met many of the great figures of the day, from Rodin and Anatole France to Edith Wharton and Queen Marie of Romania. She became a friend of Misia Sert and Stravinsky. She used to claim that her brain was "international," indeed "universal," though her heart remained resolutely Spanish. Mercedes's film career included being fired by Irving Thalberg for refusing to write a scene in *Rasputin and the Empress* (1932) about a meeting between Princess Irene Yusupov and the Mad Monk that had never taken place in life. Mercedes was that rare creature in Hollywood, a purist.

She did not have an easy life. She was the victim of depressions that in childhood led her to lie in the corner of a room, moaning, and when she was an adult she had trouble sleeping and suffered from migraine headaches. Many times she endured what she called "the dark night of the soul."[9] She believed in "astral traveling," when "the spirit or ego leaves the body while one sleeps and yet remains connected to the life force." She explained the sudden awakening with a jerk that everyone has experienced as "a too sudden parting of the astral from the physical body."[10]

Mercedes was a vegetarian who thought that "meat eating makes a tomb out of our living bodies for the corpses of dead animals."[11] She was an explorer of Eastern religions, a disciple of Krishnamurti. She began life as a devout Roman Catholic, often kneeling for hours with arms extended in the form of a cross. She put nails and stones into her shoes and walked till her feet bled. Later she rejected much of Catholicism, telling Elsa Maxwell, "I don't believe in dogmas, I believe in taking the essence from all religions, in arriving at your own creed."[12] She was an ardent feminist and loved Isadora Duncan for helping to liberate women from the burden of layers of clothes, making corsets and stockings obsolete and introducing sandals.

Until the age of seven, Mercedes was convinced that she was male. Her family encouraged this belief, referring to her as a boy and dressing her in Eton suits. Her mother had wanted a son, and would have called him Rafael, and so she called Mercedes "Rafael" instead. Mercedes played boys' games and played with boys as a boy. But one day "the tragedy occurred."[13] Mercedes was told by one of the boys that as a girl she could not throw a ball as far as they. She felt insulted and challenged the boy to a fight. But instead of fighting, the boy took her behind a bathhouse and exposed his youthful penis.

> "Have you got this?" he demanded.
>
> I was horrified. I had heard about grown people and children being deformed. These stories now leapt to my mind.
>
> "You're deformed!" I shouted.
>
> "If you are a boy and you haven't got this, *you* are the one who is deformed," he shouted back.
>
> By this time the other boys had joined us, each boy speedily

> showing me the same strange phenomenon the first boy had exhibited. They were like menacing and terrible judges! They demanded that I produce the same "phenomenon."
>
> "Prove that you're not a girl," they screamed.[14]

This was a shattering experience for young Rafael. "In that one brief second everything in my young soul turned monstrous and terrible and dark."[15] She ran home to her nurse, then challenged her mother, and it was admitted that she was a girl. In due course, as she recorded in an unpublished draft of her memoirs, Mercedes was sent to a convent to learn feminine ways, but she ran away. She continued to deny that she was a girl, explaining to the bewildered nun: "I am not a boy and I am not a girl, or maybe I am both—I don't know. And because I don't know, I will never fit in anywhere and I will be lonely all my life."[16]

Some years later, Mercedes mused on how this had affected her life and her attitude toward men and women:

> It has made me see and understand the half tones of life, and like the half tone light of dawn and twilight, whose vibrations are ever the most mystical and romantic, so too I have come to regard these half tones of life and the people who walk their rhythm, as the most beautiful. . . . To the outward form of sex which the body has assumed, I have remained indifferent. I do not understand the difference between a man and a woman, and believing only in the eternal value of love, I cannot understand these so-called "normal" people who believe that a man should love only a woman, and a woman love only a man. If this were so, then it disregards completely the spirit, the personality, and the mind, and stresses the importance of the physical body. I believe in many cases this is why the "normal" people are usually much less inspired, seldom artists, and much less sensitive than the "half-tone" people. They are held down and concerned so much with the physical body that they cannot see beyond the outward form of male and female. The Greeks understood so well that there is no pure masculine or pure feminine in one person, and in order to bring the body up to the level of this spiritual understanding, they did not hesitate to sculpt on the physical plane the hermaph-

> roditic type in their works of art; and in the poetry of their lives they accepted homo-sexuality and bi-sexuality, whose impulse they regarded as just another stream which flowed toward the same great sea—the eternal source of love![17]

The young Mercedes loved her eccentric, aristocratic mother. She said she suffered from a mother complex, and when her mother died Mercedes guarded the body so zealously that she tried to stab her brother when he came near. Her father was handsome, poetic, intellectual. When he was a young man in Cuba, he had survived a battle in which twenty of his companions had been shot. In later life he brooded over this constantly, and when Mercedes was fourteen and he was an old man, he killed himself by jumping off a high rock. "I knew this gesture was, in his mind, an expiation at last to his comrades for having escaped with his life so many years before," she wrote.[18]

Mercedes herself was capable of dramatic and violent action. She owned a small Colt revolver and took comfort from the idea that if life became too difficult, she could point it at the roof of her mouth "and pop myself off this baffling planet."[19] One day it disappeared, and Mercedes discovered that her sister Baba had removed it for safety, throwing it into the East River. She was outraged:

> "You took it," I said, and leaped at her. The weight of my body knocked her over backwards and we fell down. I grabbed her throat and banged her head over and over again on the floor.[20]

Like many New Yorkers in the twenties, Mercedes loved the smoky nightlife of speakeasies and drag clubs.

> What we all saw in it is difficult to understand now. I suppose it was the newly found excitement of homosexuality, which after the war was expressed openly in nightclubs and cabarets by boys dressed as women, and was, like drinking, forbidden and subject to police raids, which made it all the more enticing. Youth was in revolt, and outwitting the government and getting the better of the police lent a zest to our lives.[21]

Mercedes wrote in a draft of her memoirs, "How am I to convey to the reader the diverse people I feel within me—a reader who probably also has as many diverse people as I have within him or within her—as the sex may be. And here too, is another problem. Who of us is only one sex? I, myself, am sometimes androgynous . . ."[22]

Between 1920 and 1935 Mercedes was married to the painter Abram Poole, but she refused to be described as Mrs. Poole, remaining resolutely Mercedes de Acosta. Nor did her marriage prevent her from pursuing various ladies. She even claimed to have taken a girlfriend with her on her honeymoon. She had remarkable success in this regard. Alice B. Toklas wrote of her, "A friend said to me one day—you can't dispose of Mercedes lightly—she has had the two most important women in US—Greta Garbo and Marlene Dietrich."[23] Shortly before her death at the age of one hundred, "Dickie" Fellowes-Gordon, Elsa Maxwell's lifelong friend,* recalled that Mercedes used to boast, "I can get any woman from any man,"[24] and there is considerable evidence to support this claim. Truman Capote was one of those fascinated by Mercedes's sex life. "Truman thought up a game he called International Daisy Chain, the point of which was to link people sexually, using as few beds as possible," recalls the art historian John Richardson. "He used to say that Mercedes was the best card to hold. You could get to anyone—from Cardinal Spellman to the Duchess of Windsor."[25]

*Dorothy Fellowes-Gordon (1891–1991), scion of a Scottish family, shared Elsa Maxwell's life and sometimes wrote her column for her. She lived for many years in a beautiful villa in the south of France but died in penury in London.

Mercedes: "A slender body, hands soft and white . . ."

Mercedes always dressed in either black or white, or a combination of the two. She favored cloaks, and tricorn hats, and well-cut jackets. She operated with champagne, lilies, and caviar, and if necessary would fill a room with such delights, giving no thought to cost in the cause of seduction.

She was variously fascinated by many famous and complicated women—the Italian diva with the tragic face, Eleonora Duse, whom she first saw passing in a gondola in Venice when she was eleven and who died in Pittsburgh and whose body she arranged to have lie in the Dominican Catholic Church on Lexington Avenue; the Russian ballerina Tamara Karsavina; and Isadora Duncan.

Mercedes first met Isadora in 1916 and, during the course of a long friendship, arranged for the payment of many of her bills and the editing and publishing of her memoir, *My Life*. "Many days and nights we spent together," Mercedes recalled, "eating when we felt hungry, sleeping when we felt tired, regardless of time or the hour."[26] Isadora often danced for her, and did so once while humming much of *Parsifal*. In the last year of her life, Isadora wrote a poem to Mercedes in her almost illegible hand, a fragment of which reads:

> A slender body, hands soft and white
> for the service of my delight . . .
>
> Two sprouting breasts
> Round and sweet
> invite my hungry mouth to eat.
> From whence two nipples firm and pink
> persuade my thirsty soul to drink
> And lower still a secret place
> Where I'd fain hide my loving face

My kisses like a swarm of bees
Would find their way
Between thy knees
And suck the honey of thy lips
Embracing thy two slender hips.[27]

Other women in Mercedes's life included Marie Doro, a Charles Frohman* star, a small, alert, and intelligent creature with spectacularly dark eyes and thick brown hair. Marie wrote popular songs and was an authority on Shakespeare's sonnets and Elizabethan poetry. She shared Mercedes's fascination for religion and studied at the Union Theological Seminary in New York. "She had a way of weaving in and out of my life," wrote Mercedes, adding, "If you never knew Marie intimately—and this was almost a lifework—you could never have known all her tricks for hiding her beauty. I was immediately aware of her, even when she dressed herself up like a pixie to conceal it!"[28] Marie used to go into hiding "to contemplate" and once changed her hotel four times in one week to escape her friends. When she died in 1956, she bequeathed $90,000 to the Actors' Fund.

Mercedes's great early friend Elisabeth (Bessie) Marbury, the companion of the interior decorator Elsie de Wolfe and agent for H. G. Wells, Somerset Maugham, and Oscar Wilde, provided entrée to another romantic attachment, the Russian actress Alla Nazimova. Nazimova was dark and intense, slender and exotic-looking, and when she appeared in the United States she had a clearly defined mustache, fashionable in Russia but not in America. This she was eventually persuaded to remove. Mercedes met her after a large benefit at Madison Square Garden in which Nazimova had run around the arena dressed as a Cossack, carrying a Russian flag and leaping into the air every few steps. Mercedes called on her in her dressing room and was at once transfixed by her large violet eyes. Nazimova held out her hands: "We took to each other instantly. I felt completely at ease and as if we had always known each other."[29]

*Charles Frohman (1860–1915), American theatrical manager who sponsored the first London production of *Peter Pan*. The first manager to realize the possibilities of interchange between London and New York shows.

Mercedes de Acosta, 1934.

Nazimova had come to America in 1906. She learned English and performed in many Ibsen and Chekhov plays as well as creating the role of the murderous wife in Eugene O'Neill's *Mourning Becomes Electra.* When she received applause, she did not bow but gave "the Roman salute," which later acquired sinister overtones from Mussolini and the Fascists.[30]

Nazimova lived in a large Spanish house on Sunset Boulevard amid three and a half acres of tropical plants. At one time it was thought she was having an affair with Rudolph Valentino, but she preferred her considerable entourage of women friends. However, she was not pleased when Valentino fell in love with her protégée, the costume and set designer Natasha Rambova (née Winifred Shaughnessy), an exotic self-creation in veils, turbans, and dazzling earrings to whom Nazimova herself had introduced him. She set about warning Valentino of the doom that would be his lot if he married the ambitious hussy, but he remained resolute. After the marriage Valentino's career floundered, and his friends went so far as to believe that the tensions of the couple's subsequent divorce led to the stomach disorders that killed Valentino in 1926.

Nazimova turned her house into a hotel, the famous Garden of Allah, in 1927, but at first it was badly managed. When she sold it, she was cheated out of what she had put into it, and the stock market crash of 1929 took the rest of her money. She died of cancer in 1945. She held one further curious distinction: she was Nancy Reagan's godmother.

Eva Le Gallienne

Shortly before she married Abram Poole on May 11, 1920, Mercedes met Eva Le Gallienne. Eva was twenty-one and Mercedes twenty-seven. They met again in November 1921, when Eva was playing Julie in the first American production of Ferenc Molnár's *Liliom*. Mercedes wrote her a formal letter of admiration: "My dear Miss Le Gallienne . . ." and invited her to dine. They found themselves soul mates, drawn to each other not only physically but by shared hopes for the theatre and their intense adoration of Duse.

Eva Le Gallienne was the daughter of the British literary critic and poet Richard Le Gallienne (a friend of Oscar Wilde's) and his Danish wife, Julie Nørregaard, a journalist. Her parents separated in 1903, when she was four, and she was brought up in Paris. At the age of seven she was taken to see Sarah Bernhardt play Prince Charming in *The Sleeping Beauty*. She later said that Bernhardt's arrival on stage was "like an electric shock." She made her acting debut in London in 1914 and set off the following year for New York. She had a difficult time in America at first, and the part of Julie was a particularly important step in her career. The critics loved her.

Eva was on tour much of the time, and when she was not on stage she tended to lead a solitary, almost reclusive, existence. Early in their relationship she acknowledged that she was in love with Mercedes, who was ostensibly living a conventional married life with her husband. Eva had begun a tour of *Liliom* in February 1922, three months after their first dinner, and she wrote to Mercedes almost every day, sometimes more than once. In the archives of her papers there are almost a thousand sheets of letters covering the years 1921 to 1927.* She saw Mer-

*The information in this section is largely derived from Eva's letters to Mercedes. They are now in the Rosenbach Museum in Philadelphia, which kindly

cedes occasionally when she came to New York for a rehearsal or on a Sunday, but their meetings were furtive, and the fear of censorious gossip lay heavily on both of them. The insecurity of separated lovers was made the more intense by Mercedes's bouts of ill health, neurosis, and lack of confidence.

Their meetings took place at Eva's apartment, for which she apologized for its not being more glamorous. It should perhaps have been banked with white camellias and a few gardenias. Having given herself totally to Mercedes, she was terrified of losing her. She wrote that the thought of Mercedes's husband or anyone else lying in Mercedes's arms was unbearable.

In May, Mercedes fell ill, and Abram Poole wired Eva with the news. Now the essential conflict came to the fore: Eva's jealousy of Abram, who had a legal and moral right to take care of his wife. The touchy situation was exacerbated by the arrival of an ex-girlfriend of Mercedes's called Billie McKeever. But Mercedes soon recovered, and on June 4 she sailed for Europe on the *Olympic,* accompanied by a series of notes from Eva to be opened each successive day on board. They professed her insane love and the hope that Mercedes had not made any romantic conquests on the moonlit deck.

Eva herself left for Europe two days later on the *Mauretania,* traveling to London to stay with her mother in Gloucester Place. Mercedes worried about the propriety of sending letters there, but Eva reassured her that she locked them away instantly and then read them over and over in the night. The lovers met in Paris and stayed together for some weeks. Their love nest was the Hôtel Foyot in the Rue de Tournon (where Casanova had once lived). While in Paris they visited "Dickie" Fellowes-Gordon, who recalled the visit nearly seventy years later and confirmed that they appeared very much in love.[31]

On July 22, Mercedes left for Munich, pursued by adoring messages from Eva, whose mother had come to stay with her. The mother was read aloud to from *Jehanne d'Arc,* a play written by Mercedes for Eva. When Eva was alone, she entertained herself by visiting the Moulin Rouge in Montmartre and dancing with girls.

---

permitted me to examine them thoroughly. The Le Gallienne estate did not permit me to quote directly from them.

Finally, a note from Mercedes arrived via the sculptress Malvina Hoffman. Eva at once set off on the Orient Express to join her. Together they traveled to Genoa, Venice, Munich, and Vienna. Molnár, the author of *Liliom,* met them in Budapest, where Eva was warmly greeted by banners reading "Welcome Julie," given flowers by strangers, and in general fêted. But soon Eva had to leave Mercedes with Abram. While she made her way back to London via Paris, the Pooles went to Constantinople,* where they stayed at the Pera, the celebrated hotel whose guests have included Kemal Atatürk and Agatha Christie. In her memoirs, Mercedes left a vivid account of a "poignant memory":[32]

> One day in the lobby of the Pera Palace Hotel I saw one of the most hauntingly beautiful women I had ever beheld. Her features and her movements were so distinguished and aristocratic-looking that I decided she must be a refugee Russian princess. The porter said he did not know her name but he thought she was a Swedish actress who had come to Constantinople with the great Swedish film director, Maurice Stiller.
>
> Several times after this I saw her in the street. I was terribly troubled by her eyes and I longed to speak to her, but I did not have the courage. Also I did not even know what language to use. She gave me the impression of great loneliness which only added to my own already melancholy state of mind. I hated to leave Constantinople without speaking to her, but sometimes destiny is kinder than we think, or maybe it is just that we cannot escape our destiny. Strangely enough, as the train pulled out of the station which carried me away from Constantinople I had a strong premonition that I might again see that beautiful and haunting face on some other shore.[33]

Mercedes insisted on this version of her first encounter with Garbo, but, sadly, it cannot have been Garbo that Mercedes saw, or thought she saw. Garbo and Stiller did indeed travel to Constantinople, but not until December 1924, at which time Mercedes was certainly in New York.

Interestingly, the first draft of Mercedes's memoir tells the story rather differently, giving ample evidence to its subsequent embroidery:

*Mercedes's passport records her presence in Constantinople from August 8 to 18, 1922.

> In this strange and amazing city I moved about, stirred by a thousand emotions but quite unconscious that at that moment, moving too perhaps in this stream of human life and living even in the same hotel at which I was then staying, was a person who would one day mean more to me than anyone in the whole world.
>
> And yet, looking back on those days and nights now, I seem to feel that I lived holding my breath, and as though straining to hear a voice or catch a glimpse of a face—both of which I had been waiting for all my life.
>
> When I left Constantinople I wept bitterly. I could not say why but it was as though I were being torn away from my own heart. Did my sub-conscious already then know that in leaving this city I was turning my back on my true Beloved, Fate intended still to hold away from me, but whom I was destined to meet on a far distant shore many thousand miles away from this Eastern land![34]

While Mercedes was busy fantasizing in Constantinople, Eva was at her mother's home in England, worrying about how to sort out this complicated relationship, with its domestic scenes and Mercedes's threats of suicide. When Mercedes finally arrived in London, Eva almost immediately left for New York. Mercedes did not follow until October, while Eva returned restlessly to her *Liliom* tour. The ensuing separation brought the usual agonies, reprimands, and jealousies. Eva was wholly faithful to Mercedes, and was frequently wounded by her gibes that she might have found someone else. She was lonely and alone, which Mercedes was not. One night she telephoned from Toronto and Mercedes replied from a room filled with guests.

The affair continued through 1923. That spring, the producer Sam Harris turned down *Jehanne d'Arc* but asked Mercedes if she had something else he could do for Eva. She quickly put together *Sandro Botticelli,* a curiously ill-developed play. The plot was simple enough. In the first act Simonetta Vespucci, the inspiration for *The Birth of Venus,* agrees to pose for the artist. Then in the second act she does so. Eva was to pose nude before a somewhat bashful audience. This was achieved by the device of throwing off her cloak while hiding her nakedness behind flowing locks and a high-backed chair. Alexander Woollcott condemned the performance as a muddle, the stage overcrowded with actors "with somewhat the jostling effect of men colliding in a Pullman washroom."[35] Years later Mercedes wrote that the play had been panned, and rightly. At the time, Eva concluded that it was an example of what she should not do.

In the summer, Eva was again in London with her mother, while Mercedes was at Trouville. The two lovers escaped together to Brittany on a walking tour, dressed as Gypsies, and then went to Paris, where they made a pilgrimage to the Hôtel Regina, the home of their idol, Duse. They both began to cry when they spotted her wrapped in a blanket on her balcony. The following autumn, while Eva was on tour once more with a much-acclaimed performance in Molnár's *The Swan,* Duse was making her final, ill-fated tour of the United States, and Mercedes and Eva met her at last.

Throughout 1924 their relationship was deteriorating. Eva was continually on tour, and Mercedes was pursuing her various affairs, amusements, and enterprises. At one point, however, Eva began to make progress with the long-held plan to stage *Jehanne d'Arc.* She had found a French producer who was in quest of plays to stage in Paris the following spring. Eva pursued this, and early in 1925 the two women, along with the set designer Norman Bel Geddes and Eva's dog, sailed for France. The play was to be staged at the Odéon, which would fulfill Eva's childhood dream of performing there. (When she was six she had passed the theatre regularly on her way to school.) But numerous complicated changes of plan transpired. One problem was that Paris proved too exciting for Bel Geddes. He went berserk and was forever returning home drunk and having his head bandaged from brawls or falling out of taxicabs. "Our young American genius discovers sex, night life, vie de Bohème and Paris!" wrote Mercedes.[36]

The play was finally performed in June at the Théâtre de la Porte-Saint-Martin, where it attracted much attention. Eva's portrayal of Joan was praised for her "fine perception and extraordinary talent,"[37] and the sets were deemed "ingenious and of rare beauty."[38] Eva took numerous curtain calls. Despite all this, *Jehanne d'Arc* never went to the United States.

The three-and-a-half-year affair between Mercedes and Eva ended soon after. It did so partly because Mercedes befriended a young playwright, Noël Coward, who was about to make his name in America. His team was traveling to the United States to stage *The Vortex,* a provocative play about drugs. They went by the *Majestic,* and both Mercedes and Eva were on board. Coward noted the failure of their expedition: "I think they were sad about it; at any rate they alternated between intellectual gloom and feverish gaiety and wore black, indiscriminately."[39]

In Coward's group was his designer, Gladys Calthrop. She and Eva formed a liaison, which caused something of a stir. "Dickie" Fellowes-Gordon went to see Coward and asked where Gladys was. "It's all very embarrassing," came the reply. "She's gone off with Eva Le Gallienne."[40] Mercedes is less than informative in her memoirs. She writes, "About this time I found that Eva and I for a variety of reasons were growing apart."[41]

Gladys Calthrop was a serious diversion, but there were other reasons for splitting. Eva was ambitious, and Mercedes had now involved her in two stage flops. The more lasting break came when Eva met Alice DeLamar,* heiress to a considerable mining fortune. Cryptically, almost bitterly, Mercedes noted in her memoirs that "a circumstance" during the run of *Jehanne d'Arc* "opened the way for Eva to have her Civic Repertory Theatre** and made this project financially possible for her."[42] This was an injection of funds from Alice, and also from the financier Otto Kahn. The DeLamar connection was later strengthened when Alice bought property in Weston, Connecticut, and Eva took a house there.†

*Alice DeLamar (d. 1982) lived in an apartment on the Île Saint-Louis and had a home in Palm Beach. Her father, Joseph Raphael DeLamar (1843–1918), was known as "the Wolf of Wall Street." He made a fortune when gold was discovered in Colorado, and left Alice $10 million.

**Eva founded the Civic Repertory Theatre in 1926. The idea was to produce meritorious noncommercial plays. Low admission prices and the Depression contributed to the theatre's demise in 1933.

†George Balanchine and others also lived on this property. Eva remained there happily for the rest of her life, surrounded by raccoons, skunks, and possums, which she fed at night. She was still appearing on the stage as late as 1983. She was given

There was little communication between Eva and Mercedes after March 1926. Eva wiped Mercedes out of her life. While she normally kept letters and remained friends with old lovers, she destroyed those of Mercedes and eschewed her company. In 1965, Eva published a tribute to Eleonora Duse* in which she charted the course of her friendship with the diva without so much as a mention of Mercedes.

---

the National Artist Award by President Gerald Ford in 1977 and the National Medal of Arts by President Ronald Reagan in 1986. She had been active all her life in attempting to form a national theatre in America. Eva died in Weston on June 3, 1991, at the age of ninety-two.

**The Mystic in the Theatre, Eleonora Duse* (Carbondale and Edwardsville: Southern Illinois University Press, 1965).

Garbo and Mercedes:
"I bought it for you in Berlin."

In the late summer of 1925, soon after returning from Europe on the *Majestic* with Eva and Noël Coward, Mercedes received a message from a photographer friend, Arnold Genthe, saying that he was making a portrait of the most beautiful woman he had ever seen and wanted Mercedes to meet her. But Mercedes was leaving to visit Eva's father in Woodstock. On her return to New York, there was a package from Genthe, saying that he was sorry that Mercedes had not been able to meet his model, Greta Garbo, now on her way to Hollywood with Mauritz Stiller. Mercedes recalled:

> I opened the package and took out a large photograph. There before me, in profile, was the beguiling face of the haunting person I had seen in Constantinople.[43]

Stiller and Garbo had been in Constantinople a few months earlier, hoping to make a film in Turkey, and Mercedes's romantic version of events conflated that trip with her own, earlier one, with her husband. In any event, the Fates were drawing Mercedes toward the great obsessive love of her life.

—

Garbo had been taken under the wing of Mauritz Stiller in 1923, when she was an eighteen-year-old drama student, awkward and unsure of herself. Stiller's role in Garbo's career was that of Svengali to her Trilby. A giant Russian Jew who was often seen in a yellow fur coat, he had ground his way to the top, making more than forty motion pictures in Sweden. Long determined to find the raw material from which to create a world star, he set about molding Garbo's appearance, her acting, and her character. He even chose the name Garbo. For £160 she took a leading part in *Gösta Berling's Saga,* based on the novel by Selma Lagerlöf. It was released in 1924. But the film that got Garbo the most notice was *Die freudlose Gasse* (*The Joyless Street*), directed by G. W. Pabst.

Garbo and Stiller had stopped off in Germany on their way back to Stockholm from Constantinople for the filming with Pabst, and it was in his picture, a somber study of postwar society, that Garbo's sensuality first came over on celluloid. In the meantime, Louis B. Mayer had seen *Gösta Berling's Saga* and invited Stiller and Garbo to Hollywood. Thus in 1925 the pair set sail, expecting instant stardom and fame. Disappointment followed. Garbo's rehearsed lines for the American press were greeted by one solitary reporter. They were abandoned in New York by MGM until the photo session with Genthe landed Garbo in *Vanity Fair* and Mayer's attention was drawn to his neglected acquisition. She was summoned to Hollywood and afforded star treatment. Stiller didn't fare as well. Like Salka Viertel's husband, he was one of the European imports who didn't make it in Hollywood. Stiller completed two films there, both for Pola Negri at Paramount. The other projects he worked on were partly directed by others. He soon returned to Sweden, where he died in 1928.

Garbo's first American film was *The Torrent* (1926), a part she secured when another actress fell ill. Her reviews were far from the usual accorded to fledgling stars: "Miss Garbo is not beautiful, but she is a brilliant actress."[44] Her next film, *The Temptress* (1926), turned her into a valuable property. There then began the celebrated and romantic partnership between Garbo and John Gilbert, which extended from *Flesh and the Devil* (1927) until silent films became talkies. Gilbert's squeaky, high-pitched voice belied his matinée-idol good looks; he came to grief. Of the Gilbert-Garbo films, all but *The Divine Woman* (1928) survive. They reveal Garbo expressing a seemingly effortless languor that makes her coactors appear wooden. The somewhat thin plots were not helped by the censor, who insisted, for instance, that "syphilis" should become "embezzlement" in *A Woman of Affairs* (1928), the adaptation of Michael Arlen's celebrated novel *The Green Hat.* Frequently, suggested screenplays left the temperamental star cold, causing her to dismiss one project with her famous line: "I t'ink I go home."

Even in those days Garbo eschewed the more tinselly aspects of film life. She seldom attended parties, while adhering to a strict dietary regime, invariably eating chopped beef with fried potatoes and an egg followed by a piece of cake, and drinking fresh fruit juice. Her love of solitude encouraged her growing reputation as a mysterious lady. Tallulah Bankhead said her mystery was "as thick as a London fog."[45] At times throughout her life the fog lifted and she became unaccountably gay, the life and soul of the party, before retreating once more.

In *Anna Christie* (1930), Garbo's rich, deep Scandinavian voice hypnotized audiences. While in real life she was big boned with a heavy nose and boyish stride, the camera converted her into a creature of elegance and beauty. She was not set in a previously tried mold. The poet Iris Tree spoke of Garbo's eyelids. She said that when Garbo closed her eyes, her eyelashes were so long that they got tangled up and there was a great fluttering like the noise of butterflies moving their wings before she could open them again.[46] The voice completed the image. Some years later Kenneth Tynan wrote, "What, when drunk, one sees in other women, one sees in Garbo sober."[47] Tynan wrote too of Garbo's unchanging effect on screen: "She could still (and often did) fling her head flexibly back at right-angles to her spine, and she kissed as thirstily as ever, cupping her man's head in both hands and seeming very nearly to drink from it."[48]

The critic Arthur Knight mused on Garbo's appeal in a love scene:

> Came that superb moment common to all the Garbo films, when her reserve broke down, when all the arguments against love that her script-writers could dream up were flung aside, and with a sound that was half sob, half ecstasy, she ran to the arms of her lover. At such moments, every man in the audience felt that he alone was holding this exquisite woman, who, suddenly defenseless, revealed a depth of sexuality that would require a lifetime of delightful appeasement.[49]

Garbo was filming *Susan Lenox: Her Fall and Rise* in 1931 when she met Mercedes de Acosta at Salka Viertel's house. Mercedes had just arrived in Hollywood, or "Follywood," as some people called it, to work on a screenplay for Pola Negri. She soon found that the town's main problem was "stupidity, vulgarity, and bad taste"[50] rather than the depravity that was its common reputation. Nevertheless, she was to stay there for many years. Although obliged to go to the studio from time to time, Mercedes eschewed "film people" and naturally gravitated to the more sophisticated European milieu of the Viertels' circle. She was invited to their house on Maybery Road in Santa Monica for "tea" one afternoon, and as they sat and talked the doorbell rang. Outside in the hall there was a low voice speaking German that Mercedes recognized at once from *Anna Christie.* Garbo came into the room. "As we shook hands and she smiled at me I felt I had known her all my life; in fact, in many previous incarnations."[51]

> As I had expected she was remarkably beautiful, far more so than she seemed in her films then. She was dressed in a white jumper and dark blue sailor pants. Her feet were bare and like her hands, slender and sensitive. Her beautifully straight hair hung to her shoulders and she wore a white tennis visor pulled well down over her face in an effort to hide her extraordinary eyes which held in them a look of eternity. When she spoke I was not only charmed by the tone and quality of her voice but also by her accent. At this time she spoke English quite incorrectly with a strong Swedish accent and her mispronunciations were enchanting. That afternoon I heard her say to Salka, "I trotteled down to see you." Oddly enough, the words that she said were often more expressive than the correct ones.[52]

Little conversation passed between Garbo and Mercedes, but at one point they were left alone briefly. "There was a silence, a silence which she could manage with great ease. Greta can always manage a silence."[53] In due course Garbo noticed a heavy bracelet Mercedes was wearing. Mercedes handed it to her with the line "I bought it for you in Berlin." Presently, as ever, Garbo went home in order to spend the evening having dinner alone in bed. But the first meeting had been a success.

Through Salka Viertel they met again, and Garbo clearly took a liking to Mercedes, trying to prevent her from going to a lunch party given by

Pola Negri. Garbo even rang her at the lunch and summoned her to her home, at 1717 San Vicente Boulevard. Welcoming her new friend across the threshold, a rare treat, Garbo scattered blossoms for Mercedes to walk across. Mercedes even saw the bedroom: "It was more like a man's room. I thought it a sad room."[54] But it was a short visit, since Garbo was tired, and presently she used words that would become a much-repeated joke line as they parted in the future: "Now you must go home."

Their friendship was forged on revelations about early life and discussions of dreams, with long talks about matters both profound and trivial, often lasting through the night. Mercedes never minded: "Although I had not been to bed all night I felt refreshed."[55]

Not long after this, Mercedes and Garbo took the holiday that Mercedes described as such a perfect idyll. It began in typically disorganized Garbo fashion. She summoned Mercedes to inform her that she needed total solitude and would be retreating to an island in the Sierra Nevada. She got into her car and swept away. Mercedes retreated home, disconsolate. A few days later, Garbo telephoned. She had reached the island, felt that the beauty of it should be shared, and had decided to come back to collect her. Thus Garbo endured a three-hundred-mile drive back through the Mojave Desert in grueling heat. On her return visit she stopped every few hours to telephone: "I am getting nearer, I am getting nearer."[56] The last call came from Pasadena. Garbo arrived, and Mercedes put her to bed on the sleeping porch, though neither slept much. Next day Mercedes rang the studio to say she was departing. There was nothing for her to do there, so they were delighted. It took a further three days to reach the island once more, and then the idyll began.

James, the chauffeur, was dismissed. Garbo then rowed Mercedes across Silver Lake to the small island and its tiny log cabin. She explained that the boat was their only way of getting there. "We must be baptized at once," said Garbo, throwing off her clothes and diving into the water. Mercedes followed. Garbo cooked simple dinners of poached mountain trout. And they talked. The photographs Mercedes took show Garbo, bronzed and healthy, wearing a beret and shorts, gym shoes and white socks. In some of them she is topless, and in others she has a shirt thrown over her head, just covering her breasts. Mercedes was discovering a different side of Garbo.

> It is generally accepted that Garbo is morose and serious. This is one of the things said of her in the legend that has been built up around her. All legends are built on rumors and hearsay. Of course she is serious if there is something to be serious about and she does not run around with a broad grin on her face like most American executives, but that does not mean that she is morose and lacks humor. As a matter of fact she has *real* humor and a remarkable sense of it. During those six weeks in Silver Lake, as well as many times since, she has shown her sense of fun to me.[57]

Mercedes wrote more about this holiday in the early drafts of her book. Garbo had her "literally rolling on the floor with her sense of comedy." She told the story of her uncle in Sweden and how she continually asked him, "Does Uncle care a lot about Jesus?" Though he affirmed this several times, at length he became irritated, jumped up, throwing down his newspaper, and declared, "No! Uncle doesn't give a damn about Jesus."[58] This became a catchphrase for Mercedes and Garbo whenever something bored them.

To friends, though, Mercedes expressed her occasional irritation. Garbo was always on a diet, and Mercedes said that Garbo would bore her with lengthy descriptions of the food she was *not* going to eat. During the months in Hollywood after that holiday, Garbo and Mercedes were much in each other's company. And Mercedes began to notice other traits that bothered her. Mercedes was a devoted animal lover and vegetarian, and Garbo did not measure up to her standards of interspecies relations:

> She had an appalling habit then of burning insects she found in the house or in the grass. She would burn ticks, spiders, daddy-long-legs and water bugs. The first time I saw her do this we were sitting on her lawn and she found a tick on her leg. It was trying to dig in and bury its head as they do. I saw her pick it off her leg, strike a match and burn it. My stomach turned over. "How can

> you take life so easily?" I asked. "These insects have just as much right to live as you have. Why don't you just carry them off to some other part of the grass? You don't have to kill them, much less torture them by burning. They probably have a large family waiting for them somewhere. Have you ever thought of that?" She bowed her head and said she never thought much about the insect world at all—but that now she would consider it and change her ways. Not long after this she telephoned me quite late one night to say that she had found a spider on her bed and had carefully picked it up and put it out the window. "Bravo," I said, "now you are learning not to be a murderer."[59]

Mercedes observed Garbo closely when she was working, and she saw that, like Duse, she was more of a medium than an actress. Though Garbo barely read the script of a film, she was able to draw the essence from it. Though she had never been to court in Sweden, or to a ball, she knew exactly how to act such a scene. She never went to see her rushes or to any previews.

Garbo was making *Mata Hari* at this time, and the film was released at the end of 1931. Mercedes thought the story poor. Mata Hari had been the mistress of Phil Lydig, Mercedes's brother-in-law, so she knew a lot about her. She could not have looked less like Garbo, and Ramon Novarro, playing opposite, was so small that his shoes had to be built up, which was all too apparent. Mercedes liked Garbo only in the execution scene: "In the long black cape with her hair brushed straight back and her face unrelieved, she never looked more beautiful or more stirringly dramatic."[60]

Soon after Garbo finished work on *Grand Hotel* in 1932, her bank failed and she lost all her savings. She had to make stringent economies while not alerting MGM to her financial straits, since she was negotiating a new contract and did not want to appear vulnerable. She moved into Mercedes's house during the filming of *As You Desire Me* (also 1932), possibly her finest film, and then left for New York and Sweden, the first of several well-publicized trips home. It was after she left that Mercedes became the friend of Marlene Dietrich, who bombarded her house with dozens of roses and carnations.

Mercedes may have enjoyed a perfect idyll with Garbo on the island in the Sierra Nevada, but throughout her life, however well she came to know Garbo, she never succeeded in being sure of where she stood with her—though she did acquire a good understanding of Garbo's character and her various dilemmas. "To know Greta," she wrote, "one must know the North. She may live the rest of her life in a Southern climate, but she will always be Nordic with all its sober and introvert characteristics. To know her one must know—*really know*—wind, rain, and dark brooding skies. She is of the elements—*actually* and *symbolically*. Forever, in this present incarnation, she will be a Viking's child—troubled by a dream of snow."[61]

Garbo and Cecil:
"I would do such things to you."

At the end of March 1932, while Garbo was living with Mercedes, Cecil Beaton was staying with the Gouldings in Hollywood. A few months earlier, Eddie Goulding had married Marjorie Moss, a dancer from New York who had accompanied Mercedes to California. John Gilbert, Garbo's costar and purported lover, was their best man. Cecil was aware that Garbo sometimes visited the Goulding house, and since he was obsessed with meeting and photographing her, he hoped she would come over during his stay. Indeed she telephoned, but, on hearing that Cecil was there, said she would not come: "No. He speaks to newspapers. I don't want to meet him."[62] Cecil was furious. He telephoned a friend who knew her, so that, if he could not meet the star, at least he could talk about her. Even in this he was thwarted. There was no reply, so he retreated upstairs to have a long, hot bath.

He dressed in a new white kid coat, snakeskin shorts, and white socks and shoes. Then he looked out of the window, and there to his surprise was Garbo, sitting cross-legged on a garden seat with the Gouldings, smoking a cigarette. She too was wearing white.

Cecil went down to try to telephone once more. Then he ambled into the drawing room, where he found Garbo and his hosts. He gasped, "Oh, sorry," and turned on his heels, but Marjorie called him back. He recalled later, "This time I walked across the drawing-room on air."[63]

Cecil described their meeting fully in his published diary *The Wandering Years.* He concocted the details from some rough pencil notes that he made at the time, and which survive among his papers. Of all their meetings, this is the most curious to unravel. He related how Garbo had turned the full barrage of her magnetic charm on him; how she complimented him on his youth and beauty, his white Indian shoes; how the Gouldings "hardly existed in the presence of their guests"; how he and Garbo "crab-walked with arms around each other's waists, and much friendly hand-squeezing." It was on this occasion that Garbo picked a yellow rose from a vase, held it high, and declared, "A rose that lives and dies and never again returns." There followed a scene worthy of Proust, Swann pressing Odette's rose to his lips and then locking it in a secret drawer of his desk. (Cecil took the rose, pressed it in his diary, took it home and framed it, and hung it over his bed. At the house sale held after his death a photographer from New Zealand bought the rose for what then seemed the exorbitant sum of £750.)

The party continued. The two couples ate, played charades, and drank Bellinis. Garbo accepted Cecil's invitation to go to his room and see photographs of his house in England. In his unpublished notes, Cecil claimed to have kissed her. He wrote that she said to him, "You are like a Grecian boy. If I were a young boy I would do such things to you."[64] Everyone stayed up until dawn. "The lights were turned out and our bacchanalia became wilder in the firelight."[65] As the sun rose, Garbo got into her large motorcar and departed. Cecil panicked about not seeing her again. "Then this is good-bye," he cried plaintively.

"Yes, I'm afraid so. C'est la vie!"[66]

Cecil concluded, "The Gouldings were rather too baffled by the evening to talk about it. I could hardly believe what had happened. The only concrete proof was the yellow rose that she had kissed."[67]

Whatever Cecil thought about this meeting, it is worth remembering Anita Loos's letter and her stories about rows between Garbo and Mercedes; how, very soon after this, Garbo left for New York without saying good-bye to Mercedes and then went to Sweden. But by the winter of 1933 Garbo and Mercedes were reunited, and Mercedes was writing to Cecil, whom she had met in New York in the late twenties and become friends with: "Greta told me yesterday that she had met you when you were out here last. You didn't tell me about it."[68]

Cecil Beaton, self-portrait with Anita Loos at San Simeon, 1931.

CHAPTER 2

CECIL

Getting On in Society

In 1971, David Bailey made a documentary film about Cecil Beaton called *Beaton by Bailey.* In one scene Truman Capote and Diana Vreeland, the editor of *Vogue,* are talking about him. Mrs. Vreeland says:

> Cecil is a character who's completely made himself because—from the beginning, I've known him all my life, he's a friend of a lifetime—he always wanted a very good life, and he realized there's only one very good life and that's the life that you know you want and you make it yourself. That's what he's done. Don't you think?

TRUMAN: Yes, well, he's a total self-creation . . .

D.V.: Mmm, total . . .

TRUMAN: And there are very few people in the world that are total self-creations and he certainly is one, because nothing in his background and nothing would in any way lead one to suppose that this person would emerge out of this cocoon of middle-class English life . . .

Cecil's grandfather Walter Hardy Beaton (1841–1904) made his way to London from the family home in Somerset and founded the firm of Beaton Brothers when he was very young. It imported wooden cross ties for railway tracks. He described himself as a timber merchant and agent. He had various businesses that did well, and he spent his latter days, portly and prosperous, in a splendid house in Abbots Langley, Hertfordshire, with many servants, including a gardener and a butler. When he died in 1904, he left the then-considerable fortune of £154,475 12s. 6d.

Cecil's father, Ernest Beaton, married Ettie Sisson, the good-looking daughter of a Cumberland blacksmith. He brought up his young family in Hampstead and was able to send the children to good schools, Cecil himself going to Harrow. But the timber business failed, particularly when steel and concrete took over and timber blocks were no longer used in road construction. The family, which had moved to Hyde Park Street in an hour of prosperity, was forced to retreat to Sussex Gardens, near Paddington Station.

Cecil himself was born in Hampstead in January 1904. He was the eldest of four. There was a brother, Reggie, who followed his father into the family business. He was a conventional young man who in 1933 committed suicide in a time of depression by throwing himself under a subway train. Cecil had two much younger sisters, of whom he was very fond. As they grew up he dressed them identically and took numerous photographs of them, which he often succeeded in selling to newspapers. Cecil hoped for good matches for them, and did his utmost to act like Svengali and Pygmalion combined. In due course Nancy married Sir Hugh Smiley, a baronet in the Grenadier Guards. The younger sister, Barbara, or "Baba," as she was known, married Alec Hambro, who served in the Second World War and died of wounds in Tripoli in 1943.

Cecil and his father had little in common, though they were both devotees of the stage. Ernest Beaton was a benign figure, a man of sound common sense and simple tastes, a stolid man. His favorite book was *Vanity Fair,* which he read thirty times. He took part in amateur theatricals and played forty-six seasons of cricket for Hampstead.

Cecil's early life was dominated by his adoration of his mother, whom he believed to be an important society lady. He was disappointed when he realized that she was no such thing, but he was determined to rectify the situation. He also loved his exotic aunt Jessie, his mother's elder sister, who had married a Bolivian diplomat. Here again Cecil rather exaggerated her importance. She was neither rich nor very glamorous, and her connection with court life was only a minor one. Nevertheless, she opened Cecil's eyes to a glittering world beyond the confines of Hampstead.

Cecil's first love—and his most enduring—was the theatre. He collected postcards of glamorous actresses and, inspired by theatrical photographs, began to experiment with a small Brownie box camera.

Cecil went to school at Heath Mount in Hampstead, where Evelyn Waugh, a lifelong enemy, delighted at sticking pins in him. He went on to a grim establishment, St. Cyprian's, where his colleagues included Cyril Connolly and George Orwell, the latter making the school notorious in his essay *Such, Such Were the Joys.* Cecil won the drawing prize in the Christmas term of 1916 and was commended for his designing of the *H.M.S. Pinafore* program. His thespian abilities received early recognition: "The 'Little Buttercup' of Beaton made it difficult to realise that it was Beaton and not a sister. His acting was absolutely natural and could not have been improved upon in any respect."[1] A year later his acting in *Mikado Minor* was likewise commended in the school magazine: "Beaton, as Nanki Poo, sang with sweetness and acted with feeling. His 'Tit-willow' was a pleasure to hear."[2]

Harrow proved more congenial to Cecil, and he passed his time engaged in amateur theatricals and painting in the art school. In 1922 he went up to St. John's College, Cambridge, where he did not distinguish himself academically but became a key figure in the acting world, taking part in the Cambridge Amateur Dramatic Company and the Marlowe Society and working hard designing sets. He established some advantageous friendships during this time, veering to the smart set of Trinity.

A major preoccupation during his Cambridge years was his cultivation of publicity. In those days publicity was frowned on. It was almost the case that a gentleman appeared in the newspapers on three occasions only—when he was born, when he married, and when he died. Surreptitiously, and haunted by the fear of discovery and the disgrace that would certainly follow, Cecil bombarded London newspapers with stories about himself. On several occasions he was nearly found out, but he lied to avoid exposure. He lost sleep over this, but no sooner had the immediate panic passed than he began to dream up new publicity schemes. He enjoyed acting, but the photographs in the papers were the key things.

By such methods he made his name. He realized that however talented anybody was, there was no hope of success unless the results of the work were seen. The more publicity a play received, the more people would wish to see it, and thus there would be more money and the sets and costumes could be more expensive. It was the same with photography. He was not always the inventor of the elaborate and at times exaggerated ideas for photographs in the early 1920s, but there is no doubt that he was the man who made a success of them. For example, it was Maurice Beck and Helen MacGregor who first posed their sitters reflected in the lid of a piano. It was Cecil who made the pose famous.

After coming down from Cambridge with a series of failed exams to his credit and, more important to him, having made a spectacular success in a Footlights production of *All the Vogue,* Cecil was a lost soul. He entered London social life with some energy, willing to participate in any dreary charity project if he felt it would advance him. Before long he was propelled into his father's dull office in Holborn, where he lasted but a week, and was then sent to the office of one of Mr. Beaton's partners, Mr. Schmiegelow.

Cecil was still busy trying to get on in society and spent his lunch hours going to publishers' offices in the hope of designing book jackets. This quest had some success. Then he managed to scrape together enough money to join two editors from *Vogue* on a trip to Venice, which opened his eyes to a world he would soon join. He watched Lady Diana Cooper on the Lido, spotted the fashion photographer Baron de Meyer, and managed to show his portfolio to Diaghilev. But nothing positive emerged, and Cecil returned home feeling guilty.

It was not until the end of 1926 that he broke into the world he had always sought. This came about principally due to a fortuitous meeting with the Adonis-like aesthete and Bright Young Thing Stephen Tennant. Cecil's manipulation of his own publicity meant that Stephen and his entourage knew exactly who he was and what he had achieved, and they welcomed him into their circle. He was, in a sense, a new toy. Soon every chic young lady in London wanted to be photographed by Cecil, and *Vogue* was happy to publish the results. Cecil capitalized on his success by staging various exhibitions. When he felt London had been conquered, he crossed the Atlantic to try his luck on the other side.

Mercedes first met Cecil Beaton in New York on December 13, 1928, at a party given by Muriel Draper* that consisted of "several Lesbians and arty young men."[3] Mercedes left with him, and two days later she took him to an exhibition of sculptures by her friend Malvina Hoffman. Cecil did not want to go:

> I didn't think I liked her very much & I had no desire to see an exhibition of sculpture by a woman friend of hers. But when I actually saw Mercedes de Acosta I was pleased & delighted & found her a very kind & clever friend & guide without any false show of affection & effusion. She is a friendly creature, & she gave me my first glimpse of the Grand Central Station & I was amazed!

Cecil did not enjoy the exhibition: "Most of the work was excruciatingly bad but there were two lovely negro heads in bronze which were beautifully designed." Mercedes took Cecil home and surprised him greatly by revealing that Osbert Sitwell was a homosexual. By the end of tea, Cecil wrote, "Mercedes was charming, talking jerkily in a hollow voice. She is very mannish but charming, kind, clever & interesting & I know she will be one of my greatest friends in New York."[4]

So it proved, for the following night, she invited Cecil to join her at a talk by Muriel Draper, and he then invited her back to see his work:

> It was a lovely evening & Mercedes delighted me by being so wildly enthusiastic. For her earnestness & enthusiasm I admire her terrifically. And I was delighted that she liked some of my work

*Muriel Draper, née Sanders (d. 1952), hostess and interior decorator. In her heyday she entertained Chaliapin, Henry James, Stravinsky, and Diaghilev. Years later she was accused by Senator McCarthy of being "pink." Ostracism followed. She was the sister-in-law of the monologist Ruth Draper and the mother of the dancer and artist Paul Draper. She published her memoirs, *Music at Midnight*, in 1929.

> so much. Her criticisms were very apt. . . . She is charming & birdlike & vividly quick. She doesn't mind contradicting me flat. She never curries favour. She is very like a child. After I had shown her photographs & little paintings we sat down to smoke & talk & the clock ticked on for hours, I learning so much about Mercedes. She has glorious enthusiasms, glorious friendships & I like her so much for not being afraid of saying "Oh yes he wrote me a perfect, a lovely letter saying I was his friend, he'd never been so happy with anyone before. He felt he could trust & confide in me, that I gave him more happiness & security than anyone he had met." She talked superhumanly, enthusiastically about her work & a play which may be coming on soon which she thinks is a very wonderful play & with which she had had bad luck because it was written for Duse "whom I adored more than any human person & Duse was crazy about it & just as she was about to do it she died & I put it away & wouldn't let anybody else have it." But now it appears she has found the right person & the play, the first to deal with the Mother of Christ after the Crucifixion, will either be a terrible failure or a triumphant success. This funny, thin, hawklike little woman stayed talking in quick starts & jerks until very late. We were both worn with exhaustion & although I was in no hurry for her to go, I was very happy to be able to sink into bed, to stretch one's limbs out full & relax.[5]

In Mercedes's account, Cecil was then "extremely slender and willowy . . . this resemblance to a swaying reed or willow tree gave an impression of fragility. . . . Cecil and several other young men carried this vogue almost to the point of an art."[6] Mercedes was to remain a lifelong friend of Cecil's and judged him thus:

> Little by little he has expressed a diversity of talents unique in one person. He possesses that rare combination of creativeness and artistic sense which also includes the daily living of his life. In physical appearance he has become more distinguished and handsome and in time I believe his books, paintings, and photography will be considered as some of the most sensitive expressions of our age.[7]

This first trip to New York resulted in a good contract with Condé Nast, many new sitters, and many meetings with the luminaries of the day. Cecil's gimmicks were a great success. The ladies could not wait to lie on the floor while Cecil perched on a ladder to take their pictures.

Cecil was then preparing his *Book of Beauty*. Thus, in the winter of 1929 he went back to the United States in search of suitably famous beauties to photograph. This time he went to Hollywood, declaring that above all he was determined to put Garbo in his book: "Oh, she's going in regardless of her measurements. She has personality, and she has perfect lines, aside from academic beauty."[8]

Anita Loos accompanied Cecil to California and gave him his first introductions. He soon found his feet and was busily photographing stars such as Mary Astor, Fay Wray, Kay Francis, Gary Cooper, and Dolores Del Rio. But Garbo was nowhere to be seen, and he became obsessed with snaring her:

> She is the only person with glamour. She is flattered and pleased that she is an amazing success but she does not want to meet her fans. Women send her orchids every day, men telephone on long distance calls to try and hear her voice. She is so casual and dreamy. She doesn't give a damn and the fact that she doesn't give a damn and will not come out of hiding only increases the frenzy and as with me they are almost driven insane with desire to see her and incidentally she gets more publicity in this way than if she were at everyone's beck and call.[9]

Cecil had made friends with the former child star and musical-comedy actress Elsie Janis and enlisted her help in telephoning Garbo's home. A very foreign voice answered and informed them, "Mees Garboh awaye for weekend."[10] Cecil then beseeched the famous director of publicity at MGM, Howard Strickling, to arrange a meeting. He reached Garbo on the telephone and relayed Cecil's message. "Oh I don't know about it. Oh well," was the unpromising reply.

During Cecil's last week in Hollywood there appeared to be a chance, but hopes were finally dashed, as he noted in his diary:

> I at last got through to Strickling and, after having my hopes raised so high yesterday in answer to my "What about getting Garbo?" there was the deadly "Not a chance." Hell. Damn. Blast

> the bitch. I almost wept with fury, exhaustion, pique. Hell . . . She's got nothing else to do.[11]

Cecil left Hollywood in January 1930 a disappointed man. Soon after this, in Palm Beach, he ran into Mercedes. Cecil enjoyed gossiping with her about "the dreary crowd of New York Lesbians & we made fun of their boring loyalty to one another, their earnestness, squalour, poverty & complete lack of humour. Mercedes . . . could not be less like her outrageous appearance which is formidable in the extreme."[12] More important, Mercedes, although she had not yet had her fateful meeting with Garbo, furnished him with some extraordinary tales about the elusive star:

> Mercedes was charming, intelligent & could not have been more amusing & witty. I related stories of Hollywood & she told me a great deal about Garbo which thrilled me so much that I felt like taking the train to Hollywood once more just to see her. When still only a child in Sweden Maurice Stiller took her up, gave her books to read, educated her, fell in love with her & she became his mistress & adored him. He was already quite fifty years old & stood for glamour, intelligence, all that was intellectually stimulating in life. He took her to Hollywood. She had an affair with John Gilbert. It was the first time she had come into contact with anyone young. Stiller was furious that she should fall for anyone so half-witted as Gilbert & leave his household. He left Hollywood, he died, & Garbo almost killed herself from remorse & grief. She never looks in the mirror. She is like a boy, takes long strides. The only time that she became noisy with excitement was when the tailor sent her a new pair of riding breeches made with flybuttons. She rushed about unbuttoning them & buttoning them up again, showing them to every body. She is very silent. She talks little. She isn't so far a Lesbian but might easily be one. Well, that was Mercedes' story gleaned from a great friend of Garbo's.
>
> Later in the day Rosamond* told me a different version. She was what men call an ideal woman, supremely intelligent, lovely, rivetted with sex appeal, the perfect lover. She is supposed to kiss

*Rosamond Pinchot (1904–38), American actress and beauty who committed suicide.

better than anyone. She has a long line of lovers the whole time. Her eyelashes are the longest there have ever been. Rosamond said the spontaneity & exquisite precision of her performance in *Joyless Street* was the most lovely acting she has ever seen on the screen.[13]

Back in England, a period of financial security followed for Cecil. He found a mysterious, deserted house, Ashcombe, lost in the Wiltshire downs, and secured a fifteen-year lease. The derelict building, secluded and almost impossible to find, sat proudly on top of a hill with a winding valley stretching ahead of it. Unique for such a site, the back of the house was at the foot of a horseshoe of hills. Cecil promptly set about converting it into an enchanted domain.

In 1930 Cecil had an exhibition at the Cooling Galleries, and he published *The Book of Beauty.* Though he had failed to secure a photograph of Garbo, she was included in a sketch, and he wrote:

MISS GRETA GARBO

A few years ago a pouting, sullen blonde could always be seen having lunch by herself in a film company's cafeteria in Hollywood. She could hardly speak a word of English, she hated nearly everybody, she was thoroughly miserable and looked it. She had only lately arrived in Hollywood and possessed two dresses, two hats, one set of underclothes and no friend. Her name was Greta Gustaffson [*sic*]—Garbo for short. She was often by herself and lonely, she came from Sweden and, like many Swedes, was of an almost albino blondness with pale eyelashes; her hair was tousled, she showed no signs of being *soignée,* but she photographed well and the company would use her for publicity pictures, posing in grotesque situations and clothes, and absurd animals belonging to the property man's paraphernalia would come in useful to make a "stunning" caption. In the photographs this young woman possessed a rare, eerie quality, and soon she improved her appearance a hundredfold by painting her face in a very definite and unusual, though to her very becoming, way, with the eyelids blackened heavily and the brows plucked in the shape of a butterfly's antennae. She looked like some pale being that belongs beneath the water, some ephemeral sprite or naiad to be seen for one fleeting glimpse in a greenish, unearthly light, with flowing, waving hair, holding cornucopias of shiny shells. To-day this young woman—The Garbo, as she is known—is the most glamorous figure in the whole world; there is no one with a more magnetic, romantic or exotic personality, there never has been a film star with so wide an appeal. . . . Greta Garbo is Queen of Hollywood, her salary is fabulous, her word law. She has pointed features in a round face, her mouth is wide and knife-like. Her teeth are large and square and like evenly matched pearls; her eyes are pale, with lashes so long that when she lowers her lids they strike her cheeks; her complexion is of an unearthly whiteness and so delicate that she looks to have one layer of skin less than other people, and the suspicion of a frown is sooner perceptible. Her sinuous movements are panther-like, mermaid-like, and though she is tall, with massive arms, hands and legs, she is an ethereal wraith. How mysteriously beautiful she was as the pale orphan in her first big role in the German film *Joyless Street.* Surely there never has been such beauty before. She was like a rare, white convolvulus, and her acting was so simple and poignantly touching that one wondered why no other actress had been able to act like that before; her smile seemed so spontaneous and candid that it looked easy to smile like that.

Hollywood then claimed her and discovered that she could be the world's most voluptuous lover, that she could kiss better than anyone else, and possessed more sex appeal. . . . She appeared in such films as *The Flesh and the Devil, The Temptress, Love, The Kiss, A Woman of Affairs, The Mysterious Lady.* The young officer, in Ruritanian uniform and wearing gloves, would bow formally and kiss her hand; they would look at one another with half-shut eyes, half-opened mouths and trembling nostrils; and this would lead to close-ups of smouldering embraces. . . .

Her whole film career is but a passing phase in her existence, which one feels began and will end with time itself. With her slightly insane look, eyes that are thinking strange thoughts, and weary smile, she is Leonardo's Gioconda, a clairvoyant who, possessed of a secret wisdom, knows and sees all.[14]

"I'm really much more fond of men."

Cecil Beaton's sex life began with a comradely friendship with Edward ("Boy") Le Bas at Harrow. Cecil later confessed that he was effeminate at school and had worn powder and lipstick. He told Garbo that his father was so angry when he caught him made up that he locked him in his room for a whole day. After leaving Harrow, Cecil met Kyrle Leng. This was to be another of Cecil's many doomed friendships, since Leng had already met his lifelong companion, Robert Gathorne-Hardy.

Cecil had various sexual experiences at Cambridge, particularly when acting in plays. He was the object of considerable attention from a tall rowing man named Ben Thomas, who went on to occupy the respectable position of Controller of the Central Office of Information. There were the inevitable riotous undergraduate parties, described in detail by Cecil, who in the sobriety of the dawn would consign to the pages of his diaries every aspect of the previous evening's bacchanalia. Most of the other undergraduates who thus indulged themselves went on to enjoy heterosexual lives, marrying glamorous, sometimes predictable, wives and having affairs with the ladies of the day.

In his diaries Cecil mused on the subject of his own sexuality. He hated to accept his homosexuality, but equally he was appalled at the idea of having any physical relationship with a woman. In October 1923 he wrote:

> My attitude to women is this—I adore to dance with them and take them to theatres and private views and talk about dresses and plays and women, but I'm really much more fond of men. My friendships with men are much more wonderful than with women. I've never been in love with women and I don't think I ever shall be in the way that I have been in love with men. I'm really a terrible, terrible homosexualist and try so hard not to be.

> I try so terribly hard to be good and not cheap and horrid . . . it's so much nicer just to be affectionate and ordinary and sleep in the same bed but that's all. Everything else is repulsive to me and yet it's awfully difficult.[15]

Cecil's inherent shyness and confusion over all this was well illustrated when, in December 1966, he considered the effects of the Wolfenden Report and legislation in Parliament that advocated some freedom to consenting homosexuals over the age of twenty-one:

> Of recent years the tolerance towards the subject has made a nonsense of many of the prejudices from which I myself suffered acutely as a young man. Even now I can only vaguely realize that it was only comparatively late in life that I would go into a room full of people without a feeling of guilt. To go into a room full of men, or to a lavatory in the Savoy, needed quite an effort. With success in my work this situation became easier. But when one realizes what damage, what tragedy has been brought on by this lack of sympathy to a very delicate and difficult subject, this should be a great time of celebration. . . . For myself, I am grateful. Selfishly I wish that this marvellous step forward could have been taken at an earlier age. It is not that I would have wished to avail myself of further licence, but to feel that one was not a felon and an outcast could have helped enormously during the difficult young years.[16]

It was in America that Cecil experienced his first tentative relationship with a woman. In December 1929, during his second visit to New York, Cecil noted in his diary, "I had had a very momentous week. I'd hardly slept at all and for the first time I had been to bed with a woman. With one on Wednesday and another, a longer and more serious affair, on Friday." Evidently he had told his friend Marjorie Oelrichs, a Newport socialite and later the wife of bandleader Eddy Duchin, that he had never been to bed with a woman, and the generous-spirited girl offered to initiate him. Adele Astaire, Fred's sister and dancing partner, then took the torch and invited him to her bed, being surprised only at his modesty. As Cecil approached, he held a towel chastely in front of his person. Leaving for Hollywood a few days later, Cecil was seen off at the station by Adele, who gave him a gold pencil as a souvenir of his endeavors.

Cecil remained friends with both women, deeply mourning Marge when she died in childbirth in 1937 and staying in touch with Adele (later Lady Charles Cavendish) until his death. Adele appealed to him in many ways, not least in her outspoken manner of talking. "It gives me pain where I should have pleasure" was one of her noted lines.[17]

The heterosexual initiation was not to lead to much. The dress designer Charles James was one of the first to accuse Cecil of pretending to be part of the heterosexual world. Cecil wrote that he found himself making rude remarks about "fairies" because "they frighten and nauseate me and I see so vividly myself shadowed in so many of them and it only needs such a little grip and dash to get oneself out of that sad and ridiculous predicament."[18] Yet but a few days later he was to be found "undermining" a virile black boxer named Jimmy, and when he returned to London, he fell victim to one of the most important love affairs of his life—with Peter Watson.

Cecil met Peter Watson in Vienna in 1930. In the course of a summer holiday that led them to Venice, Cecil discovered that Watson had become the lover of the designer and decorator Oliver Messel, from then on a lifelong rival, and he resolved to win him over. Thus he entered a four-year period of deep frustration, a mixture of elation and intense despair, that ultimately came to nothing and during which he had his first encounter with Garbo.

Peter Watson was a difficult, complex character, much admired by later generations for his haunting good looks but equally for his inspired patronage of the arts. When Cecil met Watson, the latter had just inherited a considerable fortune and was spending it on frivolous items such as Rolls-Royces and smart suits. While Watson and Cecil traveled extensively together, Watson behaved in a cruel manner to his soppy admirer, allowing him proximity on a don't-touch basis. The long extracts in Cecil's diaries make painful reading, as he made every mistake possible for an aspirant lover to a detached, relatively flattered, but ultimately disinterested friend. Deeper and deeper into the abyss did Cecil fall until he sank to that state of love so well described by Stendhal as one of "the final torment: utter despair poisoned still further by a shred of hope."[19]

At one point in their tortured relationship, Peter Watson suggested to Cecil that he should take a lover. Cecil did so in another excursion into heterosexual territory with the glamorous Viscountess Castlerosse, who in her naughty innocence loved him very much and duly seduced him in a room full of tuberoses at Faringdon, the eccentric Oxfordshire home of the eccentric musical peer Lord Berners. Bemused guests in that house where anything went climbed upstairs to listen outside the door. "Oh! goody, goody, goody,"[20] came Cecil's elated cry from the sanctity of Doris's room. Doris coaxed him in amatory matters, urging him to think of his sister's wedding during lovemaking in order to slow down. This affair amused London society very much, and one night Lord Castlerosse was dining in a restaurant when he spied Cecil entering with his estranged wife. "I never knew Doris was a lesbian,"[21] he said.

Another woman with whom Cecil went to bed was Lilia Ralli, the Greek childhood friend of Princess Olga (Princess Paul of Yugoslavia) and her sister, the Duchess of Kent. She too loved him dearly, and they were lifelong, intimate friends. This romance also boosted his career, since it led him to photograph the Kents, then Princess Olga, and soon afterward Queen Elizabeth (the Queen Mother).

During these years Cecil sometimes boasted of other conquests. He spoke of having had an affair with Gary Cooper in Hollywood, which could have been true, and certainly over the years he indulged in many sexual encounters of a most forgettable kind as a way of giving satisfaction to a passing sex urge. There are those who talk of having accompanied him to orgies or to Turkish baths, and he was certainly freer in such exploits abroad than in London, where he was an increasingly well known and thus vulnerable figure.

During the war there occurred another memorable heterosexual coupling. Sir John Gielgud, discussing Cecil's sexual habits, announced, "An actress friend of mine said Cecil was the best lay she ever had."[22] Coral Browne certainly liked to talk of Cecil's enthusiasm and said that he was commissioned to photograph her and to her considerable surprise pounced on her in the dressing room of her theatre.* When the stories of Cecil's affair with Garbo emerged in his diaries, Coral said, "Everyone in Hollywood was laughing about it. It was a trip down memory lane so far as I was concerned."[23] This affair was more complicated than it need have been, since Maud Nelson, Cecil's lesbian secretary, took too keen an interest in it and spread stories about it that caused Coral Browne more than a little trouble with the man with whom she was then living. Evidently there was almost a suicide. (At one time Coral Browne considered making this the subject of a drama along the lines of her successful rendering of the Guy Burgess spy saga, *An Englishman Abroad.*)

Many of Cecil's friends took the line that he would have had no idea what to do with a woman. Even today his detractors and some of the homosexual community with whom he associated refuse to believe it. Yet many of those who knew him well attest to his involvement, and there is evidence that, in a curious way, he had more success with women than with men.

*Coral Browne (1913–91), a much-loved actress noted for her outspoken wit. She once bet an actor friend £1 that she could get a response from an evidently homosexual youth she fancied. The next day she called out, "I owe you twelve and six."

"In the presence of this mystery . . ."

Cecil was a youthful twenty-eight when he finally met Garbo at the Gouldings' that curious night in Hollywood in 1932. Garbo was a year and a half his junior. He succeeded in remaining silent for a time about their encounter, but then, in the summer of 1934, he published some profiles of film stars in *The Sketch,* one of which was about her. Cecil began his piece with one of those disclaimers that all Garbo's friends used before writing about her: "Since her distaste for publicity about her private existence is so great, for fear of offending her susceptibilities, I shall curb my pen. But surely she will not mind if I tell you what she looks like off the screen . . ."[24] This profile was reproduced more or less identically in *Cecil Beaton's Scrapbook* in 1937. Since it is now hard to find, since it is perceptive, and since it was to be the belated cause of a major row between Cecil and Garbo, it is worth reproducing in full:

GARBO

> She is as beautiful as the aurora borealis, but to compare Greta Garbo on and off screen is to compare de Laszlo with Leonardo. The personality the public sees is magnetic, gay, tragic, sensitive and wise; but other actresses appear magnetic and sensitive, until the projector stops, and the illusion created by the director and his *aides* is dispelled. Only Garbo, when the properties are back in the back, puts on nobility with her mackintosh. In real life she possesses such a wealth of qualities, which the screen is technically incapable of reproducing, that, even if she had not the most beautiful face of our time, yet all other modern beauty would be ephemeral beside hers.
>
> Her skin is smooth as marble, generally burnt lightly to an apricot honey colour; her hair is biscuit coloured and of the finest spun silk and clean and sweetly smelling as a baby's after its bath;

her nose is so delicate and sensitive that she seems to be conscious of perfumes too subtle for others to enjoy—the perfumes perhaps of her own beauty; her teeth are large and more glistening than pearls; her generous mouth is more delicately controlled than it seems in photographs; as for her eyes, there have never been such before; in expression so quizzical, compassionate and languorous, so deep-set and of such unforgettable blue; they have large, dark irises, and boast lashes so long that it is impossible to believe that they are real, for only a few children have such a poetic growth. She has the tragic quality of a child.

Lipstick and nail varnish are put to shame by her; she uses no make-up save a dark line like a symbol on her eyelids—a symbol of no period or fashion, original to our civilisation, a symbol which only instinct created and yet which the world has copied. She is like a Debureau, pale, forlorn, ethereal, or fecklessly gay. Her hands, though she calls them kitchenette hands, are long and strong with square-ended fingers; she inhales cigarettes proudly, two fingers held high. Indeed she makes great use of her hands, and, inborn actress as she is, accompanies all her speech with gesture and mime. Tall, she is proportioned to scale, and her feet are long and slender as in Hellenic sculpture; she is agile and supple, even a gymnast. Her clothes, which are never of the feminine fluffy kind (in fact, she possesses no evening dress), have real elegance. She buys them from the local Army and Navy store, where workmen, sailors, and the like come for overalls and sweat shirts.

And yet all these qualities might be found in beauties who are not Garbo. The magic which intrigues and baffles the imaginative is not trapped and docketed. Her most inveterate worshippers despair of analysing her allure. In a quick turn of the head, in a frank look, in a boyish pout, in that proud glance from lowered lids, so pitying and yet so distant that in others it would be supercilious, in all those expressions of conscious beauty, which when imitated become clumsy, or arrogant, or ridiculous, there is a manifestation of what Hollywood cannot destroy. In the presence of this mystery all that is second-rate can be forgotten.

She despises the level of the films in which she has to appear. The dialogue deadens her and she grumbles at having to portray the symbol of sex. She would like to play romantic parts, St. Joan, or Hamlet, or L'Aiglon, and her secret ambition is to be a Dorian Gray. She would wish to play with actors who had some spark of originality or inspiration, but the director shows her the receipts for "Mata Hari" and each ensuing film, and from his point of view there is no reason to alter the policy and so after a half-hearted skirmish she grudgingly submits.

She has a sense of humour, a sense of fun, but she is unhappy, neurasthenic, morbid, for she has become, by accident, in spite of herself, something she never wished to be. A healthy peasant girl has been publicised as an exotic spy. She must lose weight, not even touch carrots—so that not only her health but her nerves have suffered from the worries of publicity. If she is seen hurrying down a side alley, she is chased for a story, and this perpetual hunting so haunts her that, being highly strung, she starts to cry and will lock herself away from even the maid for days on end. She is even too nervous to read.

For these reasons she cannot develop as a person. It is well and good to safeguard herself against the bad influences of Hollywood life, but Garbo has now become unreceptive to anything except herself, so that even when she takes her periodical holidays they are not experiences for her. She is not interested in anything or anybody in particular, and she has become as difficult as an invalid and as selfish, quite unprepared to put herself out for anyone; she would be a trying companion, continuously sighing and full of tragic regrets; she is superstitious, suspicious and does not know the meaning of Friendship; she is incapable of love.

She believed in the part of Queen Christina and was roused from the apathy with the result that we saw Garbo, not as a phantom, but as a real and noble character. During the years that followed we began to wonder why this enigma with her romantic ideas and spiritual thoughts had made no further effort to break the fetters she professed to despise. Then came "La Dame aux Camellias." Her performance as Marguerite instilled humour and vitality into a flyblown romance. It was the inevitable formula for another Garbo film, but out of it all, unexpectedly, came this astonishing performance. Every shade of emotion was present in her characterization; the gaiety of the earlier scenes was not the old aloof gaiety; Garbo had become a loving, suffering, human being. When she was dying, she had the appearance not merely of being ill, but of having lain in bed for months; in her weakness she could not smile, but retained the pride of a Bernini statue. At moments she seemed to take on herself the wisdom of Lilith, and it was because of these moments that afterwards we wondered whether she had been acting with real understanding or by instinct alone. If she is capable of such creation, she should be appearing on her own account in the roles which she alone can play. But perhaps her magic is only a freak of nature which leads our imagination to make of her an ideal she can never be.[25]

Marlene Dietrich, photographed by Beaton, 1932.

CHAPTER 3

DIETRICH: "SHE HAS SEX, BUT NO PARTICULAR GENDER."

Garbo's career was at its height between 1932 and 1941. Thereafter the long years of retreat from the world began, and she never made another film. As early as 1932 Garbo had formed her image, and it did not change much in later years. In a rare interview she said:

> I have been like a ship without a rudder—bewildered, lost and very lonely. I am awkward, shy, afraid, nervous and self-conscious about my English. That is why I built a wall of repression about myself and live behind it.
>
> A film-star's career is a full-time job and I am in deadly earnest when I say that.[1]

Garbo's films of 1932 were *Grand Hotel* and *As You Desire Me.* No sooner was Garbo free of them than she disappeared to Sweden for eight months. This was shortly after the encounter with Cecil at the Gouldings' and during the period when she and Mercedes were having a lovers' quarrel. Reporters tracked Garbo down at a hideout an hour from Stockholm, where she was staying in a luxurious villa, cradled by trees overlooking a lake. Here she enjoyed the traditional Garbo pursuits of long walks, rowing on the lake (her eyes sheltered by a tennis visor), and eating porridge, boiled eggs, bread and butter, coffee, and filibunke (thick sour cream). After her trip an interview was published with a journalist, Julia Svenson. Garbo said:

> Many people have said that I am stuck-up and unapproachable, because I haven't "gone Hollywood," because I do not mingle much with the movie colony. That is not true at all. The reason why I keep to myself is that I must recuperate from hard work and gather new strength to be able to keep going. It is absolutely true that I find much more pleasure in reading an exciting book than in going to parties. All my real friends know that. And when one has a good radio with which one can travel all over the world in one's imagination, then one can be satisfied with life. It has always been my great desire to live in peace by myself. You know, even a film star may have problems, perhaps not material ones, but—haven't we, too, a soul?
>
> Do you know, I have never enjoyed anything so much as these few months in Stockholm. It has been wonderful. One night I went to the Salvation Army. I should love to play in a moving picture where I would be a Salvation Army lass. I believe there are many themes that a good scenario writer could find in a manuscript of that type, don't you? One day I also went to the Riksdag to listen to a debate. That, too, was interesting, even if one could not use it for a movie. I have been to many lectures. I was happy that nobody recognised me. If they had, I could not have gotten anything out of an evening spent that way.
>
> I am supremely happy—mostly because I feel so well as I do now. Never have I felt so strong.[2]

Mercedes had pursued Garbo to New York in July 1932 and had returned empty-handed to Hollywood when Garbo sailed to Sweden. Thus she was left to her own devices during Garbo's eight-month absence, though she later claimed that her power to engage in psychic experiences had enabled her to "project" herself into Garbo's room in Sweden, while remaining physically in the United States.

Mercedes noted in her autobiography, "After she left, Hollywood seemed empty to me."[3] Not for long, however. While Cecil was still in Hollywood, he invited Mercedes to join him one evening to see a performance by the celebrated German dancer Harald Kreutzberg. Mercedes was not feeling well, so did not dress up. Even so, she created a striking appearance in white slacks, white turtleneck sweater, and white topcoat. As she and Cecil took their seats, Mercedes noticed a striking blond woman in front of them, who looked at her shyly. It was Marlene Dietrich.

Dietrich had been in Hollywood for two years by this time. She was thirty-one years old and just at the beginning of her great fame. The Viennese director Josef von Sternberg had recognized her raw sexuality and seductiveness and had cast her as the alluring Lola Lola in *The Blue Angel* in Berlin in 1930. Sternberg had transformed her from a rather brawny girl into a creature of glamour. He saw the conflict within her: "Her personality was one of extreme sophistication and of an almost childish simplicity," he once commented.

Despite her success in *The Blue Angel,* UFA did not renew her contract in Germany, so Dietrich signed with Paramount and emigrated to Hollywood. She made *Morocco,* which was the first of what would be a string of celebrated collaborations with Sternberg in America. Dietrich played a cabaret star in love with a French Legionnaire (Gary Cooper). Probably the most famous scene in the movie is one set in a cabaret where, dressed as a man, she plants an unchaste kiss on a girl's mouth. The film brought massive fame and adulation, which made it possible for Dietrich to endure the virtual martyrdom inflicted on her by Sternberg's precise, relentless direction. *Dishonored* followed. In it she played an Austrian spy who fixes her makeup in the reflection of an officer's saber and applies her lipstick while a German officer rants at her. The firing squad then shoots her dead. She was described as "a vamp with brains and humour"[4] and paid $80,000.

A few years ago, Dietrich's association with Sternberg was the subject of an analytic study, *In the Realm of Pleasure,* which discussed the "masochistic aesthetic." The author, Gaylyn Studlar, concluded, "Dietrich is frequently mentioned as an actress whose screen presence raises questions about women's representation in Hollywood cinema. She has also acquired her own cult following of male and female, straight and gay admirers. The diverse nature of this group suggests that many possible paths of pleasure can be charted across Dietrich as a signifying star image and across von Sternberg's films as star vehicles."[5]

Marlene herself was outspoken on the subject of sex. She told the writer Budd Schulberg, "In Europe it doesn't matter if you're a man or a woman. We make love with anyone we find attractive."[6] Kenneth Tynan pursued this theme in a celebrated profile of the star: "She has sex, but no particular gender. Her ways are mannish: the characters she played loved power and wore slacks, and they never had headaches or hysterics. They were also quite undomesticated. Dietrich's masculinity appeals to women, and her sexuality to men."[7]

The day after her first sighting of Dietrich, Mercedes was working quietly at home when her maid came into the room bearing a large bunch of white roses and announced that Marlene Dietrich was in the hall. Mystified, Mercedes went down to see if it was really she. The same shy look greeted her. Mercedes put out her hand and Dietrich took it "and in an almost military manner* bent over it and firmly shook it."[8] Dietrich told Mercedes that since seeing her the night before she had wanted to meet her, that she knew few people in Hollywood and had brought her the flowers—"white flowers because you looked like a white prince last night."[9] Mercedes thanked her and said she was delighted to have this chance to talk about the two films she had so much enjoyed.

"Oh, let's not talk about pictures," said Dietrich. "I would like to tell you something if you won't think I am mad. I would like to suggest

*In the original version of her memoir, Mercedes wrote, "rather a German manner."

something." Dietrich thought Mercedes was too thin and white, and that she looked ill. Dietrich also thought Mercedes sad. "I am sad, too. I am sad and lonely. It is not easy to adjust oneself to a new country. You are the first person here to whom I have felt drawn. Unconventional as it may seem, I came to see you because I just could not help myself."[10] Soon Dietrich was offering to cook for Mercedes.

Dietrich bombarded Mercedes with flowers. The story goes that first she sent tulips, which Mercedes rejected as being too phallic. Then she sent dozens of roses or carnations, sometimes twice a day. Once she had ten dozen rare orchids flown in from San Francisco. Mercedes would return home from the studio to find her maids "wringing their hands in despair," unable to find enough vases. "I was walking on flowers, falling on flowers, and sleeping on flowers," wrote Mercedes. "I finally wept, flew into a rage, and sent Anna [her maid] off to the hospital with every damn flower in the house."[11]

Mercedes complained to Dietrich, threatening to throw her into her own pool if she sent another flower. Dietrich was hurt but then conceived the ingenious idea of sending Lalique vases and other gifts instead. Box upon box arrived from Bullock's Wilshire containing dressing gowns, scarves, pajamas, slacks, sweaters, lamps, and lampshades. All these were duly returned to the store. Again Dietrich was crestfallen, but in the end the matter was resolved in laughter. And thus Dietrich and Mercedes became friends.

Despite seeing her almost every day, Dietrich sent more than thirty letters and fifteen telegrams to Mercedes, documenting a love affair that raged between September 1932 and May 1933, when Dietrich went to Europe for the summer.* Her first telegram, on September 15, declared that her room was a white dream, and that now that she knew Mercedes, Hollywood would be hard to leave.[12] The next day they were in each other's arms for the first time. When Dietrich was dropped off at her house by Mercedes, she jumped hurriedly out of the car, fearing that her infant daughter, Maria, might see Mercedes and wonder where her

*Marlene Dietrich's letters to Mercedes are at the Rosenbach Museum in Philadelphia. They were sealed until Dietrich's death in May 1992, but thereafter the Rosenbach allowed me to examine them.

mother had been all afternoon. Dietrich said that she hoped Maria would learn to love Mercedes as Dietrich loved her.[13]

A few days later Dietrich wrote once more, this time in her particularly idiosyncratic French. Dietrich declared that she had been on the point of leaving Hollywood but would now stay on. She would live with the hope that she could see Mercedes from time to time—to see her eyes, or her hands, which she now adored. She told her that the moment Mercedes tired of her, she would descend into her tomb without inconveniencing her with the shedding of a single tear. She signed off with much metaphorical kissing of hands and thanks for the happiness that Mercedes had given her.[14]

Mercedes complained of Dietrich's assertions that their love would last "always": "Don't say 'always,' for in love it is blasphemy. One never knows if from now on one truly loves or if one is making oaths and one simply forgets them. Don't say always, for in love nothing binds you."[15]

In October, Dietrich bought Mercedes some buttons and sent them to her with a letter, which ended with the bestowal of a kiss on Mercedes's hands—and on her lips, which had changed, she said, since they had met hers.[16] In November, Dietrich sent Mercedes a dressing gown and some handkerchiefs from the men's department of Bullock's. Watches, hair ointment, cakes, and other tempting presents arrived. Mercedes and Dietrich were often together. One afternoon Dietrich sent Mercedes a note saying that Sternberg had arrived and needed to see her that night. She had no choice but to tell him that she would remain at home, since it had to be something important. She apologized for not joining Mercedes for dinner, but assured her that she would be with her by nine-thirty or ten o'clock. She asked Mercedes to dine alone and then wait for her in bed. She would not delay a moment longer than necessary.[17]

During these months Dietrich was living at 321 Ocean Front Avenue, Santa Monica. There were swimming parties with two actor friends, Martin Kosleck* and Hans von Twardowski,** and young Maria. Mer-

*Martin Kosleck (b. 1907), Pomeranian character actor, who played Goebbels in more than one film.

**Hans von Twardowski was married to Mercedes's friend Eleanora von Mendelssohn.

cedes noted: "On the whole we had very happy times at the beach house."[18] Mercedes called Dietrich her "Golden One." Some time later Mercedes wrote a small billet-doux to her:

> For Marlene,
> Your face is lit by moonlight
> breaking through your skin
> soft, pale, radiant.
> No suntan for you glow
> For you are the essence of
> the stars and the moon and
> the mystery of the night.[19]

It was entirely in keeping with the path Mercedes was taking through life that almost simultaneously she should absorb the time of two of the greatest stars of the age. Garbo and Dietrich were often compared; the conclusion was invariably the same—that Garbo won hands down. "Dietrich was a pro, but Garbo was an artist"[20] was the verdict of the writer Francis Wyndham, the man who helped Mercedes have her memoirs published in England in 1960. In the 1930s both Garbo and Dietrich were deemed to "epitomize the glamour of sin."[21]

Mercedes's personal life seems to have been quite extraordinary, but she was having some trouble with her job at MGM. This occurred because she refused to let Irving Thalberg falsify the film version of the story of Rasputin. Her main point was that Princess Irene Yusupov, wife of Prince Felix Yusupov, who murdered Rasputin, never met the "Mad Monk," and therefore a scene in which Rasputin seduced the princess was offensive and unhistorical. She went so far as to seek Prince Yusupov's permission to tell the real story, since he had told it to her privately. This was given, but the prince made it clear that if his wife was depicted in the film, he would sue the company. Mercedes warned Thalberg of the consequences, but he angrily maintained that she had overstepped her brief by consulting the prince. She said she had probably saved him a lawsuit and that in any case friendship was more important than the industry. Thalberg tore up her contract, and she was out of a job.

Dietrich comforted Mercedes during the difficult months that followed. She sent her money and brushed aside Mercedes's attempts to repay it. Sometimes Mercedes went to Paramount to watch her filming Sternberg's *The Scarlet Empress,* in which she played Catherine the Great. She was present when, in an attempt to alleviate the tense atmosphere on the set, Dietrich faked a dramatic fall from her horse, and equally dramatic headlines appeared in the newspapers. But then, in May 1933, Dietrich and her daughter left for a prolonged holiday in Europe.

As with many things concerning Dietrich, the trip was dramatic. Her head ached and her heart too. She described to Mercedes how she stood on the deck, feeling lonesome and watching the crowds waving black handkerchiefs and screaming her name across the widening gulf of water between boat and shore. Her sadness left her virtually unable to breathe. As she sailed toward France, she felt she was no longer Mercedes's golden one, but her blue one.[22]

Mercedes sent flowers whenever possible, including orchids to the Trianon Palace at Versailles, where Dietrich was staying with her daughter.

Meanwhile, Garbo had returned from Sweden in April 1933 and resumed friendly relations with Mercedes. She wrote her a letter from the boat she took to San Diego, and shortly after her return Mercedes became occupied in helping her to find another house. This news Mercedes passed to Dietrich, adding that Garbo was to film *Queen Christina* under the direction of Rouben Mamoulian. In a rare reference to her rival, Dietrich cabled that she was happy about the "Scandinavian child," and sure that she would like working with Mamoulian.[23]

In a letter to Dietrich, Mercedes tried to explain the conflict of her feelings for the two women:

> To try and explain my real feeling for Greta would be impossible since I really do not understand myself. I do know that I have built up in my emotions a person that does not exist. My mind sees the real person—a Swedish servant girl with a face touched by God—only interested in money, her health, sex, food and sleep. And yet her face tricks my mind and my spirit builds her up into something that fights with my brain. I do love her but I only love the person that I have created and not the person who is real . . .[24]

Mercedes went on to point out that she had lately transferred her devotion for Duse to Garbo and that her love for the divine star did not prevent her from loving others. Later she expressed her love for Dietrich in what she hoped was a more practical form: "I will bring anyone you want to your bed! And that is not because I love you little but because I love you so much! My Beautiful One!"[25]

—

More or less oblivious to Mercedes's torn feelings, Garbo began working on *Queen Christina,* a project that had been suggested by Salka Viertel, her close friend and the woman who had introduced her to Mercedes at "tea" in 1931. She had met Viertel one evening at the home of Ernst Lubitsch, who was entertaining a celebrated German film star. It was a typical Hollywood party. "Beautiful women were clustered in one corner of the room, while the men talked shop in the other."[26] The Belgian film director Jacques Feyder (who had directed Garbo's film *The Kiss* in 1929) preferred to be with the ladies, and he took Salka over to a couch, upon which sat not only the German guest of honor in a billowing skirt but the lone figure of Garbo. Unlike any of the other guests, she wore "an austere black suit."[27] There being no room on the couch, Feyder led them out to the veranda, where the three talked with great animation. Salka Viertel found Garbo both beautiful and intelligent: "There is something unexpected in the loveliness of this face; it is always as if one were seeing it for the first time . . . she asked about my work in the theatre. She was intelligent, simple, completely without pose, with a great sense of humor, joking about her inadequate German and English, although she expressed herself very well."[28]

A new friendship was forged when Garbo appeared at the Viertel house the next day to continue the conversation. Simply dressed, she wore well-cut slacks and no makeup, except that "the famous long eyelashes were thoroughly blackened with mascara."[29] Later the Viertels discussed their impressions of her:

> What had charmed us was her great politeness and attentiveness. She seemed hypersensitive, although of a steely resilience. The observations she made about people were very just, sharp and

objective. "Probably all that fame prevents her from living her real life," I said.[30]

This new friendship sustained Garbo in the remaining years of her film career. The two women communicated easily, and when Salka had an idea, Garbo was inclined to listen. Salka thought Queen Christina would be the perfect part for Garbo, and Garbo, who knew a lot about Queen Christina, agreed. Mrs. Viertel described the queen:

> The preposterous child of the heroic Gustav Adolph, she was eccentric, brilliant; and her masculine education and complicated sexuality made her an almost contemporary character. Also her escapism, her longing for a world outside puritanical Protestant Sweden, to which she was chained by her crown, fascinated me.[31]

They hoped the film could be made in Europe, but Thalberg insisted it was easier to do it in the studio in Hollywood. Gradually it began to turn into exactly the sort of Hollywood film Garbo was so keen to get away from.

Garbo's return had done nothing to alleviate Mercedes's depressions, and during a particularly acute bout she went out in her car with one of her maids, saying, "I wish to God a car would hit us and kill me."[32] Her foolish wish was almost granted, and she was at that instant the victim of a serious accident, being propelled from the car and landing on her head. She found herself in Santa Monica Hospital and only just escaped permanent disfigurement. Dietrich telephoned from Paris and offered to pay Mercedes's expenses. Later Dietrich inquired, "How are my scars?"[33]

Mercedes recovered from her accident, though she needed considerable plastic surgery on her face, often necessitating her going around with bandages on. She suffered more depressions. As she wrote:

> Greta was filming *Queen Christina* and was at the studio all day and too tired at night to be with me. Marlene was still in Europe where she continued to write unhappy letters.[34]

Dietrich found that Europe was no longer a home, and wondered if Hollywood could become home for her. She was thankful it was there, and that Mercedes was there also, since she understood her sadness so well.

In due course a friend sent Mercedes to Sri Meher Baba, an Indian spiritualist who had taken a vow of silence. He convinced her by writing on an alphabet board that suicide was a bad idea and that she must seek salvation in "God Realization." This was the beginning of Mercedes's long interest in Indian philosophy and spiritualism.

In the winter of 1933–34, Mercedes and Garbo went to Yosemite together and got dangerously lost walking in a dark forest. Soon afterward, the Rasputin film came out and Prince Yusupov duly sued MGM. Mercedes was given her job back. She then tried to get Thalberg to make a film with Garbo as Jeanne d'Arc. He commissioned her to create the scenario. Mercedes became so obsessed with the idea that she began to visualize Garbo as the savior of France: "So complete was this transference in my mind that when I walked with her in the hills or on the beach I often saw her in medieval costume or in armor."[35] Alas, Garbo declined to take the part.

In 1934, Garbo starred in a film version of Somerset Maugham's *The Painted Veil.* It too received typical Hollywood treatment. Salka Viertel had but this to say of it: "I only recall that the producer, wanting to stress the Chinese background, insisted on scenes with a statue of Confucius under a tree. For some strange reason he always called him Vesuvius."[36]

In November 1934, Mercedes and Garbo made a shopping trip in Hollywood, and Garbo emerged from the tailor's wearing corduroy slacks. A cameraman waited for three hours on the running board of a car to capture the scene, which was then published worldwide. Mercedes took credit for instigating this fashion, particularly since she had earlier taken Dietrich to the same tailor's, from which Dietrich had ordered sixteen complete men's outfits. She too was photographed in them. Mercedes wrote:

> From that second on, women all over the world leapt into trousers. This was the beginning of the Great Women's Trouser Era!

> I am afraid that I am the culprit who started the whole thing. Fat women, thin women, tall women, short women, young and old women the whole world over thought that by jumping into trousers they could look like Marlene. Every photograph that appeared of her sold thousands of pairs of trousers to more women and swamped the shops with their sales. The war not many years later spread the habit further as women war workers everywhere took to slacks.[37]

Mercedes loved California and the freedom to be on her own. She loved wearing pants and not being in New York running a large house with servants. But she was feeling guilty about her husband, Abram Poole:

> I was deeply fond of him and it worried me that he was alone. Knowing that he had a model that he much liked I wrote him and suggested his making her his mistress. Far from taking this the way I meant it, he wrote me back a furious letter saying my suggestion was immoral. But not long after this I heard he had already carried it out.[38]

In 1935, Abram petitioned for divorce, having decided he wished to marry the model. Mercedes was taken aback:

> After all, we loved each other. We were friends and had been married fifteen years. That we could no longer make a success of our sexual life seemed to me no reason to separate. I was too European to feel, as Americans do, that the moment the sex relation is over one must fly to the divorce courts.[39]

Mercedes also noted in her draft autobiography, "It was as though my father or some close friend had written to me that he wanted me out of his life."[40] She sped to New York in order to discuss the matter, convinced that Poole did not genuinely wish to remarry. However, when this proved to be the case and Abram told her he did not really want a divorce and was counting on her not giving him one, Mercedes did a volte-face, insisting that he divorce her and marry the girl. There was then an unenlightened discussion about how this should be achieved. Abram wanted Mercedes to go to Reno and divorce him. She refused, which horrified him. "A man simply cannot divorce a woman," he declared. But Mercedes was adamant: "I answered that I did not care a damn what was done or not done and that, since he was the one who had started the whole idea, he could jolly well go and get it."[41]

Soon after this, Mercedes went to Italy and spent some time absorbing the atmosphere of a convent containing twelve nuns. She went on to Paris, where she reluctantly resumed her worldly ways, and then went to Kammer in Austria to stay with Eleanora von Mendelssohn.* As usual, the castle was filled with the likes of Raimund von Hofmannsthal and his wife, Alice Astor, Lady Diana Cooper, and Iris Tree, in addition to Max Reinhardt and Toscanini. Then Mercedes returned to New York.

Again, she was not to be there long. Garbo suddenly cabled her, summoning her to Stockholm: "I will meet you for dinner a week from Tuesday at eight o'clock in the dining room of the Grand Hotel," read her wire. Ever the adventuress, Mercedes took up the call and managed to get to Sweden, arriving in the bitter cold at 1:00 A.M. on the bidden day.

Only Mercedes could have relished what followed, and only Garbo would have put her through it. She rang Mercedes at 6:00 A.M., waking her and announcing, "I'll be right over." Then she insisted that Mercedes join her on a visit to the zoo. Four hours of darkness and freezing cold were to follow, but Mercedes suffered not a jot. "I was far too excited. I had always dreamed of being in Stockholm with Greta and now it seemed I was in a dream within a dream," she wrote.[42] They had their dinner as planned: "The evening was a sentimental one," with caviar, champagne, and the orchestra playing their favorite tunes. They went on to stay with Count and Countess Wachtmeister, and Garbo took Mercedes to see the house where she had been born:

*Eleanora von Mendelssohn, granddaughter of the composer and member of the wealthy German-Jewish banking family. She owned Kammer but had to abandon it during the war, when she fled the country. Mercedes met Salka Viertel through her. She committed suicide in New York shortly after Christmas 1949.

> She made no comment as we stood looking at it—nor did I. I was very much moved. I was moved because it was her birthplace and also by the fact that she had brought me there to see it. I knew that such a gesture meant much to her. As we moved away neither of us spoke.[43]

Back in Hollywood, later in 1935, Garbo starred in *Anna Karenina.* She made what is perhaps her greatest film, or at any rate gave her greatest performance, the following year in *Camille,* directed by George Cukor. Years later he described how much he admired the understated way in which she conveyed her tuberculosis on the screen, not with great coughs and splutters but with a sudden loss of breath. And how her eroticism was implied:

> She didn't touch Armand, but she kissed him all over his face. That's how you create eroticism. It's the uncensored thought the actor flashes to the audience. Garbo had this rapport with an audience, she could let them know she was thinking things, and thinking them uncensored. There was no "body contact" in that scene, which didn't matter. Garbo had that other quality in her character, and without it you can't generate a real love scene. She was rather cool, but seething underneath. You know that she's reckless and nothing will stop her; she has those fires underneath.[44]

He spoke of the real-life Garbo to Cecil: "Of course she's a sensuous woman, will do anything, pick up any man, go to bed with him, then throw him out, but she reserves her real sensuousness for the camera."[45] Mercedes, on the other hand, thought Garbo was too cooped up in the studio and that she had taken on the tubercular nature of her heroine.

—

Twenty-five years later, Mercedes was to make life difficult for herself by publishing her memoirs. While Garbo had been aware that Mercedes was busy writing, she ignored the process and almost certainly never referred to the book in Mercedes's presence. Dietrich took a different approach, avidly reading the galleys, offering numerous helpful hints, and finally approving Mercedes's text. "She liked it very much," affirmed Mercedes at the time of publication. "In fact, she wanted to rewrite it—Marlene is always like that."[46]

Cecil would not have appreciated some of Dietrich's comments. At one point Mercedes spoke of visiting the Frick Museum with him and quoted an observation he had made as they paused before an elaborately gilded clock: "No wonder we of our generation are neurotic. To have passed so quickly from the gentle ticking of this clock to jet planes, atomic bombs—it has all been too rapid. The transitions of our age have been too violent and too great."[47] Dietrich suggested that Cecil's name be omitted on the grounds that nobody knew who he was.[48]

Cecil Beaton by George Platt Lynes, 1938.

CHAPTER 4

STOKOWSKI, ONA MUNSON, GEORGES SCHLEE, AND VALENTINA

Cecil Beaton enjoyed more successes than failures during the thirties, although he suffered family bereavements and love problems and saw his career at *Vogue* shattered by an act of great stupidity. His love for Peter Watson was as fraught as ever, and he was variously "rapturously happy and suicidally miserable."[1] This was a period in which he was traveling extensively, broadening his artistic experience, becoming a friend of the artists Pavel Tchelitchew and Christian Bérard. He worked for *Vogue* in Paris and entered the world of Jean Cocteau. His sisters married, his brother and father died, and he assumed the mantle of head of the family.

Cecil began to take photographs of the Royal Family. He was invited to take the official portraits for the Duke and Duchess of Windsor's wedding in France in 1937 and two years later was summoned to photograph Queen Elizabeth at Buckingham Palace. He designed for the ballet, produced books, continued to photograph a series of stars and members of the British aristocracy, and undertook numerous fashion sittings. His work became more mature, and with the aid of technicians and lighting men he was able to create elaborate images in a style influenced to some extent by the Surrealists.

Just as everything seemed to be going so well, he made the mistake that cost him his job at *Vogue* and put him out of work for a period of eighteen months. Cecil often illustrated articles for *Vogue*, adorning the printed page with a number of ink line drawings. In the issue for February 1938, Cecil produced illustrations for a piece on New York society by Frank Crowninshield, and partly through ignorance of the full implications and partly through arrogance, he added some unpleasant anti-Semitic words to his sketch in minute writing.

The particularly offensive word he used was "Kike." Later he claimed that he did not realize he had done it, that the work had been undertaken when he was in a state of great exhaustion, that he assumed the words would be edited out by an eagle-eyed editor. The opposite happened. The drawing appeared, and the slogan was picked up by the press. Presently Cecil was under siege. He was summoned to the house of Condé Nast himself and dismissed on the spot. Meanwhile, 130,000 copies of that edition of *Vogue* were withdrawn from circulation. There were to be repercussions from this incident for many years to come. "He paid heavily, very heavily," Irene Selznick noted later. "He was punished."[2]

Cecil's career was saved by two things. First, there was the invitation to photograph Queen Elizabeth, which was the beginning of a long association with the Royal Family. The other saving factor was the coming of the Second World War, which opened up many new possibilities for him. Cecil was basically quite tired of photographing young debutantes gazing wistfully through bowers of flowers. Now he had the chance to travel to the Middle East and Far East, recording images of war. His photograph of an injured child in a hospital was an instant success in the United States, where it was put on the cover of *Life* magazine, leading *Vogue* once again to use his work.

—

In the mid-thirties, Salka Viertel had suggested to Irving Thalberg that Marie Walewska, Napoleon's mistress, would be a good subject for Garbo. Since the story involved adultery and an illegitimate child, there were objections from the censor's office, but Thalberg persisted. Then, late in 1936, Thalberg died, at the age of thirty-seven, and the new producer insisted that the script be rewritten to make the story sadder and more "uplifting." The film opened at the end of 1937 as *Conquest,* with Charles Boyer playing Napoleon.

Just before she began filming *Conquest,* Garbo met the next important man in her life, the charismatic conductor Leopold Stokowski, who had come to Hollywood to work in films. They met at a dinner party at the Santa Monica home of Anita Loos, and a few months later they were traveling in Europe together, staying first at the Villa Cimbrone in Ravello, on the Italian coast. "I wanted to see some of the beautiful things of life with my friend Mr. Stokowski," she said to reporters. "I have never been about and seen very much. I want to see beauty. My friend, who has seen much and knows about the beauty of life, offered to take me and show me these things." There was a great flurry in the press about an impending marriage, but Garbo made a statement denying this:

> There will be no marriage for at least two years, owing to contracts and engagements in Hollywood. After that I will be a plain woman and do what I like regarding my private life. I hope I will be forgotten and will not be bothered again by newspapermen.[3]

"Stoky" and Garbo traveled together for several months, then went to stay at an estate Garbo had recently bought in Sweden. Soon afterward he married Gloria Vanderbilt.

There was a plan for Garbo to star in the life of Marie Curie, based on her daughter Eve's book, but instead, in 1939, Garbo ventured into comedy with *Ninotchka.* Mercedes felt that it was a great pity that MGM had not discovered Garbo's capacity for humor on film until then. Garbo starred opposite Ina Claire, whose part as the Grand Duchess was considerably cut lest she upstage Garbo. In old age, Ina Claire recalled that Garbo was anxious to meet her but kept postponing their lunch. One day when Garbo rang, Claire said, "Let's postpone it indefinitely," after which the lunch took place.

Claire recalled that Garbo made a pass at her, which she declined. Then Garbo said, "Now I must go to the little boys' room." The next time Claire went to her bathroom, the lavatory seat was up.[4]

—

Around this time Mercedes made friends with the Hindu dancer Ram Gopal, who shared her interest both in Garbo and in matters spiritual. They met at a party in Hollywood. In July 1938, Mercedes joined him in Warsaw, where he was giving some dance recitals. During her somewhat traumatic journey, she spent a night in a hotel bedroom with a large photograph of Hitler looming above the bed. She was in Paris when the Munich crisis occurred (and when Chamberlain made his hopeless pact). Almost every American in Paris fled, including Mercedes's sculptress friend Malvina Hoffman, leaving only Mercedes and Marlene Dietrich in the hotel.

Instead of fleeing west, Mercedes went east, visiting Sri Meher Baba in India. Her old guru expected her to stay with him for five years, but she left after one night. Baba had promised her a room of her own, but when she arrived she found herself in a dormitory full of women. Always a bad sleeper, Mercedes was miserable. Besides the heat, many of the women snored, and they had pots under their beds that they did not hesitate to use in the small hours. Mercedes departed the next morning on a tour of India, visiting Ramana Maharshi, whom she believed to be the inspiration for the Sage in Somerset Maugham's book *The Razor's Edge.* After much discussion about religious thought and philosophy Mercedes departed for Egypt, returning to Hollywood in the spring of 1939. Garbo came to live near her on North Amalfi Drive in Brentwood.

It was at this time that the film star Ona Munson came into Mercedes's life. Ona was best known as the voluptuous scarlet lady Belle Watling in *Gone With the Wind,* which opened in 1939. Their first encounter had been at the Santa Monica home of Ernst Lubitsch, on a Sunday afternoon in 1932, when Mercedes and Garbo dropped by.

Lubitsch, an unattractive figure with his inevitable big black cigar, was entertaining Ona, at the time his girlfriend. It was the day of Garbo's spontaneous visit with Mercedes. Ona later recalled:

> As I came out of the kitchen with a champagne cocktail in each hand, I heard a feminine voice. And in walked Greta Garbo. Was it a thrill? How I escaped dropping both cocktails I'll never know. I had presence of mind to offer her one of them and she promptly embraced me.
>
> "I know who you are," she said. That was thrill no. 2.
>
> The great actress, whom I had never expected to meet, was dressed in masculine shorts, sweater and beret. She had been taking a long hike on the beach and had come in to talk shop with Mr. Lubitsch, who hurried with his dressing to greet her.
>
> Miss Garbo, I discovered, was more personable and magnetic off the screen than on. Her presence filled the living-room. And such eyelashes.
>
> She talked most of the afternoon, mostly about screen-shots and her difficulty in finding one that suited her.[5]

Ona Munson was born Owena Wolcott in Portland, Oregon, in 1906. She danced in New York as a child, then learned ballet. She went into vaudeville and was such a success that she bought her first diamond at fourteen. Her first big theatrical success was *No, No, Nanette* (1925), in which she earned a dozen encores for "Tea for Two" and "I Want to Be Happy." So popular was it in Quakertown, Pennsylvania, that a visit to the play was recommended to those suffering from nervous ailments. Ona was described as "a thoroughly delightful sprite . . . an adorable combination of youth, beauty and grace."[6]

Ona was the first girl to sing "You're the Cream in My Coffee" (in *Hold Everything!* in 1928). Later she acted the maid to Alla Nazimova's Mrs. Alving in *Ghosts,* proving her ability as a serious actress. She was intelligent, taking an interest in interior design and collecting modern works of art by Picasso, Dalí, Braque, and the Russian artist and designer Eugene Berman (later the last of her three husbands). She loved the ballet, knew the entire scores of many old musical comedies by heart, and played the piano by ear.

Ona eloped with the actor-director Eddie Buzzell and married him in San Francisco in 1926. By 1930 they were living in Hollywood, and in October of that year there was a three-cornered battle at a party given by Mary Pickford and Douglas Fairbanks at the Embassy Club. Ona was dancing with Lubitsch. Mrs. Lubitsch was dancing with the motion picture writer Hans Kräly, an old friend of Lubitsch's, imported by him from Germany. This pair followed Ona and the director about, taunting them in German and calling them rude names. Finally Lubitsch hit Kräly, and Mrs. Lubitsch hit her husband. The scene delighted the other guests. "It was so thrilling," said one. Soon afterward, Ona divorced Buzzell on grounds of extreme cruelty. Her romance with Lubitsch then became a feature of Hollywood life for more than a year.

In her autobiography, Mercedes was not forthcoming about her relationship with Ona, merely noting that Ona said she had always wanted to meet her, having heard a lot about her from Nazimova. "I thought her extremely pretty," wrote Mercedes, "but the thing that struck me most were her eyes. They were very sad, and there was something about them that touched me deeply."[7] After their first meeting at Lubitsch's house, they did not meet again until 1939. "This meeting made us great friends. After this she often came to my house, and as she was living in Hollywood and loved to come down to the sea, she came many weekends to stay with me. She was living with her mother at the Villa Carlotta in Hollywood, where I had other friends. Marie Doro was staying there with her mother; Marguerite D'Alvarez, the singer, was there; Kathleen Howard, another singer; and so was the painter Eugene Berman. Ona had a contract shortly after this with Republic Studios in the San Fernando Valley. When she started shooting, she often came from the studio directly to my house and spent the night. She used to say that she slept better in the country than in Hollywood."[8]

Ona's letters to Mercedes reveal more of their love. "I long to hold you in my arms and pour my love into you," she wrote in 1940.* She

*In a letter to Mercedes at Christmas 1946, Ona elaborated on the significance of their relationship, writing of having "shared the deepest spiritual moment that life brings to human beings" and "created an entity as surely as though [we] had conceived and borne a child."

related an ugly incident with Marlene Dietrich that occurred not long after the opening of *Gone With the Wind.* Ona had gone to Ciro's to dance when Marlene and her crowd came in. "Marlene turned the eyes of everyone on me until I blushed up to the roots of my hair. She stared continuously & I got so uncomfortable I had to leave."[9] Mercedes did not find this entertaining and responded jealously. In her next letter Ona dismissed Mercedes's wrath as a silly notion, assuring her she was "not interested in any chi-chi with Marlene or anyone else."[10]

—

In the late 1930s, Dietrich became the lover of Joe "Toughie" Carstairs, the millionaire motorboat racer for Britain, who sported a blond crew cut and tattoos. Miss Carstairs, the daughter of a Scottish colonel and an American oil heiress, had settled at Whale Cay, an island in the Bahamas, which she ran with a staff of black servants who were virtually slaves. The island had a certain appeal to dominant lady friends of Carstairs, but when, in 1939, she invited Dietrich to come and live there as a princess and doyenne of the tropical island, Dietrich was not tempted. "Toughie" Carstairs, her secretary, and Dietrich were all at the Hôtel du Cap in the late summer of 1939, and all set off back to America together.

Dietrich continued to be generous to Mercedes, even in later life. Sometime in the 1940s, Mercedes accidentally poured cleaning fluid into her eyes instead of eyewash, and it was again Dietrich, ever knowledgeable about matters medical, who came to her aid. Dietrich saved Mercedes's sight.

—

Garbo was in Hollywood at the beginning of the war, engaged in filming *Ninotchka.* "Greta was a changed person," Mercedes observed.

> She used to come for me as usual after shooting, and we walked in the hills. At least I walked, but she more often ran and danced. She laughed constantly and she used to repeat the question "Why?" as she did in the picture. She would imitate Lubitsch's accent and ask over and over again "Vhy? Vhy?" She acted out scenes for me from the picture, and some days she would really

> be Ninotchka. It was fascinating to see how by playing a gay role rather than a sad one her whole personality changed.[11]

Mercedes stayed in Hollywood during most of the war years, when all sorts of people like Stravinsky and Sir Charles Mendl and his wife, Elsie de Wolfe, took refuge there. But she was getting little work, and there was some hostility toward her because she employed a German housekeeper. So when she heard that the Office of War Information was publishing a propaganda magazine called *Victory* in New York, she applied for an editorial job, got it, and settled in New York at 471 Park Avenue. Her arrival coincided with Garbo's move to the Ritz Towers, and the two friends would signal to each other with lighted candles despite the wartime blackout regulations. Mercedes continued to write plays, including *Mother of Christ,* for which Stravinsky wrote the music.

In 1943, Mercedes's old friend Elsa Maxwell interviewed her and asked her about religion. Mercedes told Maxwell she had started out as a Roman Catholic, but that "if I had to be anything, I would be a Buddhist."[12] Ever the feminist, she was considerably impressed that Indian women had the vote and thought them much more involved in politics than American women. Maxwell said it made American women sound old-fashioned. To which Mercedes replied:

> Exactly what I thought when I returned from India. How secluded our women really are! How untouched by the realities! It's laziness, really. Do you think we can ever shake ourselves out of this lethargy, even by a war, even to have a place at the peace conference?[13]

Mercedes visited France often during these years, enlarging her circle of romantic relationships but generally entering on a steady decline in her work, her health, and the tolerance level of her friends.

—

Garbo's last film was the ill-fated *Two-Faced Woman,* made in 1941. There were some funny scenes and S. N. Behrman's dialogue was full of its usual panache, but Garbo was miscast. Contrary to what is often said, Garbo did not then decide never to make another film. She considered many other ideas, but for one reason or another none came to fruition. It was after the fiasco of the Walter Wanger plan to star her in a film version of Balzac's *Duchesse de Langeais* in 1949 that Garbo gave up the idea of films forever. As Salka Viertel put it, "The display of dilettantism, inflated egos, incompetence, and a hypocritical, indecent disregard for the sensibilities of a great actress had been unsurpassed, even in the history of films. It made Garbo once and for all renounce the screen."[14]

A while before this she had been involved briefly with Gayelord Hauser, the health expert, whom she met through Mercedes. He believed that the best cure for most things was to do what least appealed. A headache, for example, was best driven away by a bracing walk. He did not always find Garbo the most stimulating companion. On first nights in Hollywood, when he longed to be out at the premiere and party, he was invariably home alone with the most unlikely embodiment of a famous film star.

Nor did he always have an easy time with Garbo. In November 1939 he wrote to Mercedes:

> The lady went through one of her "depression weeks," and hasn't been able to do a thing, which may explain why she has not called you again. . . . Do take my advice and not write to her address, as that is one of her "pet peeves."[15]

Hauser was forever trying to alleviate Garbo's feelings of melancholia and loneliness. He thought her spirits would be lifted if she had some new clothes; thus, on a visit to New York, he took her to the Sherry Netherland Hotel, to the shop of the Russian designer Valentina. They were accompanied by Eleanor Lambert, the New York publicist. Valentina's husband, Georges Schlee, was also present, and he was surprised when his wife's new client posed stark naked for a simple fitting. Gradually the three became great friends, and it was not unknown for Schlee to escort both ladies, dressed identically in blue sailor suits, to a party.

After Garbo's film career ended, Schlee persuaded her to spend the winter on the East Coast. He hoped that she might get out and about a bit more. Presently she settled in Manhattan, returning to Hollywood only in the summer. In New York she was probably freer and more anonymous than in most other cities, and it was the ideal place for a drifter.

It was not long before Garbo was an integral part of the Schlees' world. Schlee conducted a curious, rather European *ménage à trois* and is said to have explained to Valentina, "I love her, but she will never want to get married, and anyway you and I have so much in common."[16] The Schlees are now remembered principally in connection with Garbo, but their own story is as strange as hers. They were both Russians, who had lived in Russia until the Revolution. Georges Matthias Schlee was described by Salka Viertel in her memoirs as "educated, intelligent and hospitable in the old Russian manner . . . well liked in society, and literary and artistic circles."[17] But not all opinions were favorable. Diana Vreeland recalled that "his breath smelt,"[18] while Truman Capote declared:

> Georges Schlee was an absolute bastard. He was so unattractive, he was grotesque, he was extremely ugly. I could not understand what it was all about, yet he had a hold on Valentina and Garbo.
>
> Then there was Mercedes de Acosta. Garbo was to Mercedes what Georges Schlee was to her. Mercedes was devoted to her while Greta treated Mercedes the same way Georges Schlee treated her.[19]

Schlee was a lawyer, born in St. Petersburg on June 1, 1896, to a rich family in the Crimea whose property had been confiscated. Driven south by the Revolution, he endowed a university in Sevastopol and ran a newspaper there. Then he served in the White Army until its collapse. He was said to have been a full general at the age of twenty-one. In the process of fleeing Russia, so the story goes, he saw Valentina Sanina, then a fourteen-year-old orphan, standing on a railway platform looking bewildered. She was beautiful, with a long mane of flame-red hair. Schlee approached her and offered to take care of her. Years later he revealed:

> I met her first when she was a little orphan girl without a cent in the world fleeing the Bolsheviks in Sevastopol. I was at headquar-

ters and so I sent her to my house. A few days later I called the servants and asked how she was. "She complains," they told me, "about everything." Even when she had nothing she was a perfectionist.

No wonder she became such a fantastic designer.[20]

Valentina Nicholaevna Sanina had been born in Kiev in about 1899. She was a deeply religious and superstitious woman. She said that at her birth she saw blood and knew there would be suffering—the Revolution.[21] She claimed to be descended from Catherine the Great and said that many of her relations had been killed. Until she met Schlee, Valentina was studying drama in Kharkov. She explained:

> My husband said he wanted to marry me and I said, "I can't give you love. I don't know how to love, but if you want friendship, then I'll marry you." He said, "If you marry me, I'll look after you for the rest of your life." Which he did for twenty-two years.[22]

The Schlees fled from Russia to Greece, where life was hard. Valentina used to joke, "To survive, we ate our diamonds."[23] They married and moved on to Rome and Paris. Schlee produced a popular revue called *Russe,* and Valentina appeared in a film as an angel, a part that well suited her waist-length hair. In 1923 they went to the United States with their theatre troupe. Valentina loved it from the start: "New York was so beautiful, the skies and the river so exciting."[24] Valentina acted in a play with Katharine Cornell. But later she gave up the stage for the world of fashion.

One of the first people Valentina met on her arrival in New York was Mercedes. Lucia Davidova* took Mercedes and Abram Poole to the house of the actor Tom Powers in Gracie Square to meet the Schlees. Mercedes recalled:

> She made me then a black dress with white Russian embroidery which I loved and well remember. When I met her she had thick

*Lucia Davidova, an elegant Russian with sorrowful eyes, at that time a young singer, who had fled Russia with her husband before the Revolution. Later she became a sponsor of Balanchine ballets and a generous patron of dance.

golden hair that when she loosened it trailed the floor. She wore it in a great knot at the back of her neck and I saw her once wear it wound around her neck like a collar. She was dressed in black the night I met her and was striking looking. I liked her and George and, I think, we felt sympathetically toward each other. With Lucia we left Tom's house together. It had been snowing and there was deep snow on the ground. Although it was already late and approaching the face of morning we all walked back to my house and made tea.

Abram painted two fine portraits of Valentina—one, a full length one, where she is posing on a rose patterned hook rug, which I brought down from my bathroom for her to stand on. Her hair is dressed straight back and wound in a great knot. She is wearing a white blouse and a black skirt and in her hand she is holding a gold cross and chain which I gave her. It is a forceful portrait and very Russian. The second portrait, only half size, is perhaps even more interesting. The principal motif in this portrait is a red glove.*[25]

In those early days in New York, Valentina was a striking figure. While other ladies wore short skirts, she wore floor-length outfits. While others wore conventional evening dress, she was more decorative with "the singular head-dresses, the pale white face, the chignon of blond hair . . . as timeless as an archaic Greek dancer."[26] She was also fond of wearing large straw hats and claimed to be the originator of that style, which was later made famous by Lady Diana Cooper on the Lido in Venice. One night at the opera she wore a simple dress she had created from three yards of soft black velvet, which caught people's attention and contrasted with what she called the "appalling paillettes, . . . their waistbands at their derrieres."[27] People asked her where she got her clothes, and she admitted she designed them herself.

Valentina's introduction to the fashion world was as a mannequin on Seventh Avenue, but she left when a salesman pinched her bottom. Then she worked in a dress shop called Sonia's on Madison Avenue. In 1928

*Abram Poole also painted portraits of Katharine Cornell, Greta Kemble-Cooper, and Ruth Gordon.

she opened a shop on Madison Avenue with thirteen dresses from her own closet. This business went bankrupt when a backer let her down, and one of those who helped her out of her financial straits was Leopold Stokowski.

Her new business was called Valentina Gowns. Irene Selznick said there was nothing grander than a simple Valentina dress. Not only was it timeless from a fashion point of view, but Valentina was the first person to design clothes in which a woman could throw her arms around a man's neck without her dress riding up her back. Once a woman saw Valentina at the opera and said, "Valentina, I want an exact copy of that dress." Valentina took the woman over to a mirror and said, "Chère Madame, what have you and I between us?" She refused to make her one.[28]

Valentina was not on show in her shop. She was hidden away, but if some lady came for a fitting and Valentina agreed to see her, she would ask her to move a bit so that she could get an impression of her. She had an uncanny instinct about how clothes move on the body. She thought of the human body as a machine, and each machine was different. Ideas would begin to form as to what was needed. She hated restriction of movement, favored low necks and little headpieces.

Valentina made only to order, though she did create an annual collection for I. Magnin for a while and launched a perfume called "My Own." She went on to dress Katharine Hepburn, Mary Martin, and Gloria Swanson. Clients included Paulette Goddard, Rosalind Russell, and Norma Shearer. She was her own best publicist, wearing clothes so that others wanted to wear them. She designed costumes for Judith Anderson in *Come of Age* in 1934. These were better received than the play. She also undertook *Idiot's Delight* with Lynn Fontanne, who copied her mannerisms and speech, and the stage version of *The Philadelphia Story,* which was so stylishly popular that she was inundated with orders for clothes like those worn by Katharine Hepburn for five years after.

Valentina aimed for simplicity, her day clothes being capes, skirts, and blouses. "Simplicity survives the changes of fashion," she said in the late 1940s. "Women of chic are wearing now dresses they bought from me in 1936. Fit the century. Forget the year." Other maxims included

"Mink is for football," which she said to a customer to whom she was selling a sable coat. She also said, "Ermine is for bathrobes," and, pleased with this form of idiom, added, "Children are for suburbs."[29]

At night she aimed for dramatic severity. She attacked the idea of women adorning themselves like Christmas trees. Many of her dresses clung to the body, and her colors were earth tones, shades of white, yellow (from chartreuse to ocher), olive browns and greens, and finally black. She made these up out of crepes, chiffons, damasks, failles, and mousselines de soie. She also liked the peasant look and, in contrast to that, the mandarin coat. In the 1930s Cecil wanted to photograph her, but she was reluctant. However, Grand Duchess Marie of Russia, then making her living as a journalist, said to Valentina, "As a grand duchess of your country, I command you to sit for Cecil."[30]

—

By the forties the Schlees were socially prominent in New York, rich and successful. They lived in a spacious apartment on the fourteenth floor of 450 East Fifty-second Street, on a block Dorothy Parker called "Wit's End" because Alexander Woollcott lived there. No. 450 is a well-known building opposite the River Club and overlooks the East River and Queens on the other side.

Garbo began her stay in New York at the Ritz Towers on Park Avenue, in a two-room apartment, the blinds of which were seldom raised. Later she moved to a four-room furnished apartment in Hampshire House, on Central Park South. In 1953 she moved into her last home, at 450 East Fifty-second Street, a few floors below the Schlees.

CHAPTER 5

GARBO AND CECIL: "MY BED IS VERY SMALL AND CHASTE."

The world of international society in which both Greta Garbo and Cecil Beaton were well established by the late 1940s was much smaller and more enclosed than it is today. And thus in New York, in the spring of 1946, Cecil met Garbo at a small party given by his friend Margaret Case, an editor at *Vogue.* They were both forty-two years old.

Garbo arrived in the company of Georges Schlee. The occasion was the consumption of some caviar from a delicatessen discovered by Schlee that imported direct from Russia. Vodka was at hand. Cecil had not seen Garbo since 1932, and he was taken aback by how beautiful she still was. She gave him a cracker and said, "I didn't wear lipstick when you knew me before."[1] Reassured that Garbo remembered him, he looked at her more closely. She was thinner, with a spikier nose, and lines appeared when she smiled.

> The uncompromising beauty of mouse blonde hair, the scrawny hands a bit weathered, the ankles and feet a bit poor and bumpy-looking. Has no look of luxury. The hat like a pierrot—Callot—the highwayman shirt. The incredible eyes and lids, and blue, clear iris. Historic beauty.[2]

Realizing that Garbo was about to leave, Cecil steered her onto the roof terrace, and they stood talking as the cold night bit into them and the lights of Park Avenue twinkled below. In this not unromantic atmosphere, Cecil was determined to "strike a chord of intimacy," he wrote later. "She talked, talked, talked, gabbled ever hard, like an excited child, in order to cover her embarrassment at the things I was blurting out to her while discovering the nobbles of her spine and smelling the new-mown-hay freshness of her cheeks, ear and hair."[3] In private notes he kept, he recalled, "talking hard like a child during kissing."[4] Before rejoining the others, Garbo promised to phone him.

Somewhat prematurely, Cecil proposed marriage to Garbo. She had announced, "My bed is very small and chaste. I hate it. I've never thought of any particular person in connection with marriage, but just lately I've been thinking that as age advanced we all become more lonely & perhaps I've made rather a mistake—been on the wrong lines." This gave Cecil his chance: "Well, why don't you marry me?"

Garbo was, reasonably enough, startled. "Good heavens," she said. "I don't think you should speak so frivolously."[5]

Sometime after meeting at Margaret Case's, they both went to a party given by Mona Harrison Williams,* where they danced in a dark

*Mona Harrison Williams (1897–1983) was the daughter of Travis Strader, a groom on a stud farm in Lexington, Kentucky. In 1916 she married Henry J. Schlesinger, owner of the stable. They had one son and divorced in 1920. She then married James Irving Bush, a millionaire football player from Wisconsin, and divorced him in 1924, with a settlement of a million dollars. In 1926 she married Harrison Williams, the multimillionaire president of the Empire Corporation. Mona was invariably on the lists of best-dressed women and frequently photographed by Cecil for *Vogue*. Harrison Williams died in 1953, and she married the interior decorator Count "Eddie" Bismarck, who died in 1970. Her fifth husband was Bismarck's physician, Dr. Umberto di Martini, who was killed in a car accident in 1979. Mona's Paris home, 34 Avenue de New York, is now the Bismarck Foundation.

Garbo by Beaton, the Plaza Hotel, New York, 1946.

room, the furniture of which was stacked under dust covers and the only light that of the streetlamp below. Afterward Cecil waved to Garbo as she retreated down the sidewalk to the Ritz Towers.

The pair exchanged badinage and walked in Central Park. These were far from leisurely strolls. They went at a brisk pace, circling the reservoir and then walking from Ninety-sixth Street down to Fifty-ninth Street and the Plaza. Cecil was a happy man. During one such excursion, Garbo suddenly said to him, "If only you were not such a grand and elegant photographer . . ." To which he replied, "Then you'd ask me to take your passport photograph?" A prolonged session followed, from which came the pictures of Garbo as a harlequin, among others—a "prized collection," as Cecil put it, adding, "though few of them were suitable for passports."[6]

Cecil described Garbo as a sitter in a lecture, of which his notes survive:

> She stood stiff against the wall. By degrees I said "Will you turn your head this way, then that, then in profile." As she is a naturally histrionic person, she entered gradually into the spirit of the performance; gave a very beautiful, balletic performance; her expressions were varied and full of life. She is such a good actress; her medium, her metier, should be acting all the time; this was an impromptu performance; the photographs that afternoon were beautiful; it was an illustration of what she could do as a spontaneous, histrionic exercise in plastic poses and in gesture and mood.[7]

Cecil always maintained that Garbo marked with a penciled cross the photos she gave him permission to publish in *Vogue.* He delivered these to the art director, Alexander Liberman, who was delighted with them, describing the pictures as "a precious windfall."[8]

Garbo left for California on May 21, leaving Cecil in tears. A few days later he sailed for London, and on his arrival he wrote to Garbo, inviting her to visit him on her way to Sweden, in what would be her first trip there since 1939. She responded in a friendly vein, explaining that she would not be traveling alone. (This was the first big trip on which Schlee would be accompanying her, more or less unnoticed by the press.) The best she might manage would be a tiny visit to Cecil in his London house. She had been unwell and had no particular wish to travel. Hotels in Sweden were proving a problem, but she urged Cecil to write to her care of Max Gumpel (a Swedish property magnate who liked stars) in Stockholm, addressing his envelopes to "H. Brown." She hoped possibly to see him in September. The letter was signed Harry, short for Harriet,[9] written upside down.

Garbo's next letter to Cecil was no pleasure to receive. He found himself plunged into a new *Vogue* drama, this time concerning the publication of her pictures. First there arrived a sinister cablegram from Garbo in California, making it clear that if Cecil published more than one photograph, she would not forgive him.[10] Soon afterward came a letter written the day before. Garbo maintained that she had given permission for him to publish only one picture. She had now heard that it was to be several and was extremely distressed. She never wanted anybody to see the ones of her in costume, which she deemed bad, and she ordered that they be destroyed. She felt they would show her in a frivolous light. She appealed to Cecil to frustrate their publication if at all possible.[11]

Cecil was thrown into a state of panic, but the publication process was too far advanced to stop. The magazine was virtually on the newsstands. In later diaries Cecil claimed that he sent frantic cables to try to prevent publication, but his overriding wish would have been to see them in print. Cecil consequently spent some time in disgrace, exercising his considerable capacity for guilt: "I felt as if I had committed a murder,"[12] he wrote.

—

Garbo sailed for Sweden on July 6. She boarded the S.S. *Gripsholm* at 9:15 A.M., three hours before sailing time, using a cargo gangway. It appeared that immigration inspectors were going to force her to observe "checking off" procedures like other passengers, but in the end the formalities were attended to in her hideaway cabin. She posed briefly for photographers, wearing a beige suit and hat, but all she would say was "I am awfully tired. I had to get up very early this morning."[13]

Garbo arrived in Göteborg eleven days later, and a crowd of a thousand fans was waiting to see her disembark. She was smuggled ashore by friends and conveyed to Stockholm in an express train, occupying her own private coach. Sweden was awash with rumors that she might be going to make a film there, settle there for life, or even produce religious films. One comment extracted from her was "I was tired when I left New York and I am still more tired after participating in celebrations aboard."[14]

During her stay it was said she had been signed to play an immigrant girl in New Sweden, a seventeenth-century Swedish colony on the Delaware River. Nothing came of it.

Garbo left Sweden again on August 24. There were so many spectators crowding the dockside roofs and windows that she needed a large police escort in order to board the *Gripsholm,* bound this time for New York. Lillian Gish and her sister, Dorothy, were also on board.

At the other end, the liner docked at Pier 97 at 9:00 A.M. on September 3. An hour later Garbo was escorted on deck and immediately surrounded by press representatives. As the flashbulbs popped, her mood veered from tolerance to graciousness and finally to impatience. Interviews with Garbo were virtually unheard of, and she faced her interrogators as if they were a firing squad.

"I haven't been elusive," said Garbo. "Being in newspapers is awfully silly to me. Anyone who does a job properly has a right to privacy. You'd think the same if you were in the same boat." She went on to say that she had no plans for any films, and she did not know how long she would stay: "I'm sort of drifting."[15] At length she got fed up: "Now take all your friends and go home. Have coffee. Please."[16] While the interrogation proceeded, Georges Schlee remained in the background, but he did not entirely escape the cameras.

—

Cecil was also in New York in September 1946, having been to California and back. While in Hollywood he had not only worked on, but also taken the small part of Cecil Graham in, *Lady Windermere's Fan.*

Garbo was not far from Cecil's mind during this time. In California he would do things like dial her number for the dubious pleasure of hearing it ring in the empty rooms. He conceived the plan of going over and asking the maid to allow him to plant some lily bulbs in the garden, but he could not find the bulbs. At length, one romantic summer evening, he set off in search of her house. The address she had given him was No. 622 Bedford Drive. Cecil found it and was horrified by its whimsical, toylike quality:

> I tiptoed across the green velvet lawns with heart beating to see where my beloved lived. I looked with horror. No, I couldn't be this much mistaken. No one of her taste could live in such an interior. There must be some mistake. She must have rented the house to someone else. On the walls were a variety of very bad modern pictures & a few extremely bad miniatures framed by the mantelpiece. There were many large photographs around of framed celebrities—Elsie Mendl, Greer Garson, & some blonde. With disgust I left. I could not be so mistaken.[17]

Later, to his considerable relief, Cecil discovered that Garbo resided at No. 904. The one he had gone to belonged to the columnist Harry Crocker, who let her use it as a forwarding address. When he found Garbo's real house, it was predictably spartan and heavily curtained. A high wall protected it from view, and there was a magnolia tree, the scent of which filled the night:

> I imagined my friend retreating behind the wall & staying for days on end & in secrecy even from her maid. I came home feeling content that it was a suitable house for someone of so fine & independent a character. And the more I see of the suburban intrigue & invidious influence of the Colony the more remarkable it is that a character exists who has survived fifteen years of it.[18]

Cecil was haunted by a problem that lingered from his stay in London. Inevitably, he had been unable to keep quiet about his newfound love for Garbo. The news had begun to circulate, and close friends like James Pope-Hennessy and Clarissa Churchill* were concerned that he

*Clarissa Churchill, niece of Sir Winston Churchill, now Countess of Avon (b. 1920), married the Right Honorable Anthony Eden in 1952. Before her marriage she worked for Alexander Korda and also for *Vogue*.

was not conducting his affairs with due discretion. Pope-Hennessy also thought that the presence of Maud Nelson as his secretary was dangerous, since she was the lover of Oggie Lynn, a singer who moved in London's social circles with a freely wagging tongue. With Garbo due back in the United States any day, Cecil was in a state of considerable panic about the relationship. He explained to Clarissa Churchill that he felt terribly contrite:

> I feel that much of the bloom has been spoilt—Only if the whole relationship is really genuine & wholehearted on both sides can it survive the intrigue that has now built around it. Perhaps it will be useful to have such a test—Greta arrives in New York this week—& it will be interesting to know how she will receive me—if at all. She is a most easily hurt & startled creature & Lord Kemsley's reporters* have been about as swinish as possible.[19]

Clarissa advised him to lie about the gossip and swear he had told nobody—that he was just as sickened by it as Garbo.

When Cecil read reports of Garbo's arrival, he duly telephoned the Ritz Towers. He would give his name to the operator, and after a discreet interval the operator would announce, "She don't answer." Nor did Garbo relent. Thus Cecil found himself left to his own devices. Everywhere he went he thought he saw her, and he could not help torturing himself by returning to places they had seen together the previous winter. He existed in a waking nightmare of suspense and rejection. Finally, recalling cruel words that his former love Peter Watson had used on him, he sent her a note: "You cannot dismiss me like a recalcitrant housemaid." As he confided to his diary, "Even if Greta may never forgive me, she will doubtless always remember the admonishing terms that I learnt from so great a person as Peter."[20]

Cecil reported the latest developments to Clarissa once more:

> There was a lot of press bother about Greta & she was asked on arrival back from Sweden if she were going to be married. "Well

*The English tabloids.

> well well" she said to the reporters but there has been stone silence for me. She won't answer my telephone calls, letters or telegrams—she is frightened or daresay feels I have betrayed her—& I only trust this appalling silence won't continue. I am luckily so busy that I do not have much time to brood on the disappointment.* It might be quite possible never to see her again—or to find we have started again where we were three months ago.[21]

Presently Cecil was relieved to hear that Garbo had retreated to Hollywood. He allowed six weeks to pass before phoning again. Then, on October 7, a day he deemed his "lucky number," he tried again. Deceived by being told merely that New York was on the line, Garbo took the call. A desultory conversation followed: "Why, Mr. Beaton. Why, why, why. How very surprising." Gradually, however, Cecil felt that the breach between them might heal, but "in the rather cruel, playful way that is typical of Stephen Tennant,** she said, knowing that 2,000 miles separated us: 'Come on over now.' No, but can I come later? 'Now, only now.' "[22]

By dint of perseverance Cecil managed to establish a slender thread of communication between them, a hopelessly fragile one, but a thread nevertheless. He explained his position to Clarissa:

> Greta is in California & I have very unsatisfactory talks with her on the telephone—most of the time she is out—& her moods are so variable. It is maddening that she is not here or that I am not there.[23]

Having not spoken to her for a month, Cecil rang after Christmas. She said she was surprised he had not yet gone back to England.

*Cecil was at work on the sets for the ballets *Camille* and *Les Patineurs.* He won praise for both of them. The critic for *The New York Times* described him as having "emerged the particular talent in this field" (October 6, 1946). He was due to start work on the designs of two Korda films.

**Stephen Tennant (1906–87), poet, sketcher, and novelist manqué. He was Cecil's reclusive neighbor in Wiltshire, an erstwhile luminary and Bright Young Thing.

Sometimes she taunted him by asking him over, sometimes she was pleased to hear from him, and sometimes she told him not to phone. The conversations were as inconsequential as ever:

CECIL: "How do you sleep?"
GARBO: "I sleep well if I go to bed early enough. I retire with the chickens. . . . Ah we're all bound to our duty. . . . We're soldiers fighting for *les beaux arts*."[24]

Without much confidence that the problem would resolve itself, Cecil sailed home to England in January 1947.

Cecil was tied to England until the following October, working on two films for Alexander Korda—*An Ideal Husband* (starring Paulette Goddard) and *Anna Karenina* (with Vivien Leigh and Ralph Richardson). This was an exciting commission for him, guaranteeing something of a respite from the normal financial worries. During the following months he kept in touch with Garbo by writing letters to her. The originals of these letters may no longer exist, but Cecil kept carbon copies of them, which he never showed anybody. They emerged from a tin trunk under his bed after his death.

During most of 1947, Cecil experienced the problems traditionally faced by the absent or would-be lover. In his letters he gave evidence of his worth and fidelity, writing about his activities, hoping to make these sound interesting—bait for Garbo, the lure of an alternative life in another land. But he did not have any idea how these messages would be received, and as he wrote them, he knew he was very unlikely to receive a reply.

Occasionally he phoned, but in those early postwar days it was not a question of simply picking up the receiver and dialing. The call had to be booked in advance and dealt with through an operator. Then Cecil had to wait at home to see if his request would be successful. The most usual reply was "The party don't answer," which was doubly frustrating as the "party" might well have been there but elected not to bother to answer.

This period in Cecil's life covered the purchase and restoration of Reddish House, Broadchalke, his second Wiltshire home. He had been forced to leave the dreamlike Ashcombe after fifteen years in that sturdy little manor house lost in the downs. He knew enough about Garbo to be aware of the likely appeal of a Queen Anne mansion in a sleepy English village. She was solitary by nature. He hoped to make this her sanctuary.

Toward the end of January, Britain had entered an exceptionally cold spell that lasted until March 10. The country froze under bitter easterly winds, continuous frosts, snow, and snowdrifts. In the middle of all this bleakness, Cecil began to woo Garbo in earnest, writing her twenty-three letters between March and October 1947, while she remained almost totally silent. He posted most of the letters at the time but kept one or two back, delivering them to her hotel on his next visit to New York in the winter of 1947.

Sunday March the ninth [1947]

Honey,

At last the thaw! The sun is out and the ice & snow are melting & the streets are a real mess. But what a relief. It is six weeks now we have suffered & each day has been a battle to keep warm. One had to hold onto oneself to galvanise some sort of heat in ones body & it became very tiring. Incessant anxiety. I was exhausted. Most people too. It has been a phenomenally cold winter in the country, the birds on the trees have become encased in ice—like quails in aspic. The branches of the trees are covered with ice & therefore snap off with a loud report. To walk in a wood is like being fired at—ambushed. In the north of England whole villages & towns have been cut off & a million sheep have been buried in the snow. As they are mostly in lamb at this time of the year it is not only a sad story but quite grave that we shall have just that much less to eat next year.

However at last the temperature is very much warmer, & soon we shall be enjoying spring. As I write (in my bed Sunday morning) the hens in the garden next door are jubilantly celebrating by making all kinds of noises. I have got another cold. I suppose I caught it in Paris.* I went for a week & had a lovely time. I went

*Cecil paid many visits to Paris in the immediate postwar years. He was part of "La Bande," the group Lady Diana Cooper gathered round her while her

to many wonderful exhibitions & came away feeling most stimulated & inspired. It does one so much good to have these abrupt changes & I felt as if I'd had a tonic. Although the country is still in a poor way & most people are not able to afford the black market nevertheless there is a gaiety & frivolity there that blinds one to the grim squalour—also it is very nourishing to come across a people with such a high standard of taste. I went to one dress shop & it was like a revelation. There's nothing in New York that can compare—& as for poor old London—well that's laughable.

The day in the woods at Chantilly was wonderful. Diana cooked eggs & truffles. We ate caviar & cold ham & tangerines (which I had brought across the Channel in a string bag) & we walked in the snow. Apropos of that hideous face that I included in my last letter,* Diana has recently been left a windfall by an unknown admirer. For twenty years she has been receiving passionate letters from a Spanish Marquis named Emmanuele. One day when out shopping a small & elderly man bowed from the waist, doffed his trilby hat & said "I am Emmanuele." Diana thought this was the moment to clear up the situation—& said "No it's nonsense you're writing me these letters. I've never met you in my life & they must stop." The Spanish Marquis stroked his little goatee beard, looked sad & said "I'm sorry if I've been importunate. The letters shall stop." But of course they didn't stop—& continued until—this last war. Suddenly Diana was informed by Emmanuele's lawyers in Switzerland that the little man had passed on to a better world & that he had left her his very large fortune. She had no scruples about being delighted. Unfortunately I doubt if she'll be able to touch a penny of it, as there is death duty to be paid in Switzerland, Spain & England—& anything left is being claimed by his family. How strange it all is!**

---

husband, Duff Cooper, was ambassador to Paris, September 1944 to December 1947. Other members were Christian Bérard, Denise Bourdet, Marie-Louise Bousquet, Georges and Nora Auric, and later Jean Cocteau.

*The present letter is the first one of which a copy survives.

**Lady Diana was left £28,000 by a man called Manuel, Count de Luzarraga.

In Paris one night I sat next to the widow of Rostand* at dinner. You can imagine how old she is—& she looks like nobody of today. Her blonde curls (no she's not terribly blonde) are trimmed low over her cheeks to hide the scars of her various faceliftings. She is painted like a Fratellini clown—is elaborately dressed in black of all materials (satins, velvets, chiffon, tulle, etc.) & leopard skin. A wonderful appearance like a caricature of herself & she was fascinating about the great days she knew. How tremendous was the sudden fame of her husband after the first night of Cyrano—& a lot about the divine Sarah.** She was anxious to show me how well she knew the English language & said that until she was six years old she spoke only English—but then she had been sent to a convent, & had never again spoken English. "But" she said "I remember it so well" & she proceeded to recite in its entirety "Ten little nigger boys."

Seven little nigger boys picking up sticks . . .

Then there were six . . . etc., etc., etc., etc!

Another day at lunch one of the women, who always signs herself as a four leafed clover,† wrote a message on the back of the menu & sent it over to me: "Cheri, Cecil, grande nouvelle & a very interesting one: I just now realise that we look exactly alike. You are the only one I know who reminds me of myself."

Cecil's story coincides with that she told in *Trumpets from the Steep,* pp. 226–27. The story ended with the count's two sisters receiving part of the inheritance, some going to the Swiss and English governments, and Lady Diana receiving "the little residue."

*Rosemonde Gérard Rostand (1866–1953), estranged wife of French romantic dramatist Edmond Rostand (1868–1918). Descendant of Comte Gérard, Marshal of France, and of the Comtesse de Genlis. A poet and dramatist, her *La Tour de Saint-Jacques* was presented at the Comédie-Française. A well-known figure in Paris society and a keen first-nighter. Mother of the poet and novelist Maurice Rostand. "The inseparable pair became one of the sights of Paris; and devotion to her bleached and painted son went hand in hand with Rosemonde's estrangement from her famous husband" (Francis Steegmuller, *Cocteau* [New York: Little, Brown, 1970], p. 45).

**Sarah Bernhardt played in Rostand's *La Princesse Lointaine* in 1895.

†Louise de Vilmorin (1906–69), author, poetess, and mistress of Duff Cooper.

I was very flattered and proud.

So much for that trip to Paris. I am going back there again next Friday for a short visit. Maybe I will let you have a letter from there.

Meanwhile there is other news here. A friend arrived at the house. "I have got something downstairs I think you'd like to buy" he said. I leapt out of bed. A white marble bust of an eighteenth century woman (French) was brought upstairs. My heart stopped with the beauty of it. It is a great work of art. I am as happy as can be. My day was made. It was like being in love—something nice to come home to. Although I cannot afford her in view of other more pressing needs (read later on) I had to take possession of her. So I have become (for three hundred pounds) the possessor of a really wonderful treasure. If ever my heart became as cold as the marble of which the lady is made then I could sell her for ten times as much as I have paid.

More news: Well in my last letter I wrote about an expedition to the country in search of houses. I think I was rather secretive of information concerning the trip as I have learnt that it is bad luck to talk much about things that are not definitely signed & sealed. Well it so happened that we saw two houses. One supposedly built by Sir Christopher Wren (who you know was the architect of St. Paul's). It had a lovely pale yellow & grey stone facade—with columns each side of the main window, a magnolia tree & a wonderful view overlooking a lyrical valley. But inside the house possessed no charm at all. But we saw another house. Reddish House, Broadchalke, Wiltshire. That is the address. I had once seen the house long ago & thought it one of the loveliest I had ever seen. Suddenly a friend of mine who lives nearby—one of the boys—telephoned to say the woman who owned the house had just died & that the house would be sold. There is a terrific dearth of such houses in England just now, & this being small enough to be "conveniently run" is just what so many people want. So we could not delay a moment for fear lest someone else should snap up the treasure: for treasure it is. I went there with my mother—& my secretary [Maud Nelson]—one of the girls—& we were all ravished by the loveliness of the place. The house is made of mauve brick, 1660. There is a bust over the front door—a village street is kept at bay by a low curved brick wall that is flanked with a screen of yew trees cut like poodles tails & pompons. Inside the house is somewhat rambling but with very nice rooms, & elegant windows & doors. There are just enough rooms & the garden & grassy slopes stretching from the house are quite extraordinarily romantic. I am thrilled. It is almost certain now that I shall possess the house for my bid (£10,000) has been accepted. The surveyors go there next Friday & unless any unforeseen tragedy occurs I shall take up residence there in June. So then I shall be a country squire. Just for a spell at any rate. So then I am the owner of a country seat. So then I am a man of property. Did you ever think your friend would turn out to be that?

I think you will agree that the place is enchanting. It reconciles me to the loss of my other home—which I loved so much. And this has the advantage of being extremely convenient. The other was very difficult. I am only so sorry that our wonderful gardener Dove has not lived to look after this garden. It is so sunny & the walled kitchen garden is a delight. There are two summer houses, ilex trees, a wood at the summit of the hill, a paddock & a rose garden. I possess a small suite of my own, a big bedroom with Georgian fireplace, a small sitting room or dressing room cum sitting room—or dressing room (in which I shall put an extra bed) & bathroom. This is apart from the other sleeping quarters. Quite private & detached with pretty views from every window. If you come to be my wife I trust you will allow me to sleep in the sitting, or dressing room, if not in the larger room.

Footnote: There are also two thatched cottages which are part of the estate & they look like something out of Hans Christian Andersen.

Further Footnote: I have masses of furniture in storage but won't want to use some of it—because it isn't nice enough*—& will want lots more—because these rooms will need more furniture than the Ashcombe rooms. Therefore I shall want to buy a lot of useful things. Therefore it is sheer extravagance to have bought the bust—but I couldn't help not buying the bust.

*Cecil had furnished Ashcombe with numerous improvisations: drums used as tables, curtains made from hessian stitched with pearl buttons, and a bed made from a circus carousel.

New Topic: Professional life. I motored through the squalid purlieus of London, through the ice & filthy snow to the film studios to see the sets being built.* In spite of war time conditions they have done some good jobs of recreating grand houses of the Victorian period—& the House of Commons made of plaster. Korda, with hair on end, is harassed by too many people—but however irate he becomes I never stop liking him quite immensely. He is lovable & sympathetic & got such a good sense of fun. The shooting of the picture starts in ten days time. I am also doing the clothes for *Anna Karenina* for him. He has decided to do it with Vivien Leigh in your part. A pity to try & redo something that was so wonderful—for although my memory is hazy I remember certain scenes as being so lovely . . . I am steeping myself in Russian atmosphere.

Other news of professional life . . .

Plans—but nothing definite.

Personal Items: Bad cold. Back not nearly straight enough. Am having my teeth straightened.

Love life items . . .

My Love to you
C[25]

This letter was followed with an equally long postscript in which Cecil mentioned anything that happened to occur to him, and occasionally asked a question:

Do you remember it was on the third time of our meeting again that I told you I wanted to marry you, & you said it was extremely frivolous of me—but it wasn't—& it isn't. Don't you think we are good for each other? I know I shan't be happy until you make an honest man of me.

Do you remember?

Do you remember you said you were going to tell me a secret & I felt terribly small & inexperienced & ashamed of myself as a result of the secret . . .[26]

In the next weeks Cecil dwelt on many topics. He informed Garbo that he wore no underclothes, and that he had dreamt she was four

*For *An Ideal Husband.*

inches shorter than she was, and he related his frustration at trying to reach her on the telephone. He started work on *The Importance of Being Earnest* for Alexander Korda. His activities included staying with Laurence Olivier at Notley Abbey, accompanying Vivien Leigh to Paris for fittings for her *Anna Karenina* costumes, struggling with his play, and becoming intensely angry with Garbo for her silence. But he persevered with his letters to the uncommunicative star, asking her whether she had visited Dr. Laszlo,* and if she missed her "ivory tower" at the Ritz. Cecil referred often to events of the past year: "doubtless I shall remember last Easter our visit to the Paley house, my bad headache—& your giving me palliatives, & there being only one reason why later I went to that awful Russian Easter gathering.** Oh Dear! Oh dear me!"[27]

In April, Cecil signed the lease of Reddish House. At last he heard some news of Garbo in a letter he received from Margaret Case in New York, describing that year's Russian Easter party at the Schlees', during which John Gielgud appeared in a red jacket identical to one worn by Clifton Webb. From 535 Park Avenue she wrote:

> Greta that evening was in a talkative and friendly mood wearing a brocaded Valentina dress with sleeves, her hair tied back with a lace ribbon making a divine but very new appearance. I introduced Mr. Gielgud to her and he was thrilled saying "What a pet." . . .
>
> Jerome Zerbe's photographs taken at the request of the host and hostess at the Easter party will appear in next week's *Life.* I hear that he saw Greta on the street, told her she was in one of the pictures to which she seemed to acquiesce. And now Valentina hysterically telephoned Mr. Zerbe saying Greta and George are angry and they must be removed from the magazine. I encoun-

*Dr. Erno Laszlo, known as "the Svengali of the Skin," opened the Institute of Scientific Cosmetology in Budapest in 1927. When the war started in 1939, Elsie Mendl helped him to come to New York, where he opened a skin-care salon on Fifth Avenue.

**A disparaging reference to an Easter party given by Georges and Valentina Schlee. Their Russian Easter parties were a feature of New York high life. (Jerome Zerbe photographed Garbo at the party in 1947.) Many years later President Kennedy attended one.

tered George and Greta in a corner at the Colony one evening. George asked "Are you dining with an Englishman? Maggie likes Englishmen." And Greta, laughing, said "Oh yes, how is your friend Sutro?* He is very nice, very sweet." I thought this was meant to be a reminder of you between us. There are rumours that she may do a picture for David Selznick. Someone told me George Schlee left yesterday for two weeks in California and this may mean La Greta has also gone away. George and Valentina are booked to sail for Europe in June. I am afraid I have only these dull trivialities to tell. Greta's existence is spent with boring people as aimless as ever . . .[28]

After a visit to Stratford-upon-Avon, Cecil raced across country in his Hillman Minx to stay with Juliet Duff** at Bulbridge, in the village of Wilton. He informed Garbo:

My fellow guest for the next three days is your friend Mr. [Somerset] Maugham—but I doubt if we shall talk about you as I never talk about you to any of our mutual friends—& treat you as a topic too dangerous to discuss. If by any chance your name is mentioned I assume an exaggeratedly casual air, or else, as when Kochno† told me about seeing you, I become very gracious: "Oh how charming of her. How very nice for you—& how exceedingly nice for her too!!"‡[29]

In August, Cecil went to Paris for a holiday to buy things for his house but found the city largely shuttered and the women all suntanned. He confessed to Garbo that he had had a dream about her and wondered if "perhaps we are happiest in our dreams."[30] Back in London, he at last received word from Garbo. In reply, he wrote:

*John Sutro (1904–85), film producer then in partnership with Alexander Korda.

**Lady Juliet Duff (1881–1965), daughter of the fourth Earl of Lonsdale and mother of Sir Michael Duff. A stalwart supporter of the Diaghilev Ballet and keenly interested in the theatre.

†Boris Kochno (1903–90), secretary to Diaghilev, later worked with the Ballets Russes de Monte Carlo, poet, and librettist.

‡This last line in the idiom of Queen Elizabeth.

> In my few days absence a lot of letters & magazines had arrived & I busied myself attending to the chores & I noticed that some kind friend in America had sent me some food packages—But it wasn't until bedtime that I unwrapped them—& when I discovered who had sent them I was filled with a rare & deep happiness. Thank you. Thank you. I have been feeling very lonely of late. I hated not being in touch with you, & there were times when I felt extremely sad & depressed that so much had happened since we last met. Nevertheless I have always had complete faith in you & know that whatever you may say to me that we have a very sincere sympathy & love for each other & that it is not something that happens often in a lifetime. I have always held you so very close in my consciousness & however busy I have been have always wanted you to be near & to share the excitements, & your present to me has come like Manna from heaven, & I know you are as understanding & true as I have always believed you to be. As for myself, I have never before wanted to devote myself entirely to any one woman, but I know one day all obstacles will be overcome & that we shall spend very happy times together. You have the lion's share in all my plans—& I am not very impatient for them to materialise—as neither you or I would be happy without complete trust in one another & I feel you have to see me again to realise how very genuine a person I am if I am permitted to be.[31]

Garbo was about to leave for London, and it was characteristic of her to show a small sign of life shortly before arriving. She stayed briefly in England before setting off for Paris, arriving there on August 17. Unbeknownst to the press, she was accompanied by Georges Schlee, the man Cecil described as "the second-rate dressmaker's assistant." England, meanwhile, basked in exceptional heat. It was hot and dry, with abundant sunshine, ideal harvest weather—in short the hottest August for seventy-five years.

But these were troubled times for Cecil. If he thought he could sleep easy, he was gravely mistaken. Two days after Garbo's ship docked, he was writing:

> So you have come to London. It is a great event—as if Venus came to Mars. Yet the papers treated the occasion as if some

> filmstar had just come on holiday. How bland & vulgar they are! You were quite right to avoid their onslaughts, but your utter simplicity is so pure & genuine that it baffles people. I thought I wouldn't call you unless you called me—but I found myself getting so restless that at last I decided to try & disturb you. Once I had made that decision then I was on tenterhooks. I had to keep rushing out of the house in the car to buy antiques—or to look at antiques for my house. It was not an adequately compensating excitement. I was sad to miss you—& sorry that I had to be away in my new house in the country when eventually you did call . . .[32]

Cecil continued:

> Will you spare me a meeting when you come back to London? Will you be able to free yourself? I don't want to see you just for a rushed minute or with a crowd of people. But I would love you to come quietly to dinner. There is so much to discuss—& everything in the world to talk about. I know you hate making plans—but I want to know when I can see you for a long stretch during the coming winter. Once January is over I am back in the Korda grindstone—& that's as bad as being in the army—for it is then only a question of "leave."[33]

Garbo traveled from Paris to the south of France, where she stayed at Villa la Reine Jeanne, Bormes-les-Mimosas, with Commandant Paul-Louis Weiller,* whom she had originally met through Elsie de Wolfe. Here she was able to pass a holiday of total seclusion, swimming naked and unobserved before any of the other guests had arisen. The rambling villa was perfect for one who loved to hide. So remote was Garbo during her stay that Pandora Clifford, staying in the same house, was aware that she was there but never once set eyes on her.

*Commandant Paul-Louis Weiller (1893–1993), much-decorated aviator of the First World War. Industrialist, one of whose companies was nationalized and became Air France. Benefactor of many French charities, owner of many houses. Dubbed "Poor Louis" by Nancy Mitford. Garbo called him "Paul-Louis Quatorze." Awarded Grand Cross of the Legion of Honor in 1989 at age ninety-five. Was still windsurfing with prowess in his ninety-ninth year.

Later Garbo and Schlee made their way along the coast to Cannes and the Château de la Garoupe, on Cap d'Antibes, which had been rented by the Chilean collector Arturo Lopez and his wife, Patricia. There Garbo met Cecil's friends Michael Duff and David Herbert for the first time. In an interview with Duncan Fallowell, David Herbert said they walked down the rock path. "Out of the sea strode this unbelievable beauty with her hair all dripping and water on her eye-lashes and topless. Michael and I gasped. It was Garbo." Lopez introduced them and explained that they were Englishmen who had fought in the war. "How wonderful to meet two men who've helped save the world," pronounced Garbo, somewhat exaggerating their contribution to the war effort. "Up the British Empire!" Then, apparently, she dived into the sea again. Later they played charades and she was quite uninhibited, crawling around on all fours. Herbert opined, "A totally unaffected person. And she wasn't a recluse at all. She was just bored to death with the whole Hollywood thing."[34]

On September 7 *The New York Times* published a photo of Garbo strolling along a street in Cannes wearing shorts and a broad-brimmed hat. Meanwhile, in New York, Noël Coward popped in for drinks with Valentina at 450 East Fifty-second Street. The dress designer was restless and discontented. Coward wrote, "Poor dear, I am afraid she is having a dreary time."[35]

Cecil was still writing valiantly to Garbo:

> You've had quite a long bout of strange Hotel bedrooms & waiting for that old Russian sturgeon to rouse himself in the morning. Perhaps after one brief & superficial look at London you will be pleased to get back to the impersonality of New York or Beverly Hills. But really Europe is the place for you. It is quite remarkable how after all the years you bear no imprint of America on your soul. But that shows that it is far from you, that you have no real contact with any of the people there. I think you should come more & more to Europe as you would find yourself in much more sympathetic surroundings. There is no reason why you shouldn't start to make an entirely new life here. Forget about your film career, & lead the sort of life you want. It's really terrible

that you should spend your time hiding from imbecilic film fans on Madison Avenue or Sunset Boulevard. All of which is a long way of extending an invitation to you to come & build your nest here at Redditch House . . .[36]

Garbo and Schlee did indeed return to London for a further brief visit before sailing back to the United States on the *Queen Mary*. And Cecil wrote one last letter:

Dearest Greta,
I am glad you've gone. Now I can settle down & begin to feel a bit less restless. It was no good your being here & yet not here—for under the auspices of that Russian sturgeon I could have no chance. I think it was mean of him, though, to allow you so short a time in England—& of course it was intentional. It was extraordinary to think of you being in London & able to telephone to me—but I was as pathetic as Charlie Chaplin in *The Gold Rush* when you did not turn up at my house. I said I would be sitting there—but that is hardly a true picture. I did sit occasionally & would start to read a book but I couldn't concentrate & then I heard the door of a car slam outside & I expected it to be you. When I went to the window it was a woman in a grey suit visiting the house opposite. Blast her. Then I had made all sort of preparations as I wanted my house to appear its most sympathetic. I threw away all the unnecessary papers & letters & tidied up, & I bought a lot of crimson flowers & blue hydrangeas—& I even didn't have fish for my lunch—as it makes such a stink when it's cooking & I wanted the house to reveal only an atmosphere of charm. And then you never arrived—& telephoned to say you had been delayed. What a word of emotion can be contained in a formal word "delayed." I suppose Heloise & Abelard were delayed. . . .

Meanwhile your *Queen Mary* is speeding away at full throttle, & your days until arrival will be completely unreal—timeless—inhuman. Then you will arrive in Manhattan. To do what? The sturgeon will have to face appalling squalid rows with his wife—Heaven preserve me from knowing the full horror of the Schlee ménage—& by the time the *Queen Mary* returns, refuels &

charges over the Atlantic again, I trust it will be bringing me to you.[37]

It was October. Soon afterward Cecil sailed the Atlantic for his habitual three-month winter visit to fulfill contracts for *Vogue.* He was destined for a surprise.

Garbo by Beaton, the Plaza Hotel, New York, 1946.

CHAPTER 6

He was in love with her. He certainly was. Or infatuated. A better word really. Curiously enough Cecil was one of the few people who gave her any physical satisfaction.

—TRUMAN CAPOTE[1]

GARBO AND CECIL: THE AFFAIR

Though Garbo had been much on his mind during the previous weeks, Cecil's first days in New York in October 1947 were filled with other romantic interests. For some time he had entertained a yearning for the good-looking actor Geoffrey Toone, who had played Lord Windermere in *Lady Windermere's Fan.* Toone was in New York that fall, as was an Australian whom Cecil had met in Bombay in 1944 and of whom he had written, "He is the sort of person I'd like to have in my life. Sad that our ways were divergent."[2] Only after the Australian left Manhattan did Cecil try to contact "the person who has occupied my mind for the last two years."[3]

Cecil dialed Garbo's number, and the operator told him, "Miss Brown don't live here any more."[4] The following day he tried again, and

Garbo replied. Cecil had not seen her for a year and a half, but she was as flirtatious as ever. She asked where he was. As before, he was at the Plaza, in rooms 249 to 251. Garbo offered to visit him but warned, "It may not be before Monday."[5] As the conversation progressed, Cecil felt relieved that they were talking happily: "I am now at the beginning of a new campaign. I trust that by being clever and not forcing the issues I may win through to victory."[6]

On Monday, November 3, Cecil photographed Gertrude Lawrence in the morning. In the afternoon he prepared for his reunion with Garbo. He filled his room with flowers, scattered her favorite cigarettes about, and put on his second-best suit, optimistically saving the best for a later date. During his vigil he became extremely nervous. Then the bell rang and he opened the door to admit Garbo, looking thinner and more drawn than he remembered. "What a charming surprise," he said nervously. "Surprise?" she said.[7]

They talked inconsequentially. Cecil asked her if she had experienced any "great emotional or spiritual experiences" since they had met. Garbo elected not to tell him. Throughout their conversation, Garbo never mentioned the past, nor did she so much as glance at an album of photographs strategically placed by Cecil. Then, unexpectedly, she drew the mustard velvet curtains and turned to face him.

> I was completely surprised at what was happening & it took me some time to recover [from] my bafflement. Within a few minutes of our reunion, after these long & void periods, of months of depression & doubt, we were suddenly together in unexplained, unexpected and inevitable intimacy. It is only on such occasions that one realizes how fantastic life can be. I was hardly able to bridge the gulf so quickly & unexpectedly. I had to throw my mind back to the times at Reddish House when in my wildest dreams I had invented the scenes that were now taking place.[8]

The next evening Cecil returned somewhat late from cocktails at Gramercy Park. Garbo, a suitably mysterious figure in a sou'wester hat, was waiting outside his door. That evening was not a success. After this encounter, Cecil was treated to a spell of "Miss Brown" not answering her telephone.

A long week passed, explained away by Garbo as a time of illness. When they did meet, he thought she was too pale, though touchingly beautiful. And he was relieved that the atmosphere had lost its previous tenseness. Then began an energetic program of walks in Central Park. Cecil would wait, his nose turning "mauve with cold."[9] Garbo would arrive, often adorned in a dark blue coat and Pilgrim Father hat, with a large black bag over her shoulder, and Cecil would feel elated. To Cecil she was always "a divinely proportioned figure. . . . Very unlike the rest of humanity, so utterly romantic." Confident now, he relished the subterfuges and the way other walkers recognized her, and the frivolity of their conversation as they ran arm in arm through the park.

At the end of one afternoon, Cecil entered the Plaza alone, ordered tea, lit candles, and dismissed his secretary. Garbo arrived by the back stairs, although she had been caught by the hotel's public relations director, Prince Serge Obolensky.* Still cold from their walk, they sipped tea, while Garbo looked at her watch. "Isn't it awful to be with someone who is always following the clock, who is so strict and won't let you ask questions or scrutinize?" she asked. She then pointed toward the other room and asked, "Do you want to go to bed?" He described his reactions:

> Sometimes pictures & photographs are more like people than people themselves. Very seldom when I am walking along with Greta am I able to see her. Occasionally we stop to turn & look at the new moon, & I see her as she has appeared in a prized photograph or on the screen. This afternoon there were many flashes of her in the Pilgrim hat as she was in *Queen Christina* & later in the half light she was the living embodiment of her "stills."[10]

Cecil was still confused by this turn of events. He mused that for once he was being used for his body. When he confided in Mona Harrison Williams, she told him he was being "a dope."[11] She advised him to play Garbo's game: "You've got to get her mind," she said. "And her mind's

*Prince Serge Obolensky (1890–1978), Russian émigré married to Alice Astor.

got to worry about what's going on in your mind, and when you see the results working don't have any mercy. It's crucial."[12]

Thus, for four days Cecil fell silent. Then Garbo phoned and announced she would be "right over." She suggested he had been unfaithful and muttered, "I knew instinctively that I ought not to have waited so long." Cecil told her that he had been out with Mona until 3:00 A.M. and would be dining with her again that night. Garbo questioned him further and commented, "So you are stepping out in both directions?"

Cecil did not relent in his campaign. He did not ring, and when she called him, he would wax lyrical about Mona's beauty. On Thanksgiving Day he sent her a vase of white orchids with one of his unposted letters. Then, without further ado, he left for Boston for the weekend. Garbo called several times while he was away. The following Monday afternoon they met. While feigning jocularity, Garbo asked many jealous lover's questions. She looked "plain & peaky . . . there was a white look under her eyes & the lines were deep," observed the scrutinizing Cecil. In due course the mustard velvet curtains were drawn, and Cecil was mesmerized by those huge eyes so close to his:

> Eyes that continued to stare for so long, that never lowered their lids in sleep. For sleep is something that comes with great difficulty. We talked of many intimate things that it is difficult to talk about, but managed to achieve a happy understanding and mutual enjoyment.[13]

After a nip of whiskey, they dined at the Mayerling restaurant. Garbo criticized him for "draping" himself too much and for his stance when telephoning, hand on hip. She declared she wanted to make a man out of him. They went to the theatre, and during the play, Terence Rattigan's *The Winslow Boy,* she said, "I think I'll have to propose to you." Cecil replied, "Oh no, that wouldn't work any more. You wouldn't really like that."[14] He was pleased that she stared at him while he was watching the stage. He was besottedly admiring:

> Her mind is occupied only with the nobler aspects of life. It is far more amazing to me since I made these discoveries, to imagine

how any simple almost peasant-like person can have come upon this way of life. It is even more of a paradox to think that she should have been mixed up in the world of film making. In all my experience of her I have never known before the real strength of her asceticism. She is like a spartan warrior, a crusader in life. No matter how cleverly she is being beguiled & enticed from her straight & narrow path, she is resentful of ever veering to the side—& never forgets that person's misdeeds. . . .

The more I consider it the more I realise how important it is that I should have this incentive to a profounder more serious life. In one breath she will say "I never read anything. In bed I read that obnoxious *Journal American—American Journal*—but that's just because it's put outside my door. But really when I have been through it I'm no wiser. It hasn't made any impression at all." Then the next moment she will make some profound observation that shows an uncanny instinct & flair for moral philosophy . . .[15]

There were also practical matters about their sex life for them to discuss:

When she called me this morning & said she was not in good shape & had I not better get something else to do, it was genuine & out of lack of selfishness, for it seems that although she had planned our evening to be of a passionate nature & had so looked forward to it, as a result of my last embraces she was now in too delicate a state to allow herself to be further abused. I had behaved like a boor—& had hurt her & now she must await several days until she recovers before our fulfilment can be achieved. She explained: "You see a woman is such a delicate object. You have to be very careful & not abuse her. The tissues are so easily damaged. You have to be very gentle. Isn't it obnoxious!"[16]

Cecil continued with Mona's ploys, and they continued to work. During a walk in the rain, Garbo chirped:

I like you, I like you. It's not a big word. It's just a small word, but I like you, & whenever I say goodbye I want to see you again.

> I'd like to go away somewhere, where there is a big balcony & I'd come along the balcony & go to bed with you.

She joked, "I think I shall have to propose to you, make an honest man of you,"[17] and Cecil began to entertain the possibility that she might suddenly marry him. "I have pictured to myself all the possibilities and would like so much to take on the risk, to take the opportunity of having a really new start in life."[18]

One night, after seeing a raucous play, they went to a nightclub, the Blue Angel. Garbo watched the cabaret with childlike relish, whispering from time to time, "I love you, I love you." It was almost too much for him: "Of all the people I have admired to make a beeline that ends thus is almost too good to grasp. It is to date my greatest triumph."[19] Later Garbo invited him in to room 26C of the Ritz Towers for the first time. While she rustled up a simple meal, he inspected her room, no easy matter, since she would not allow the lights to be turned on. After some kissing, he left at around 3:00 A.M. On his way home he mused on how he might turn their relationship into something more lasting, yet he did not wish to "try to make something exquisite & ethereal into a humdrum reality."

One day they discussed Mercedes, currently in New York:

> Greta said there must be something wrong, otherwise she wouldn't be so alone, so unpopular and miserable. "But she's done me such harm, such mischief, has gossiped so and been so vulgar. She's always trying to scheme and find out things and you can't shut her up." . . . When I said she had asked me point blank if I was having an affair with her, G. said, "That's just like her. It's so vulgar."[20]

Garbo told him she had contemplated marrying Bill Paley, the chairman of CBS. Cecil then said, "Why don't you marry me?"

"Why?"

"Because I am not rich. I have nothing to offer you but salvation."[21]

Garbo seldom spoke of Schlee but, having again been spotted by Serge Obolensky in the Plaza, she said, "Well, I do have the rottenest luck. I bet the 'little man' will see me next and then my goose will be cooked."[22] Garbo explained that Schlee was under the weather and tired of having to look after the sixty women who worked for his wife. Nor did he like going home at the end of the day. Cecil concluded optimistically, "This is the first time she has alluded to the Schlee business. It is obviously a drab necessity that she must go through with." He was pleased when she announced she would retreat to California when he left. "There is nothing to keep me in New York," she said.[23]

Christmas approached, and Garbo became more outgoing. Before a performance of *A Streetcar Named Desire* that she was attending with Schlee she said, "How would you like me to telephone you afterwards and if the devil's in me I'll come right over and spend the night."[24] But she did not appear, nor did she ever stay the whole night or allow Cecil to do so. But, ever the coquette, the next morning she telephoned and appeared in his rooms:

> In the brilliant light she was as beautiful as ever. The eyes like an eagle's of pale mauve blue. The skin on the neck and chest of the finest grain and as shiny as marble. Her legs long and like a young girl of fifteen. The skin is deep apricot in colour. We were very happy in our mutual ecstasy. Sunday morning had been put to its ultimate use.[25]

Garbo then tied her hair back with a yellow ribbon and they shared a bath amid happy laughter. Cecil began to take his happiness for granted. As he reported to Clarissa Churchill (his special confidante) in England:

> As always I suppose I am anxious to try and make these delights more binding and permanent but I doubt if I shall really succeed although my self assurance is beginning to be something quite alarming. I have never before realized the strength of a thought. If one has this little seed planted in one's head it can grow into something that really moves mountains. For years I had put the wrong little seed in my head and it made me very unhappy.[26]

On another visit to her apartment, Cecil discussed what he should call Garbo. He hated her various pseudonyms, "Miss G." and "Miss

Brown." She hated to be called "Greta." He hit on "Wife." Pleased with this, he shouted it out. "No, no, you must be quiet," she said. "There's never any sound in the apartment. It's as if no one ever lived here. Never any noises at all." Cecil noted in his diary, "And I can well believe it."[27]

On Christmas Eve, Cecil was ill in bed with a cold, and Garbo came to visit him. The plan for Christmas Day was lunch with Mercedes (whom Garbo now called "the little black and white" on account of her austere black clothes and white powdered face). She kept Mercedes in the dark about whom she was bringing, merely saying, "You'll know soon enough so long as you've got the extra place."[28] On Christmas Day, Cecil made his way to the Ritz Towers and out of idle curiosity opened the kitchen door. Garbo was furious at this intrusion into her privacy and rebuked him. Cecil was duly crushed. They went to Mercedes's, and a "rather pathetic and silly chorus boy sissy"[29] called "Mr. Everly" (Cecil Everly, a onetime manservant, later a socialite) also arrived. Garbo was in high spirits, singing and reciting poems and bits of Heine. But at 3:00 P.M. she suddenly left, taking Cecil with her. As they neared Schlee territory she walked on ahead, urging Cecil to phone her that evening.

That evening Cecil dined at Mona's. After dinner, with the women upstairs and the Duke of Windsor lingering over port with the men in the dining room, he phoned Garbo. She told Cecil not to display the plate she had given him for Christmas as it was a favorite of Schlee's. After dinner Mona gave a ball that Cecil left at 3:30 with a splitting headache. When he awoke the next day, New York was under a layer of snow. He still felt ill but had to photograph a society bride. Cecil had arranged drinks at his apartment, and it proved no mean challenge for his guests to get there. Garbo arrived in gum boots and a seafarer's hat with Schlee. The other guests included George Davis, Salvador Dalí, Alan Porter, and Natasha Wilson. Cecil examined his rival:

> As for Georges I do not trust him at all. He seemed very ill at ease and his eyes never met mine with any confidence or honesty. He seemed to emanate a very troubled electric atmosphere and even the drinks did not give him a false confidence in me. He made one

> or two remarks that I did not think in the highest quality. On arrival he said: "You must have asked an enormous number of people here," and when accepting another drink, said "I'll just have a sip to show—there's no ill feeling." I whispered to Greta: "Is it going all right with him?" and she said with infinite conviction: "Ooh Yaais."[30]

As the party broke up and the other guests were leaving, Cecil tried to sneak a quick kiss. A look of terror crossed Garbo's face and she said, "Don't be so silly."

On New Year's Eve 1947–48, Cecil dined with the Harrison Williamses. Cecil was pleased when he received a telephone message: "It's Mr. Thompson on the line." Garbo, weepy after a difficult evening with Schlee, wanted Cecil to join her. Mona gave him permission to sneak away. He taxied down Park Avenue, with its centipede of brilliant Christmas trees, and observed the other merrymakers. He thought himself "the luckiest person in the world."[31] Soon he and Garbo were drinking 1840 whiskey, a gift from Margaret Case, in his rooms at the Plaza. He toasted their marriage, at which Garbo smiled a little diffidently, and then they fell to wild, tender embraces "and we had neither enough arms to entwine around each other's shoulders and waist."[32] The pair then stood by the hotel window as sirens sounded, car horns honked, and 1948 dawned.

—

On January 2, 1948, a telephone message was left for room 249 of the Plaza, addressed to "Mrs. Beaton." It read simply, "Mr. Thompson phoned."[33]

—

Throughout January and almost all of February, Cecil and Garbo remained together in New York. Often Garbo would say, "I must be going," which would herald sex:

> I did not know that so many fancies could be born of the moment and in so many different moods of sentimentality, playfulness,

> emotional love or sheer lust. I began to realize how much time I had wasted and how little I had learnt in the sphere of lovemaking.[34]

Garbo gave Cecil pointers about technique. "I don't like anything rough or staccato,"[35] she said. Cecil could not believe his luck: "Here I was with someone whom I'd always wanted to love me and here she was loving me."[36] Their outings were full of sexual innuendo. "Wouldn't you like to put it in your mouth and feel it growing bigger?"[37] she asked, gazing at the exposed nipple of a female figure by Michelangelo in a museum. She discussed homosexuality, saying that people "could lead their hidden lives, have their exciting secrets, that she herself was always intrigued by paths that were slightly fantastic, but public flaunting of these things was obnoxious."[38] Gradually Cecil found he was more spellbound by her "wonderful and noble" character than by her beauty.

Meanwhile Schlee succumbed to a nervous illness. Having devoted the past four years to Garbo, he did not like the recent developments.

Just before Cecil's forty-fourth birthday, Garbo became nervous while drinking vodka with him and inquired, "You don't write about people, do you?"[39] He wrote in his diary:

> I was really shocked and upset that she should ask me this for it was a hangover of the past and I thought was entirely forgotten and forgiven. I said "How could you imagine I should ever do anything that hurts you. I love you so much. I only want to do the things that will make you love me more. Surely you trust me?"—"How would I hang around the Plaza the way I do if I didn't. But people have so often used me, have hurt me by doing things that have surprised me. I've known crooks and they've wanted to use me, and they have, and though I've been shocked and . . . I still don't believe they're bad."[40]

Garbo was onto something, since Cecil's diary for the period between November 1947 and March 1948 is devoted almost exclusively to her. Neither of them then knew the trouble this would cause them, yet as a record of a star in her lonely middle age and of a man long obsessed and finally living out the reality of his dreams, it remains a vivid, important document.

Cecil hoped Garbo would soon go to California and that he could follow her. He asked if he might stay with her there, but she said the house was disorganized and it would worry and embarrass her. Then on one bad day, after a meeting with Schlee, Garbo telephoned with what she called "very sad news."[41] Schlee was making a fuss about her seeing Cecil. Therefore he must not come to California. He was desperate, but when they met he told her he had genuine business to discuss with Alfred Hitchcock. She winked and said, "Then I couldn't prevent your doing that."[42]

Cecil grew more and more confident of the sexual hold he had on her. He explained this in his diary:

> I am so unexpectedly violent and have such unlicensed energy when called upon. It baffles and intrigues and even shocks her. May this last a long time!! After a time I had a rebirth of vitality & was not at all tired when I took her back home.[43]

In the midst of all this activity, Mercedes arranged to dine with Cecil. He wrote a long account of the evening:

> Greta gave me various suggestions as to how to avoid answering any ambiguous questions that her curiosity might prompt her to ask. "Just say: 'Now really Mercedes you must be nutski' or look her straight in the face & say 'I don't know what you're talking about' "—But the evening was very different from the one I had imagined. To begin with I asked Mercedes many questions about her incredible sister Mrs. Lydig, her extravagances, her clothes, her patronage of the arts, her travelling with her own masseuse, hairdresser, valet, maid—seven in all. . . .
>
> At dinner we talked about Gandhi's death—the spiritual life in India, & it was not until well on in the meal that we talked about Greta & then it was Mercedes who talked & never once asked me any questions or seemed to be curious or indiscreet in fact to show herself as anything but the most wonderful & loyal friend of 20

years devotion—in the face of many setbacks & raw deals—for Greta is really unkind to her & gives her terrible mental beatings. Mercedes started by saying that she was really worried about Greta—felt that she was in a terrible quandary—that her life was at the cross roads—& if she continued for another 2 years to squander any valuable & fleeting time she would be finished & left without any interests in life—& few enough friends. She says that the conflict that always goes on in Greta's mind—whether about accepting an unimportant invitation she is loath to come to any decision—is the reason why she will not now work in the movies—She would like to—yes—but—then the dread comes in—& although she is a great actress with the temperament of an artist—she does not reconcile herself to films. She has always despised them & even her best ones she has felt were of no value or quality. Even when she was able to dictate about films she would like to play she was still miserably unhappy & when Mercedes drove her to the studio for the opening day's work on *Marie Walewska,* Greta was in tears all the way in the car, saying "This is prostitution."

"Yet she feels that she should act of her own happiness—that she has this fount of energy that may be given release—& what is her life now? Hunting around Third Avenue junk shops for furniture for Schlee's apartment & waiting for him to telephone. Where does it lead? His wife has a stronger character & firmer hold than Greta—after 2 years she'll get her husband back—& what for Greta? It worries me so much I can't sleep at night!" She discussed the possibilities—of going back to nothing in Hollywood—of staying under Schlee's influence in N.Y. or of going to Europe. I was very surprised when Mercedes said: "She said she might go to stay with you in England!"

I longed to get Mercedes on my side—to beg her to use that little influence she has to swing Greta towards me, but, maybe, fortunately, I spoke not one word—while Mercedes continued her diatribe against the way Schlee has mismanaged the European trip, seeing the worst sorts of Americans that she scrupulously avoids here—she told me nauseating stories of their stay in Paris. "It's so unfair—that this wonderful being should be exploited so—& doesn't realise it. She's like a child in her naivete & she's always been exploited—Look at Stokowski—they went to Italy together & she discovered there that he was sending back reports to the American papers about their forthcoming marriage—When she discovered this she left for Sweden with her sister-in-law."

Then she touched on the subject of Greta's family. "But" warned Mercedes "don't ever mention it to Greta. It's a sore subject. She doesn't like it talked about, but it makes me very sad, for she doesn't see her mother & I fear when her mother dies she will have great remorse & sadness."

"But isn't the mother dead? I thought she died 2 years ago."

"No she's here in Connecticut staying with her son—& they are very unhappy that they never hear from Greta."

I asked about the mother. "She has Greta's narrow brow but that is all." Mercedes told me a great deal that was of such fascination to me that the restaurant where we ate was emptied of Dalí & the other clients & we were the last to leave.

"Greta's much less melancholy now than she used to be. I went to see her the other afternoon & she asked me what could she do in life—& she stays awake at night brooding & getting thoroughly low. Nevertheless she is much happier than she used to be. When we lived together in Hollywood she used to come back from the studio in tears most nights, abysmally unhappy—& she would sit alone locked in the cellar & for days on end she wouldn't talk. But now she's much more stable—though she is such a perfectionist in her work that she's never happy while on a picture. She wants every scene she does to be perfect & she never comes up to her standards. That's why she would never go to see rushes. They would always disappoint & depress her, but she's a very intuitive actress, does not know what she is doing. She's very mediumistic; although she has no idea of how to behave in great ballrooms or with royalty at all, it comes quite easily to her in front of the camera. Once the Crown Prince of Sweden came to Hollywood & she was placed on his right at a banquet—& she waited all the time to see which knife & fork he would use—& she copied him & she laughed because later everyone said he had used the wrong ones—& she had followed suit. But if that scene had been played before the cameras she would have instinctively picked up the right forks & played the scene with the ease acquired of the manner born."

This alone may sound rather gossipy but Mercedes's real devo-

> tion & unselfish affection prompted every thought she uttered during the evening & she had no personal axe to grind, nothing to offer in fact except the great desire to help Greta all she can—& Greta has few people who can help her.[44]

Cecil took another series of portrait shots of Garbo sitting in his apartment. Then he began a new campaign, based on the arrival of Alexander Korda in New York that February. Because Garbo had expressed some interest in Cocteau's Elisabeth of Austria play, *The Eagle Has Two Heads*, Cecil suggested to Korda that she should be invited to star in it. Korda and Garbo had a meeting that went well, though Korda refused to let her see the recent *Anna Karenina* with Vivien Leigh, since he was rightly ashamed of the performance of Kieron Moore as Vronsky. Cecil encouraged Garbo, longing to take credit for her return to the screen and equally longing to dress her for the part. For a time he was as keen on the film idea as on that of marriage.

Inevitably, Schlee intervened in the film question, acting, in Cecil's words, as "the second agent."[45] One night Cecil, with Garbo's collusion, followed them to the theatre to spy on them. Garbo was strikingly dressed, with her hair hidden under a black skullcap. Though Cecil remained discreetly out of view, he was sure Schlee could sense his presence: "At times I felt that the vibrations sent out from me to her must surely be felt by everyone in the theatre."[46]

Although it was Cecil's firm intention to follow Garbo to Hollywood, he told her he was probably going to sail back to England. On February 20 he suffered the awareness of an unwelcome truth in a coincidence in the theatre. He decided to call Garbo during the intermission, but the phone booth was occupied. Increasingly irritated, Cecil nearly tapped on the door. Then the door opened and Schlee emerged. Cecil's initial amusement soon turned to worry: "But seeing Schlee fly to the telephone as I do, and that after seven years, gives me an indication of how dreadfully devoted he must be, and that here is really something to have to contend with—a really tough battle! But the reward is worth it."[47]

Three days later, he and Garbo met before she left for California. They were both purposefully vague about the future:

> We went into the other room and I watched her wonderful face staring at me, or turning her head "profile perdue" with the chin thrown back and revealing the incredible beauty of the line of her throat. The sun was pouring through the windows and I would have liked to have remained until it was long after dark, but once more in a hurry . . . I heard some slight scuffling in the room, like the wind blowing tissue paper. It was Greta dressing herself. When I protested she said she had only remained so that I might have some satisfaction from her tired little body.[48]

Garbo left for California the next day, while Cecil remained in Manhattan. On the evening before she left, he went to see a film with his actor friend Geoffrey Toone. Garbo telephoned him while Toone was in the room, which made conversation stilted. Later he phoned back, and they said good-bye, wondering, as she said, "what Fate has for us."[49]

A few days later, Cecil wrote to Garbo in California:

> My Angel
>
> I thought about you such a lot—at ten minutes to six while you were waiting for the train to leave—at six o'clock when it started to take you away on such a long journey—& then during the following night & day I pictured you chugging away inclosed in your very stuffy & confined metal box. For days & days I figured out you would still be imprisoned in that foul smelling grit collecting compartment & I wondered if after the first day of it you wouldn't start to have a headache. Your departure has created a great blank in my life. I have been very busy with so many things pouring down on me at the same moment,* but even so your absence has been keenly felt throughout the hours. Whenever I have been walking along the streets I have seen shops or corners or objects in the shop windows that we saw together or conjured up various meetings with you, & I have felt very grateful for so many sweet memories, but sad that now they are of the past. It

*Cecil was very busy taking photographs for *Vogue*.

has made me feel very lonely—& really bored. Whenever the telephone bell rings I don't care—because I know it won't be you. I have very little curiosity left.

You have been away four days & it seems like an eternity. Even the city looks quite different. It is no longer winter. It is even more like London than New York with dark almost black daylight, a lot of rain & unbelievable slush. Our snow clad park is unrecognisable. The last of the dirty stratas of ice & snow have melted & there's a sort of foetid balminess in the air.

I am really not interested to remain here any longer. I have been doing quite interesting things as I wanted to break out from my usual rut & I've been exploring odd corners of the city & staying out very late at night. One night I went to the small French boîte that I'd always wanted to take you to. It is between 8th and 9th avenue—has sawdust on the floor & the most delicious French cooking—wonderful pâtés, a chicken cooked whole in a red pot, excellent coarse potage & on arrival one is greeted with the welcome whiff of French tobacco. This should have been one of our haunts this winter—but somehow it wasn't. It was another of the things we never got around to. Then later that night—much later—I was taken to the Greek quarter of the city & went to very peculiar nightclubs where we drank Ouzo & watched hideous Greek women doing belly dances to Arab music. The clientele exclusively sweaty Greek & ugly & so removed from New York that one thought one had been transplanted to the poor quarters of Athens.

Last night—very late—I was taken to a place where young men looking like a lot of starlings dance together to the juke box. In its way quite a sight. Before that I had been to a private showing of a most moving & beautiful French film, *Le Diable au Corps* with Gérard Philipe, the young man we admired in *The Idiot,* playing the part of a sixteen-year-old college boy who falls in love with a girl older than himself, & has to assume the appalling responsibility of being responsible for her death in childbirth. The young man gave one of the most poignant & lovely performances I have ever seen. He looked much younger & uglier than in the Russian story. It is a film that comes once in twenty years. There is nothing wrong with it. Every detail so sensitive &

imaginative. It was a great experience & I was very touched & of course some of the tender love partings & reunions went very close to my heart.

All the people I have come across are terribly upset about the alarming news of Russia's aggression. People think that unless we make some much more definite stop to Russia now that we will sooner or later be involved in another holocaust.* It is really too ghastly to contemplate. We must remember time may be short, & that without being reckless, we must be as happy now as we can be.

Poor Alex Korda came back looking very rattled & overtired. I had a difficult session with him as he altered his point of view so often. At one moment delighted if I do the Hitchcock work—& then saying "No I won't play second fiddle to anyone. I'll give you what you want." In the end nothing definite has been decided except that he said I can always "have my berth" with him & his company. He said that if you were really serious about signing a contract** he would start on plans right away, but he regretted that your agent "had had to go to Bermuda," though he was quite funny about it. I do think the one most important thing to state very firmly at this point is that under no circumstances would you have Kieron Moore opposite you. It is my secret bet that Alex still tries to kid himself, & others, with thinking that this Irish lout can be made into a sympathetic lover. He is terribly stubborn. A friend of mine who works for him [Clarissa Churchill] in London wrote me this morning "Poor, Poor Alex. It is a tragedy that a man of such intelligence must bear the burden of such terrible mistakes without really knowing what has happened. More a tragedy that no one can, or ever will be able, to help him—no counsellor or friend—he is quite damned."

He gave me the script for the "Eagle" to read. It is just a rough treatment & there are still too many signs of it being an

*In January 1948 the British prime minister, Clement Attlee, had issued a warning about the spread of Soviet communism, describing this as a new form of imperialism. On January 23 he declared that Britain wanted to have friendly relations with the Soviets but would never accept communism.

**For *The Eagle Has Two Heads.*

adaption of a stage play—but there are wonderful scenes in it. Only you could bring it to life in the way that it must be. Romantic & mysterious, & you will give the necessary warmth & humanity. I was very encouraged. I think it can be a fine film. I told him you would like to have Mrs. Viertel work on the script & he thought that an easy thing to arrange, & he would certainly do that if it would make you happy. But he himself would not suppose the lady in question had much gift for dialogue.

I miss you so much. I trust you will be settling down in your new environment with many tender thoughts of your devoted friend.

Cecil[50]

In response to this, an unsigned telegram reading "THANK YOU AND LOVE" arrived at his hotel.[51]

—

Cecil stayed on in New York for a few more days before advancing on California:

> To make my winter's conquest complete I knew I must see her in her own home. I must be able to spend the days uninterruptedly with her, just to stay from morning until bedtime without her looking at her watch and saying "Got to go now."[52]

Luck played into Cecil's hands. Having convinced himself that Garbo wanted to see him, he made plans for a four-day visit. Nor did he rush it. Then *Vogue* commissioned him to do some work and agreed to pay all his expenses. His trip to the West Coast lasted from March 3 to 15, but he worked for *Vogue* only in the second week. As he set off, there was still the danger that Garbo would not see him or that Schlee would materialize to frustrate his plans.

Garbo met him at a bus stop in Beverly Hills and drove him to her home. Though she was nervous as to what his reactions to her house might be, he was thrilled. He looked about at the Renoirs, the Modigliani, the Rouault, and the Bonnard and prided himself on being inside "the Holy of Holies."[53]

Cecil took Garbo into his arms:

> In a bout of tenderness I gathered her into a series of long embraces. We suddenly looked at each other in startled amazement. "You really want to in the middle of the morning?" In a trance I went upstairs through her sitting-room up the circular stairs to her pale blue, pale grey and burgundy coloured bedroom. We were very happy in our fervour and something very violent had overtaken us both. We had not seen one another for so long. Our reunion was most passionate and ended in a serenity that was most beneficial. We came downstairs the tenderest of friends.*[54]

In the evening Garbo cooked for him as the night grew cold: "My teeth were still chattering as I went upstairs again to Greta's room. I was very grateful for the solace of her hot water bottles & later for the soothing warmth of her nakedness. I was in a state of enchantment & creativity, of love & lust & tenderness."[55] But even now she did not let him stay the night. Nevertheless, Cecil was perfectly happy: "It was the day on which I entered the portals of Paradise."[56]

During the next idyllic days Garbo worked in the garden, they drove to market, and in the evenings they dined together. The former hearty strolls in Central Park were replaced by energetic walks along the Santa Monica beaches. As he inhaled the scent of an orange tree, he declared, "This is everything that I came all this way to enjoy."[57] And he stored up memories for an uncertain future: "If there is another war then I shall be able to remember that I had the ecstasy of this night."**[58] Another day he sunbathed naked, finding Garbo "a little less loving and more matter of fact. But the night of bliss cannot be sustained ad infinitum."[59] When "the Dragon" (Garbo's maid) was out, she too sunbathed naked and washed herself down with the hose. But passion was never far away:

*This passage and several of those that follow were erased by Cecil from his manuscript diary but copied down identically in his own hand on a separate sheet of paper.

**Another expurgated diary entry.

"After a slight siesta we suddenly aspired to make another trip upstairs to the bedroom & to work off our animal steam. The intensity of our lust was terrific & I marvelled at the inevitable. It seemed so pure & natural."[60]

Occasionally they saw old friends, like the Mendls and Clifton Webb. On these occasions Cecil felt eclipsed by his famous friend. He preferred to be alone with her, lighting a cigar and smoking it as he lay with her on the cedar-colored sofa.

On Monday, March 8, Cecil began work for *Vogue*, which afforded him an image of Hollywood, "vulgar, cruel and relentless."[61] He welcomed his return to the haven of Garbo's home. One day bad news came when Korda wired that he could not do *The Eagle* but suggested Garbo might try *The Cherry Orchard* with Cukor. She declared Chekhov a bore.

On only one evening were Garbo and Cecil separated. She dined with the Mendls and Mary Pickford while he kept a date with Garson Kanin and Ruth Gordon. On Friday, March 12, they went to MGM to see the Garbo version of *Anna Karenina*. "Well, well," she said. "It takes Beaton to get me to the studios for the first time in six years."[62] They dined with Salka Viertel and her husband. Alone later, Garbo asked, "Do you love me?" and they went upstairs together to enjoy almost the last opportunity of being together before Cecil had to go home:

> Some time later in the dark, Greta said "Would you like me to tell you a little story?" & then explained that I had never before made love to her as I did tonight, that to begin with I'd been so rough & now was gentle & understanding & the desired result had been achieved. I felt very happy and pleased with myself and great satisfaction for my prowess as a lover. Then I must hurry home for Greta was very tired. We waved tenderly to each other in the night. As I trailed my weary body home I wondered if I had made any advance on this trip towards the goal of marriage, towards an arrangement for a film or even a trip to England, and I must admit that I had not. However this has been a most happy, idyllic interlude. I am forever amazed that I have had these long uninterrupted days with my loved one and through all the hours together

> we have always been sympathetic companions though most of the time we have been besotted lovers.[63]

Not everything went according to plan. Garbo would not allow Cecil to draw her, and the photographs he took made her look rather middle-aged and not at all his image of her. On their last day they visited Catherine d'Erlanger and the photographer George Platt Lynes and met Katherine Anne Porter. In his private talks with Garbo, Cecil was insecure, feeling that she did not deem him a serious person:

> In that there is a modicum of truth for I have never until I met her realized how little I am able to scratch beneath the surface of the meaning of things.[64]

Back at her house, they were alone again:

> I have a picture of her as a sort of Saint Sebastian laid out for suffering with her head thrown back and her arms held high with clenched fists. I have a picture of her profile outlined with a red glow from the heating light on the wall by the bed.
>
> I remember her turning her head and gazing at me very sadly. Tomorrow I leave. This is our last night together. We lingered in each other's clasp in the hall and then the pantomime of the waving from door and window. As I walked home I wondered if I was not in a way relieved that I was departing tomorrow.[65]

Cecil was exhausted by the intensity of the relationship. Garbo was lacking sleep and succumbing to the strain. Unlike her, Cecil both wanted to work and had to in order to support his mother and pay his bills:

> I have done nothing for so long and I feel I should now set seriously to my other tasks. For the past four months I have done little else but devote myself to my passion for Greta.[66]

For his departure Cecil bought a huge bouquet of mixed flowers. He took them to Garbo's house: "I felt rather as if I were about to undergo an operation, an amputation, but my voice was very clear and cold."[67] Suddenly emotion overcame him. His chest quivered, and he shook with sobs. The tears flowed freely down his cheeks. As he got into the cab, he gazed at her "looking like a tired, sad child of sixteen, looking at me with such infinite pity and sorrow."[68]

The taxi driver tried to talk to him, but Cecil could not concentrate. He was "convulsed in childlike tears and sobs."[69] He was in for a long train journey back to New York, and as he rattled across America, he recorded the circumstances of his love affair in his manuscript diary.

—

Cecil remained in New York less than a week before sailing to England on March 27. There was time for one letter to Garbo, written on a Sunday morning:

> My dearest one,
> As I can't fly out to you again just yet, I am very impatient for next Saturday, when I sail in the opposite direction. New York is beastly. It is haunting. It has changed so much since you have gone. The bracing cold has given way to a sweaty mugginess, everything looks dirty & ugly but there are too many things to remind me of the nice times we had together—the Park, 57th Street at Park Avenue, "Butler's Studio," the dribbling cat restaurant, Maria Remarque* & even that awful John Gunther** & his brand new wife† remind me of you—and then there are all the

*Erich Maria Remarque (1898–1970), German novelist, author of *All Quiet on the Western Front.*

**John Gunther (1901–70), whose best-known book was *Inside Europe.* His "Inside" reports provided bird's-eye views on the people and politics of the continents he wrote about. He was one of Garbo's intimate friends, and there were copies of his books in her Manhattan apartment.

†Jane Gunther, formerly Vandercook. She became John Gunther's second wife early in 1948. She first met Garbo in 1947 and became friends with her and also with the Schlees. They remained friends until Garbo's death, Jane Gunther writing in the Sotheby's sale catalogue, "In the last years we used to talk about nothing in particular several times a week."

places we didn't get to together. . . . No. The days that have passed since last Monday have seemed pointless. Perhaps it isn't New York's fault. The spark has gone out of me & I'm not interested in what's going on. I might as well hurry back to England & make the cut even more complete. And trust in our destiny that we shall soon again meet.

I cannot thank you enough for my visit to you. It was much more than I could have ever hoped for. It was everything I might have dreamt of. If Zoë Akins* felt she had the entree to the Vatican when she was given a glimpse of your swimming pool you can imagine how I felt at being allowed to share your existence for that brief but limitless period when there were long uninterrupted spells & we were living outside clock time—in another sphere of happiness. It was wonderful for me to feel so close & attached, & I felt we got to know one another much better. You can rely on me always to feel for you an increasing devotion & affection.

Thank you. Thank you. For the salad luncheons shared with you & the blue birds, for the walks by the Pacific ocean & in the mountains, & the expeditions to the Farmer's Market & seed shop, & for the lovely sunny days in your garden. Thank you. Thank you. Merci infiniment!

Muchas grazias.
Dunke schon.

In spite of the wee little Swedish rabbits the train journey seemed endless. There was a welcome respite of five hours at Chicago where I had an excellent luncheon with the rabbits & afterwards went to the Art Institute. Here I was lucky enough to have a final glimpse of the French tapestries. They reminded me of our visit & I had a special fondness for the pet dog & rabbit & other small animals you had pointed out.

Dazed & headachy I eventually arrived at the Plaza just as Miss Cleghorn was getting the keys for the new room. I am economising by living in a double room on the same floor so that Eugene still wheels in the breakfast but the last weekly bill will not be such

*Zoë Akins (1886–1958) had written the screenplay for *Camille.*

a burden. Already the train journey is quite forgotten as a dream. But not my ten days in California.

I have been out once or twice, to a poor effort of a play about Hollywood, to a very sexy Italian film, to a particularly boring dinner at Patcevitchs* for all the dressmakers—a worse dressed collection you couldn't imagine, & as a group they are more limited in their interests & even less kind about one another than actors.

George Cukor found a lot of wiriness & vitality in England & seems to have packed an incredible amount of activity into such a short visit. He said that Korda was enthusiastic to do any picture that you & George would like to do. So we must really put our heads together. I shall keep my eyes skinned but won't waste your time with suggestions unless I am convinced that something has possibilities. It is so discouraging & perplexing to weigh the pros & cons of something that hasn't got the real substance.

I am sad to think you have had four days of not feeling well & a chill on the stomach to boot. But now you must rest & allow your poor body a little relaxation. Don't dig or saw or paint & spread fertiliser too strenuously & don't allow any black & white troubles to get you down.

I am conscious of this being a silly & pretentious letter & it doesn't say anything that I really feel—but none the less I will send it to you, & I have had a feeling of happiness in writing it because it is to you—

With my deep love & devotion
Cecil

P.S. Don't forget I have a double cabin on the *Queen Elizabeth* sailing the 27th inst. If you can utilise the extra bunk I shall be more than delighted.

*Iva Voidato-Patcevitch (1901–93), a Russian émigré who became Condé Nast's assistant and took over as president of Condé Nast Publications after Nast's death in 1942. Married for some years to Nada Ruffer, onetime fashion editor of British *Vogue*. Nada told Cecil in 1946, "We're rich now. But who cares? It's come twenty years too late."

Don't forget that there are freighters leaving direct from California to England & I could meet you on arrival at Southampton which is not far from my home.

Don't forget!

Don't forget![70]

He signed off with a sketch of a heart pierced by an arrow.

Cecil Beaton at Reddish House, in the village of Broadchalke, in Wiltshire.

CHAPTER 7

THE BROADCHALKE LETTERS

Cecil returned home to England a happier man. In October 1947 he had been experiencing the frustrations of writing to Garbo and receiving no reply. But now they had begun a love affair. For Cecil it was a conquest, the capture of a great star and one of the most famously elusive figures of the twentieth century. It was something else for Garbo. She was fond of Cecil, beguiled by him, and they had fun together. But her attitude to sex was one of Scandinavian practicality. Their affair could never mean as much to her as it did to him.

There were other complications—the ever-threatening presence of Georges Schlee, for instance, and Cecil's uncertainty as to the nature of that relationship. History does not answer this question. Schlee had become what Kenneth Tynan described as "a sort of Kafkaesque guard, employed to escort her to her next inscrutable rendez-vous."[1] There were even rumors that there had been a relationship between Garbo and Valentina. Again, there is no conclusive evidence.

There was a dilemma in Cecil's mind as to what he ultimately wanted. At one time his ambition had been to photograph Garbo. This had been achieved, the results had been published, and Cecil had been forgiven. Now he was keen to bring her back into films, and he wanted to be the man to dress her. Had Garbo agreed to make another film, Cecil would have been to the fore. In this there was considerable personal ambition, but ambition of the most constructive and positive kind. Beaton created some beautiful costumes for stage and film, transforming many actresses into dreamlike creatures.

During his love affair, Cecil had also been more than energetic in recording her every movement, inflection, and change of mood. Lengthy conversations were transcribed. This is not the action of a besotted lover, since it distances the one partner from the other. It is of course the traditional duty of the social historian, and Cecil's diaries, with their razor-sharp portraits of his contemporaries, have indeed assured him a place in the history of his time. From Garbo's point of view, however, it was nothing short of betrayal.

Cecil sought to consolidate his victory. He believed his life would be complete if he could persuade Garbo to marry him and settle down with him. This was by no means a passing fancy. The next step in his campaign, therefore, was to get Garbo away from Schlee and safely into the Wiltshire countryside. It was a campaign that would last two and a half years.

Cecil arrived home from New York at the beginning of April. A telegram awaited him at his London apartment in Pelham Place, dated March 31. It read simply "CECIL"[2] and it came from Garbo. As in the previous year, his overtures to her were letters and the occasional telephone call. Of the letters he wrote he preserved copies. The charitable explanation for this is that he was using them as a substitute for the diary he normally kept. The letters are packed with his news, and he wrote regularly at length. The uncharitable explanation is that he was keeping a record for later publication. The letters do not constitute a regular correspondence as such. Between April and November, Garbo wrote only one letter back, though she occasionally acknowledged them with a word—literally a word.

When not preoccupied with Garbo during this time, Cecil worked with gusto on an ill-fated play, *The Gainsborough Girls.** He continued to decorate Reddish House, and he had many visitors. In his first letter to Garbo, he reported on his crossing from New York to London, addressing her as "Mon Seul Désir."

On arrival in England, Cecil maneuvered his way through customs and was soon driving through "the new wrought iron gates to the front door of my home."[3] Cecil was greeted by his mother and Aunt Jessie and observed plenty of evidence of work done and the continued presence of builders. He climbed into his new four-poster and read the proofs of his *Portrait of New York.* He wrote to Garbo, and next day he wrote again, beginning this time, "Mon Ange, Le Bébé dort bien??"[4] He reported that Michael Duff had returned from New York, and his mother, Lady Juliet, thought he looked "very gross." David Herbert was still in Morocco, but his boyfriend was living in his house at Wilton with a dog that had bitten Herbert's mother.

Cecil went to London to work, to scour the antique shops, and to go to the theatre. Back in Broadchalke, work continued:

> I wish you would come & give your expert help!
>
> Please, my dear young man, do scratch a few lines to your ardent suitor. If you haven't anything to write about please answer the following questionnaire:—
>
> Have you cut away all the ivy?
> Have you been exercising in the hangman's noose?
> Are you much browner than when I left?
> Are you sleeping long hours?
> Are you dreaming a lot?
> How is Madame Alba?**

**The Gainsborough Girls,* Cecil's much-rewritten play about the daughters of the eighteenth-century English painter Thomas Gainsborough, was staged in Brighton in 1951 and, renamed *Landscape with Figures,* in the provinces in 1959. It flopped each time.

**Garbo's neighbor in Hollywood.

Did you have any black & white trouble?*
Any Crocker interruptions?**
Any walks along the shore?
Any walks in the mountains?
Any further visits to the Nursery?
Do you remember the young man falling down?
The poor old woman falling down outside Macy's?
Do you remember the dog on Third Avenue?
the dog at Parke Bernet Galleries?
the dribbly cat

All these are important. I would also like to know if you are well & happy.[5]

Spring burgeoned gradually. Cecil sat on his terrace in the sun, reading books on Gainsborough. He wrote a bit and attended to the weeding. His routine, he thought, was very similar to Garbo's.[6]

On page after page, Cecil described his growing love for his house and his various activities. He darted from Salisbury to London, he was frequently at the theatre and the ballet. He was entertained by royalty and was continually in quest of new experiences. Some of his letters reveal the kind of life Garbo would have shared with him, had she been in London:

> I went to see a play about the love affairs schoolboys have with one another.† It was all rather naïf [*sic*] & melodramatic, but the audience, which consisted of men who had possibly had no love affairs since their schooldays, were riveted by the excitement & nostalgia. What made the evening particularly interesting was the

*A reference to Mercedes, who was expressing considerable curiosity about the romance.

**A reference to Harry Crocker (1894–1958), columnist with the *Los Angeles Examiner* for twenty-three years. Crocker studied law at Yale, acted in some motion pictures, and undertook some management work for certain top Hollywood personalities. It was his address Garbo used when in Los Angeles. He had been much in evidence during Cecil's California stay.

†*The Happiest Days of Your Life*, a farce by John Dighton, opened at the Apollo Theatre on March 29, 1948.

presence of Queen Mary, in white ermine & diamonds, in a box with her brother & Princess Alice.* The old girl has been stepping out to all the small theatres & if there's any play on with a rather provocative theme, she's bound to be there.** The other day I read in the paper "Queen Mary saw *Hog's Blood & Hellebore* at the Boltons on Friday night." On the Tuesday she was engrossed by the goings on in a public school dormitory. The nicest item in the evening was the behaviour of the audience. Everyone cheered the arrival of the Queen Mother, then the curtain went up, & for the rest of the evening until the end of the play, they never pried or stared. I am really very impressed by the manners of the most ordinary people here. The old lady waved & smiled at the end of the entertainment & obviously loved being such an attraction when she got into a brilliantly illuminated Daimler, but she was allowed to remain an ordinary human being for the main part of the evening.

Next evening I went to Covent Garden to hear Traviata—(Princess Margaret present). There is a new Lady of the Camellias called Schwarzkopf who was beautiful & with a good voice. I had never heard the opera before! an event! Next evening a group of friends organised a small dinner to repay some of the hospitality we had enjoyed when in Paris from Duff & Diana Cooper. . . . The gathering took place in a private room at the Ritz, we paid two guineas each towards the expenses &

*The Earl of Athlone (1874–1957) and H.R.H. Princess Alice, Countess of Athlone (1883–1981). The next day, April 14, was Lord Athlone's seventy-fourth birthday.

**Queen Mary had caused quite a stir by attending Elsa Shelley's *Pick-Up Girl*, a play about a fifteen-year-old girl, who had had both syphilis and an abortion, caught in bed with a middle-aged man. It was staged at the New Lindsey Theatre, and Queen Mary's visit prompted the Lord Chamberlain to give it a license (John Johnston, *The Lord Chamberlain's Blue Pencil* [London: Hodder and Stoughton, 1990], p. 151). Her official biographer, James Pope-Hennessy, discounted the popular view that Queen Mary was an isolated relic from a past age: "She would sally forth from Marlborough House to listen to the proceedings at a court for juvenile delinquents—'It was most interesting but I have never heard so many lies told in my life'—or to enjoy *Oklahoma* or *Annie Get Your Gun*" (James Pope-Hennessy, *Queen Mary* [London: George Allen and Unwin, 1959], p. 612).

Duff in a speech said he had had the best dinner since before the war before last. It was a good meal. Oysters—which are so much better & quite different to American oysters; sole done up in a "party" sauce—mushrooms, etc; a poussin—the first crop of asparagus—& chocolate soufflé. Wines flowing—cigars—witty speeches. You would have been amazed. It all had a very 18th century air & everyone seemed very leisurely & self assured. As unlike anything one could find in America as the oysters. . . .

My other dates in London: Lunch with one of the directors of the Old Vic [John Burrell]. He is paralysed down one side but swings along like an ape—& with inhuman strength in his arms. Theatre talk. Filthy food in a restaurant of his choosing, leather lettuce.

Lunch in a doll's house in Westminster [with Lady Waverley]. Big Ben echoing in one's ears. Very funny meal. Again my friend Diana. Also Evelyn Waugh who told us about "Behind the Scenes" at Forest Lawn.* Upstairs in the cosmetic department the beauticians talk about their subjects as "Loved Ones." "Three more loved ones for you to do before lunch time Miss Marbury." He was shown everything by the Publicity man but was not allowed to touch. Evelyn is a very sinister character, & I have been secretly frightened of him ever since my first morning at my first school when he came up in the "break" & started to bully me . . .[7]

Occasionally Cecil attempted to telephone Garbo, always a frustrating experience. Eventually in the middle of the second night, the call came through: ". . . although it was difficult to say anything except Tootleloo it was lovely to hear you, & to have spent two whole days full of expectancy," he wrote.[8]

Cecil was enjoying some gifts from Garbo: "The Battersea enamel dish you gave me looks very well in its new home. So does the green & white plate. The last of the white peppermint sweets has gone down my gullet."[9]

*Waugh published *The Loved One* that year.

Back in London, Cecil was delighted that Korda was no longer his taskmaster. He used the relative financial freedom earned by his Korda work to give him time to write his play. Truman Capote,* a new friend of Cecil's, came to stay at Broadchalke. Cecil reported to Garbo:

> I found him a very remarkable person—a genius—although only twenty three years old, he has the maturity of a man of sixty. I like him a lot, as well as being impressed & think if he lives (his blood doesn't flow easily in his veins—or some other such awful thing happens to him) he will make a contribution to the world.[10]

Christian ("Bébé") Bérard was another visitor soon afterward: "He has such zest & appreciation & I was warmed by his liking all that I had done."[11] The two were just about to go to bed when the telephone rang and a voice asked why Cecil was not at the Duchess of Kent's fancy-dress party. The dance was in full swing: "The Duchess à la grecque with pearls in her hair, Princess Liz** in Spanish costume, Prince Philip in a Policeman's uniform with handcuffs . . ."[12]

Cecil could not resist. He and Bébé drove a hundred miles through the fog to Coppins, the duchess's Buckinghamshire home, finally arriving after many vicissitudes in police stations and telephone boxes. He was afraid they would be too late, but the party was a riot of gallops and polkas:

> Some of the headdresses were funny. One elderly woman represented "night and day," one side of her face was covered with cold cream, & had her hair pulled back in curling papers, the other half was very much made up with one black eyebrow, half the lips rouged & the hair very ondule . . .[13]

The party ended at the first light of dawn, and the Duchess of Kent insisted they bed down on sofas: "It is not always agreeable being

*Truman Capote arrived in Britain on the *Queen Elizabeth* and stayed at Claridge's. His first novel, *Other Voices, Other Rooms,* was about to be published in Europe. But its success in the United States had made Capote famous, and he was lionized by the British establishment, both literary and social.

**The present queen.

royalty, but I am now going to avail myself of one of the advantages by commanding you to stay," she said. They were soon joined by the duchess and her beautiful sister, Princess Olga, both with their hair down, and they sat for hours eating chocolates and chatting about the party. Next day Cecil and Bébé drove home in their dinner jackets to find Mrs. Beaton awaiting them at Broadchalke. "My mother said that it had been a great shock to Elsie, the maid, not to find us in our rooms this morning: 'She is such a sensitive, delicate girl,' said my mother."[14]

In London, Cecil saw George Cukor, who was there to make the film *Edward My Son:**

> He started to tell me how much Del Guidice** wanted to make a film with you, that Daudet's *Sapho*† he thought would be wonderful—but when I said I thought there would be censor trouble we were interrupted.[15]

Virtually all Cecil's letters contained an invitation to Garbo to come to England:

> Dear Sir
> The summer is passing so quickly—blazing June already & now I am getting impatient for you to come here—won't you come & stay a couple of months here & see how you like it, & if you do like it stay on for life?[16]

Cecil had already begun to become impatient and dashed off a rather less friendly letter when, all of a sudden, there arrived a reply from Garbo, thanking him for his invitation. She told him she was very tired, probably from shopping at Bloomingdale's, where she in fact spent more

**Edward My Son,* a flop of a film based on a successful stage play by Robert Morley. It starred Spencer Tracy and Deborah Kerr.

**Filippo Del Guidice (1892–1961), Italian-born producer who ran Two Cities Films.

†*Sapho,* written in 1884 by Alphonse Daudet (1840–97), the story of a young provincial who finds a mistress in Paris but becomes ensnared by her demanding love.

time browsing than actually purchasing. She contemplated a visit to California, then perhaps back to New York and maybe abroad when the tourists were no longer traveling. The letter was vague, but it made the specific point that if she did go to California, she could be reached c/o Harry Crocker, at 622 North Bedford Drive. She ended by asking Cecil if he was one of the many who had been to Montecatini.[17]

Garbo did not come. Instead Cecil returned to the London circuit, where he met Tennessee Williams* and noted that Williams was now a man of some assurance:

> Eyes very beautiful, teeth very ugly. He is surrounded by admirers, accepts their compliments gracefully but longs to be off by himself where he can behave badly. He has a book of short stories** coming out, that are to be privately printed. I expect they will create a tremendous upset because the subject matter is all very explosive (there is one called "The Black Masseur"† which is really a terrible story) but he thinks, perhaps rather too naively, that they are only to be read by "people who will enjoy them."[18]

Interestingly, Cecil did not respond to Garbo's letter of June 25. In fact, he allowed more than three weeks to pass by before writing again. Possibly he was hurt to know that she was not going to join him and consequently recalled Mona Harrison Williams's advice to be somewhat cool. When he did write, it was to say that he had been busy weeding, something that had never prevented him from writing before.

The London season continued to preoccupy him. He gave a supper party for the Duchess of Kent at which Helen Hayes was a guest. He visited Emerald Cunard,‡ who was in the throes of death. He did not relent from his quest for a visit from Garbo:

*Tennessee Williams was in London to discuss plans for *The Glass Menagerie* with "Binkie" Beaumont and John Gielgud.

***One Arm and Other Stories* was privately printed in an edition of 1,500 in 1948, published by New Directions in the United States in 1954.

†"Desire and the Black Masseur," a gruesome tale in which a masochist is devoured by a black masseur.

‡Lady Cunard (1872–1948), leading social figure and onetime friend of King Edward VIII and Mrs. Simpson. She died on July 10.

> When will you come over? I spoke to John Sutro & he said he didn't think there was any immediate possibility of making a film, but he was in charge of the "George Sand" project, & would I like to read the script. It has not arrived. Korda wants me to work on two films next March, *Tale of Two Cities,* Dickens, and *Tess of the D'Urbervilles* with Selznick's young lady* in the leading part. Neither project sounds at all interesting to me, & maybe they won't materialise . . .[19]

Cecil contemplated a visit to Tangiers: "I may possibly go off & misbehave among the Arabs in Morocco. That is unless you would be coming over, or would rather I didn't."[20]

Midsummer arrived at last, and news of Cecil's escapades crossed the Channel. In Paris, Alice B. Toklas was "staying on alone" at the Rue Christine, receiving visitors and writing to old friends. On July 22 she wrote to one such, Samuel Steward: "Do you remember Cecil Beaton—he's desperately in love with Greta Garbo and the Duchess of Kent equally so with him. Do you like my gossip—everybody tells me a little."**[21]

While Garbo drifted, Cecil sped to Paris to stay with Lady Diana Cooper in her love pavilion at Chantilly. He found his old friend missing the excitement of the embassy. Bébé Bérard accompanied him to see Dior's new collection. Then he went to stay with Elsie Mendl at the Villa Trianon at Versailles, wondering if he occupied the room that Garbo had once "honoured."[22]

Back in England, he spent the weekend with the Marquess and Marchioness of Cholmondeley at Houghton and was as impressed with the lavish hospitality as with the good taste that prevailed. He slept in a bed draped in apricot velvet that might have done justice to the altar at St. Peter's in Rome. He wrote to Garbo, "The bed was so large that I felt quite lonely & I thought perhaps one day we might visit the place together."[23]

*Jennifer Jones (b. 1919), actress and film star. Second wife of David O. Selznick. Cecil later dressed her for the play *Portrait of a Lady* in New York in 1954.

**This particular story almost certainly came from Jean Cocteau, lately in London.

While he was in another stately home, Cecil read Salka Viertel's treatment of *George Sand*, the film everyone hoped Garbo would make:

> I am sorry to say I think it hopeless. There is no reality in it, the characters never come to life, & there is no story. I'm afraid it is a phoney—& doubt if life can ever be injected into it. What a pity! I do wish the perfect story could be found.[24]

Back at Broadchalke, Cecil was restless. He went to Paris for a few days. He contemplated his trip to Morocco. Equally, he thought he might stay home and read. Toward the end of August, Cecil wrote less patiently to Garbo:

> My darling Greta
> As you don't send me very long letters it isn't any use my asking you how is your supply of frown papers, if you have been on a trip, if you have made friends with any new blue jays at luncheon time, if your double boiler is working whole time or if the geraniums fill the vases in your blue bedroom. There's not much point in trying to find out if you've been seeing Constance Collier's companion,* or more of Azalea Mamoulian,** if you've altered the pink lamp shades, taken a photograph with the camera in the hall cupboard, if Madame Alba has been cribbing your shopping lists or if you are now enjoying the rewards of putting down all those sacks of manure . . .[25]

But life was never dull for long. Lucian Freud, an unknown painter of twenty-six, came to Broadchalke:

> Then a young painter, a grandson of the great Freud, came to do a drawing of me. I sat on the lawn for hours on end, bored stiff & not knowing what to do with my mouth, & the boy did a most wonderfully careful likeness of Vincent Sheean.† I wasn't very

*Phyllis Wilbourn, faithful companion to the British actress Constance Collier and later to Katharine Hepburn. Still with Miss Hepburn in 1994.

**Azadia Mamoulian, wife of the film director Rouben Mamoulian.

†Vincent Sheean (1899–1975), journalist and writer.

> pleased but tried to overcome my inferiority complex. The boy is charming & unexpected & it was nice to have him about the place for several days sketching the dog, the summer house, & the branches of apples in the kitchen garden.[26]

Cecil had been working energetically on his play, *The Gainsborough Girls,* and from a friend he received the first of many disillusioning criticisms about his skills as a playwright. At last Cecil heard some positive news about Garbo—if through the medium of the newspapers:

> I read in the paper* a paragraph that you had signed to do a film. Perhaps it is true. If so I expect you are in a great state of preparation, exercising your shoulder blades & hanging on trapezes. I only trust it will be a wonderful picture & that it may give you the opportunity of coming over here & spending a few endless eternities with your lover . . .[27]

Garbo was again in the news in September when she filed her first papers for American citizenship in Los Angeles. At that time the journalists had gleaned that she might be making a film about George Sand. Garbo had to appear in public to fill in the necessary forms in the Federal Building. She arrived wearing slacks and a sport jacket, filled in the papers, answered a few questions, and retreated to her home in Beverly Hills.[28]

In November, Cecil flew to New York for the first of two visits. He and Garbo met a few times, and just before he left, he called on her at Hampshire House to show her a mass of photographs of his house: "She was enchanted. She might reconsider my offer if it were still open. She was sweet and trusting."[29] He summed it up in a letter to Garbo on his return:

*It had been reported that Garbo had signed a contract with Walter Wanger to star in a film in Europe the following spring. Wanger, producer of *Queen Christina,* did not name the film but said filming would take place in Rome and Paris and that a certain Eugene Frenke would be involved (*New York Times,* August 19, 1948).

> It is almost unbelievable that now I am back in my nice country bed & everything around me is so familiar & customary, I have since I last wrote to you made the gigantic journey to New York, have had two fleeting but enchanting glimpses of you & have successfully flown the Atlantic again . . .[30]

Cecil found himself plunged into the bleak realities of an English winter. He dashed down to Brighton to see *The Return of the Prodigal,* a Gielgud play for which he had done the decorations. David Herbert arrived in Wiltshire with a new friend. Michael Duff had also found a new friend. Lady Juliet brought Somerset Maugham over with Terence Rattigan. The Oliviers were "stampeding" at Cecil's door, wanting final costume arrangements made for their Australian tour.

Cecil planned to return to New York for his normal winter visit but was delayed first by the dock strike, then by dark fog, and finally by the Royal Family. On November 14, Princess Elizabeth gave birth to Prince Charles at Buckingham Palace, and Cecil was awaiting a summons to take the first official portraits of mother and son. The summons was delayed by the King's serious illness. Cecil wrote:

> No royal baby on a crimson cushion, not a bleat from the Palace, but I suppose they're all trying to keep His Majesty occupied & amused. He never reads a book & has no resources so it's hard work sitting, baby sitting and king sitting but no photograph sitting for C.B.[31]

Meanwhile the Oliviers were pressing Cecil hard, causing him to complain, not for the first time, that theatre people were self-centered and spoiled. There was a sudden burst of enthusiasm about *The Gainsborough Girls,* and "Binkie" Beaumont asked Cecil whether he would like Ralph Richardson for one part, Vivien Leigh for another. Cecil was at last summoned to the palace and took some photographs of the young Prince Charles. His thoughts were still with Garbo:

> Now I want to ask you a question. How is your burgundy coloured dressing gown? & now another? How long will it be

before I ring the bell three times & it is opened by my little Swedish boy-friend? Will the little wisp of a moon that is decorating the sky tonight have become a full faced cheese? I trust it will only be a bit lopsided . . .[32]

Cecil sailed for New York on the *Queen Elizabeth* in mid-December. No sooner had he arrived than he phoned Garbo. At first the line was busy, then there was no reply. Cecil was livid, as he wrote in his diary: "Here at the beginning of a winter I was back three years when she would sometimes answer my call and sometimes not."[33] Later Garbo rang him, but Cecil feigned not to recognize her: "Is it some Japanese?" He chided Garbo for not taking his call, and when she claimed to have dashed out, he asked, "Do you swear?" "I never swear. Stop behaving like Mercedes."

Nevertheless, they lunched the next day at a gourmet sandwich shop, of which Cecil disapproved, and he found her "in fine fettle—very friendly and confiding and not seemingly conscious of my rather frozen attitude."[34] Gradually he thawed, and as each day passed they grew closer: "It is quite extraordinary that people can know one another as intimately as we have for so long and yet all the time develop an even closer intimacy."[35]

One Sunday morning, Cecil tried to make a plan for Monday and Garbo demurred:

"But why? You said you could."

"Well you know why I can't" (intimating Schlee's domination).

"Well it's very unkind just to see me when you feel like it and whistle me along."

"Well I'm afraid that's the only way it can be."

"Perhaps I'd better not see you again."

"It's too complicated. It's worrying me too much—it's giving me a nervous breakdown."

"Very well then—I'll go for my walk in the park," and the telephone call came to an abrupt end.[36]

Cecil went for a walk in Central Park with John Myers* but concentrated solely on ways of eliminating the influence of his rival. He did not call Garbo, but on Monday morning his phone rang: "Have you got over your bad mood?" That evening they met, and Cecil said, "I do know how difficult it must be for you and I do appreciate your loyalty to Schlee—you can't just let him down overnight—but human relationships do change and you mustn't wreck the chances of your career continuing, or give up your life to someone who bores you."

Garbo appeared to sympathize with his cause, but she left Cecil with a problem. She wanted to come to England. She would never come alone, and if she came with Schlee, Cecil's chances of seeing her were slight. He felt the visit ended on an optimistic note, however, and he sailed to London on February 11, 1949, his mind filled with happy memories:

> On 58th Street she got out of the taxi and stood in the street—holding the small bunch of carnations picked out of my vase and waving and smiling so widely—standing with feet apart in the slush of the recent rainstorm—wearing her fur coat and policeman's hat. We had had such a pleasant evening—recently she had acquired the habit of coming to my rooms at all hours even when the secretary was there, leaving her mackintosh and books.
>
> The carnation gathering had taken place just as I was about to check out of my room. Greta had come along at six o'clock. There had been packages and luggage to send to the boat. The secretary leaving—"You see" Greta said. "They all seem to like you. She liked working for you." Miss Harrison left. I put a "Do not disturb" sign on the door. G. said "I miss you." The room already looked vacated. There are always so many papers around—so much life. We were very happy and childlike. . . .
>
> An intimate dinner [at the Colony] in which she talked of the inadequacy of her career—the high hopes she had had as a girl when first under the spell of Maurice Stiller (only of course she did not mention him by name). She could never get over the great

*John Bernard Myers (1920–87), American art dealer, editor, publisher, puppeteer, and stage producer. Author of *Tracking the Marvelous.*

influence he had had over her, because in her family life there was never any interest in the things that she liked. It was a sudden revelation to know him. She talked about the manner people should conduct themselves. If their sex desires are in a certain direction they should not be obvious to the world and she was more emphatic than ever that there was only one possible human relationship of man and his mate. There was the clock ticking away. We must walk back in the cold night to the Hotel. Then to the boat . . . an idyllic winter was at an end. At one moment I was about to weep. But the delicious Château Yquem at dinner had put us into a gay humour and we both smiled and laughed and were cheerful—even in parting, I was very happy.[37]

Cecil was destined for another long period of separation. Many times he thought he was on the point of seeing Garbo in Europe, but they were not to meet again until the following October. Thus, once again, he resorted to letters:

My beloved Greta
This writing block has been waiting in the drawer by my bedside all the time I was in New York. Now it is my link with you, together with the memories of the times we have spent in the meantime. But already they are quickly becoming part of the past. It is only ten days ago since we waved goodbye in that slushy 58th street & you stood with your feet apart holding onto that mingy little bunch of carnations, & I, in the taxi, was tightly grabbing your parcel of hair lotion. Ten days ago—& it seems such an eternity . . .[38]

After a smooth, sunny voyage, Cecil disembarked in England. He went immediately to Broadchalke, where a tall row of flowering snowdrops gave the first hint of spring. There was some bad news. Christian Bérard had died in Paris:

I heard the awful reports of his death in Paris—& the horrible behaviour of that crowd who surrounded him. He had died in the theatre—like Molière, while working on his latest production (see I am trying very hard to write clearly, darling, but my fingers are getting a bit tired & the writing is not as good as it was at the beginning!) & had been taken back to his apartment, & laid in a coffin while friends & relations came to haggle over the spoils, & a bad painter took up a position & did a portrait of him as he lay on a pillow looking as another friend said "like a mad, murdered King." Poor Sweet Bébé—a person with such a big heart & such sweet sensibility.[39]

Cecil turned again to Garbo:

And now you? my sugar pie. I wonder, wonder what were the results of your Guyon tests. No appendix I trust. Are you feeling more chipper? I do trust so.

I loved our New York season together & so happy to think we achieved an even greater intimacy than before. I loved our afternoons & evenings together, the various visitations to Macy's, Peck & Peck, & the shoe shop. All the shopping was a treat & I have mats from Chinatown, & bed linen from Fifth Avenue & grey ties & silver dishes & ashtrays to remind me of many occasions. I loved our matinee in the rain, the visits to the movies (one bad—but then we were both restless) one good (maybe we were relaxed). I loved the Rameses evening & the visit to Nella Webb. Remember you have your sun in Virgo—you are analytical, discriminating, a perfectionist—a leader—an original. You have a beautiful mental rhythm (!) You are going to make a journey in May & in June you will start a seven year phase of splendid progress. On June 13th you will have a big surprise—& for the next 7–14 years all the magnetism you have stored up is going to burst forth! & remember CB & you have much in common—& will make money for you. Remember there is nothing (according to Nella Webb at any rate) against your marrying CB.

And now a list of thanks (Oh dear my fingers are getting stiff). Thank you for saying I am less inclined to drape myself than before. Thank you for discouraging me against that brown hat & swinging on awnings & for saying I've got a bit better in some ways: Thank you for helping me to choose those dresses. Thank you for letting me brush your hair. Thank you for your influence on me.

And here is a list of things I'm looking forward to:—

Hearing you are better—that you are enjoying using that bamboo pencil—that you are coming to pay me a visit here this summer; that the orange trees have survived the snow—that Madame Alba is kind to you.

And here is a list of things I miss:—
Our telephone conversations to say good morning & good night.
Our meetings at the Plaza, at Tiffany's, at 58th Street corner.
Our "gatherings" in celebration of birthdays, or New Year's
Vodka, old golds, your link bracelet & watch. You.

But these are only a few of the trivial things that I dare write about. There are so many others.

Now I must leave you for London & I trust by my bad writing I haven't put too great a strain on you.

My Blessings, my love, my love
from your friend, companion & lover
Beatty[40]

Cecil went to see Laurence Olivier and Vivien Leigh in the production he had designed of *The School for Scandal,* finding that celebrated thespian pair "rather grudging in their generosity."[41] He later exaggerated this into a major row and a lifetime of nonspeaks. He was still involved with his own play, but there were no immediate plans to stage it.

Now then. I have read "Adolphe"* as you said "they" had considered it a possibility as a film for you. It is a wonderful book & written in such a wonderfully succinct style—with only the very essentials & how marvellous the description of love, which makes me remember so much of our times together. . . .

As to the idea of your comeback to the screen as a woman who throughout the film is in this degrading & terrible situation of being more in love with her lover than he is with her, it seems to me—well very unsuitable. In fact without any of the usual qualities that a film possesses it seems hard to find any vehicle more

*By Benjamin Constant de Rebecque (1767–1830), French philosopher, orator, and politician. *Adolphe,* a psychological romance published in 1816, was one of his best-known works. Byron wrote, "It leaves an unpleasant impression."

unsuited to making into a moving picture. I trust they are not wasting any more of your time on that level.[42]

Cecil's life continued much the same, a mixture of visits to London and the theatre. He flew to the south of France to stay with Somerset Maugham at the Villa Mauresque. In Paris he called on Boris Kochno, Bébé Bérard's friend, who showed him some early Bérard portraits, and visited an exhibition of clocks at Versailles. Staying at the Ritz, Cecil was horrified to hear a couple making love in a nearby room:

> Their window must have been open onto the court for I could hear only too well their horrible moans & it was very depressing. I thought how awful that people must inflict this sort of thing on [one] another. The woman seemed terribly unhappy—or perhaps she was just petulant & silly—but for a very long time she whimpered & moaned as if in great pain, & then shouted "Stop it, Stop it." I nearly got out of bed & shouted into the court for her to stop it. It was a horrid thing & it quite put me off the hotel corridors for I imagined such horrible scenes taking place behind each door. Barbara Hutton was on the same floor & I felt if I stopped still I'd hear her petulantly complaining "Stop it, Stop it!"[43]

Cecil lived in hope that he might one day receive "a welcome message written with a gold bamboo pencil."[44] Instead he was rewarded with a cablegram from Garbo. "Good Morning," it said.

Easter was celebrated in a burst of early summer. Cecil reported some news of Mercedes:

> Black & white wrote me from Paris asking me if I had any news of you. Would that I had, but I dare say I'd keep it from her. Whenever your name is mentioned I put on a po face as if I was a Chinaman. I look in the news items to see if you have made up your mind about doing a picture, but best of all I'd like you to exercise the bamboo pencil on my behalf . . .[45]

Cecil maintained his one-sided correspondence through May, and in June he headed for Paris "just for the hell of it."[46] He knew he was likely to run into Mercedes there. Typically, when on good terms with Garbo, he saw Mercedes as a threat. When on bad terms, he saw her as an ally.

Since April 1949 Mercedes had been living in an apartment on the Quai Voltaire. Never still for long and with the habit of appearing where there was a healthy mixture of cultural and social life, Mercedes was happy being a Parisian. She had also embarked on a new love affair, this time with an American woman living in France, Poppy Kirk.

CHAPTER 8

MERCEDES AND POPPY KIRK

By the late 1940s, Mercedes was well set into stout, but graceful, middle age. The black cloaks or highwaymen's capes were habitual, the pointed shoes with silver buckles always worn, the tricorn hats her trademark. Sybille Bedford recalled her "Cuban pirate elegance," noting that she was of "startling appearance, with a kind of swagger, but feminine—no collar-and-tie nonsense." Bedford added, "She was literally a cloak-and-dagger figure. She could have been in a musical comedy. She should have worn a sword."[1]

Mercedes's affair with Poppy Kirk began in the autumn of 1948 and lasted until 1953. Poppy was born Maria Annunziata Sartori in March 1899, the daughter—or possibly adopted daughter—of Victor Sartori, the American vice consul in Livorno, a man of Italian descent originally from Philadelphia. Poppy was pushed into her first marriage in Paris, very young, by her family. Her husband was Mario Montrezza, a ne'er-do-well lawyer from Turin fifteen years her senior. They had a son, Victor, born in 1923.

In Paris, Poppy worked as a model. She was a friend of Jean Cocteau, who was always supportive despite being snobbish about her job. Later she worked for Schiaparelli and the Ballets Russes. She loved Chinese artifacts, screens, lacquer boxes, furniture, and plates, read Chinese poetry and philosophy, and took a keen interest in Oriental religions, most particularly Buddhism.

Her first marriage having failed, Poppy retreated for a while to her little villa in Santa Margherita. In 1935 she married a rather dry, intelligent English writer and journalist, Geoffrey Kirk, at twenty-eight some eight years her junior. He had served in the Secret Service, and while he could have continued a bohemian existence, enjoying the company of literary figures, he joined the Foreign Office in 1939 and rose to be a minor ambassador. Poppy spent part of the war in London, where she energetically cooked in the canteen set up in the National Gallery, she and her staff serving a record 2,400 meals in one day. Sybille Bedford remembered that Poppy was "awfully good about charitable works and having cocktail parties. She was not at all intellectual. She was a terrific flirt and always succeeded in implanting herself in people's hearts and minds."[2]

Poppy was known as "Madame Poppi" when she worked at the well-known couturier's, Molyneux. She had had several romantic relationships with women early in life, and when her first marriage failed she was rescued by the half-Indian Paulina Terry, one of the daughters of Maharajah Duleep Singh.* Then there was a lady called Gilberte, who

*Duleep Singh (1838–93), the Maharajah of the Punjab. In 1849, when the Punjab was annexed to British India by the governor-general, the Earl of Dalhousie, Duleep Singh, age twelve, abdicated and handed over the famous Koh-i-noor diamond to Queen Victoria. The deposed maharajah came under the Queen's care but privately called her "Mrs. Fagin," adding, "She has no more right to that diamond than I have to Windsor Castle." He lived at Elveden, later the estate of the Earl of Iveagh. He married a German woman, who died in September 1887. Paulina was born to his young mistress, Ada Wetherill, three months later. The maharajah married Ada in May 1889. Paulina married a Lieutenant Terry.

Poppy Kirk working in a soup kitchen during the war. She met Mercedes in 1948.

had wanted to share a dwelling with her in Italy. During this later phase Poppy lived with Princess Dilkusha de Rohan,* the daughter of a British Army officer, Major A. T. Wrench, stationed in India (hence her strange name), and an American mother. In 1922, Dilkusha married Prince Carlos de Rohan, a scion of that French princely family. The wedding photos show an uncomfortable bride with heavy, dark eyes, draped in silver lamé and Brussels lace, clinging almost furtively to her spry young husband, a dapper figure with slicked-back hair and carnation. They lived in Austria, where in 1931 he was killed when his car hit a tree. Dilkusha moved to Paris, worked in haute couture, and became part of the circle of Alice B. Toklas—who thought her "bawdy" and drank her first and last Bloody Mary at a birthday party "Dil" gave her.

Poppy claimed that Dilkusha resented her work and never wholly understood her. Their weekends were often tedious, relieved only by a concert. Poppy felt that Dilkusha was not really interested in intimacy.[3] It was Dilkusha who brought Mercedes into Poppy's life, taking her to dinner at Poppy's house. Mercedes knew about the Dilkusha affair. Of the meeting she wrote:

> When we arrived Poppy was in the kitchen and called out to us to take off our coats. As I am always very sensitive to voices, I like to hear a voice before I meet the person it belongs to. Poppy has a charming one, and her English is English, although she was born and brought up in Italy. The room we were in was lighted only by candles and when she appeared I thought for a second that I wasn't seeing clearly, or that I was dreaming again. She was wearing the same Chinese gown the woman in my Tibetan dream had worn and in fact she was the same woman.** There were the same slit, half-closed eyes, and the same faint smile. I was actually so stunned by this encounter that it was difficult for me even to shake hands with her. She was so busy preparing dinner that she was unaware of my emotion, but when we sat down at the table

*Alis Dilkusha de Rohan (1899–1978). She died in Wyoming.

**A few days earlier, apparently, Mercedes had been suffering from a high temperature while staying at the Crillon and in her delirium had dreamt of just such a woman as Poppy, who had smiled faintly as she passed by.

> and I remarked on her gown, she said, "I always wear Chinese gowns. I love everything oriental." . . . She did not have to say this to make me believe it.[4]

Poppy was on her way to New York, and Mercedes soon followed. She wasted no time in effecting a seduction, and they embarked on a blissful affair. But early in 1949, Poppy left Mercedes to join her husband, Geoffrey, who had recently taken up his post as first secretary at the British legation in Panama. This was to fulfill a promise made a year earlier that they would try to start a new life together. They met in Mexico, where there was a conference. The reality of her trip soon came to seem most unpleasant to Poppy, as she confessed to Mercedes in tender letters sent back to New York. In a hot, smart nightclub in Mexico City, she asked Geoffrey to release her from her promise. He had no choice but to agree, though he was bitter and thereafter treated her with icy politeness.

In the meantime, Mercedes had rented her apartment to the actress Carol Channing and moved to Paris. Here she found Poppy's former lover, Dilkusha de Rohan, behaving badly. Jealous of Mercedes, she began to show Poppy's letters around and to talk indiscreetly. There was, of course, some justification for her thinking that neither Mercedes nor Poppy had been a good friend to her. In any case, knowing Poppy would soon come, Mercedes took an apartment at 5 Quai Voltaire. She sent Poppy an unsigned cable to this effect, which Geoffrey opened in error. He took it to Poppy but said nothing. Then, just before dinner, he suddenly turned to her and gently asked her if she intended to marry the cable's sender. Poppy answered vaguely.

Throughout February and March, Poppy sent anxious, loving letters to Mercedes. Finally Geoffrey gave Poppy the airfare to Paris, and she flew there on Saturday, April 16. She and Mercedes moved into the new apartment, and Poppy went back to work at Schiaparelli's.

Sybille Bedford was one of Poppy's many friends to be surprised by her involvement with Mercedes. She observed that Mercedes was a person of extremes, that people either loved her or hated her. She had met her with the Huxleys and found her "unbelievably tiresome." Tallulah Bankhead nicknamed Mercedes "Countess Dracula."[5] Janet

Flanner, the famous "Genêt" of *The New Yorker,* loathed her. "You can't trust Mercedes an inch," Poppy's friend Allanah Harper* would say. "How can you be with this demon?"[6] Yet Mercedes appeared "tamed" in Poppy's company, and there were periods of happiness for both of them.

While Poppy was busy working for Schiaparelli, Mercedes was growing steadily more restless. She was used to being alone, but after her happy times with Poppy she found this harder to accept. They moved into the Hôtel Bisson,** also on the Quai Voltaire, and Mercedes grew lonelier. Her friend Eleanora von Mendelssohn committed suicide by jumping out of a window, while Ona Munson, then living in Paris in a depressed state with her husband, Eugene Berman, succeeded in transferring much of her depression to Mercedes.† Hating the dark days, the rain, and the cold, Mercedes decided to visit New York.

Poppy tried to be philosophical about Mercedes's wish to spend time with old friends in New York. She also had to be philosophical about the continued hold of Garbo. Poppy was no admirer of Garbo, falling into that far-from-small band of people who found her tiresome. While Mercedes was away, Poppy dined with Geoffrey in a Paris restaurant. He begged her to come back and gave her a gold cigarette lighter.

By early 1950, Mercedes showed no sign of returning, and Poppy suggested a new scheme. Mercedes could live in New York and see Garbo from September to June, and then spend the summers in Paris with Poppy. She made this suggestion a little resentfully, since she in fact felt that Mercedes was being selfish and wondered how she would feel

*Allanah Harper (1901–92), a socialite friend of Edith Sitwell's with literary interests, was the first person to encourage Cecil to make a career out of photography.

**Hôtel Bisson, between the Pont Neuf and the Pont Saint-Michel. The composer and diarist Ned Rorem was also staying there at the time.

†Ona Munson's career had foundered due to a row with one of the studio bosses. She put on weight and attempted to diet by taking estrogen. Depression followed. A few years later, in February 1955, she was found dead in her apartment at 255 West Eighty-sixth Street. There was an almost empty box of sleeping pills by her bedside and a note that read, "This is the only way I know to be free again. . . . Please don't follow me."

if Poppy took off to her London home in Lloyd Square whenever it suited her.

In March, a gloomy Geoffrey continued to press Poppy to return to him. Poppy could not explain her position, which was precarious, to say the least. She berated Mercedes for being ungracious and for leaving her so often. When Geoffrey returned to New York that spring, Poppy tried to persuade him to meet Mercedes. He refused. Then she became involved in a prolonged drama, paying for an Easter cake Mercedes had ordered for Garbo. Exasperated by the personalized cakes Mercedes was inclined to dispatch, she suggested that Mercedes should send the same one to each ex-girlfriend, merely changing the ribbon around it.

Later Poppy came to New York, and she and Mercedes returned to Paris together. In the summer of 1950 they shared a duplex apartment on the Quai Saint-Michel opposite Notre Dame, and Poppy bought a farmhouse at Aincourt, in Normandy. A Siamese kitten, Linda, came into their lives and was doted upon by both.

The affair between Poppy and Mercedes continued with as many separations as periods together. In 1953, Poppy was working for Schiaparelli in New York. Her son, Victor, returned from Bucharest, where he had been employed with the State Department, and he and Poppy decided to share a flat. Eventually they settled for part of the year on East Thirty-fifth Street. Mercedes kept the cat.

By August 1953 the relationship had settled into mutual affection. Mercedes spent Christmas of 1953 with Poppy, Victor, and Jennifer Neill.* Then, in the early months of 1954, matters came to a head, Mercedes frequently phoning Jenny to say Poppy would not talk to her and did not understand her. Poppy moved to her last home, Krech Martin, at Lanmodez, near Pleubian, on the north coast of France, and from time to time Mercedes went to stay with her there.

*Jennifer Neill was the daughter of a friend of Mercedes's who worked in the wartime canteen with Poppy. She married John Arnold-Wallinger in 1955. Her family liked Mercedes, who even stayed with Jennifer's grandmother in the 1960s. The latter telephoned her granddaughter to say, "Well, I'm a pretty amazing Victorian old lady with a lesbian staying with me, who is entertaining a party of queers for tea."

Poppy remained on good terms with Geoffrey, who served as counsellor in the British embassy in The Hague from 1953 until 1960. It was Mercedes's understanding that their relationship was restricted to the occasional holiday together, but in reality Poppy returned to him, though not without long breaks away.*

*Geoffrey Kirk was the ambassador to El Salvador from 1960 to 1967, and Poppy went there with him. Later they turned against each other. Geoffrey retreated to Hertfordshire and died in 1975, having cut Poppy out of his will. She fell on hard times, and Sybille Bedford arranged that she should cook for the PEN Club in London. Poppy died in a nursing home in Oxfordshire in 1986, aged eighty-seven.

CHAPTER 9

DARLING SIR: "I WISH YOU WOULD LET ME SAVE YOU."

In June 1949, a few weeks after Mercedes and Poppy moved into the Quai Voltaire apartment, Cecil was in Paris. He stayed with the Duff Coopers at Chantilly, visited the ailing Elsie Mendl at Versailles, and went to a cocktail party given by Marie-Louise Bousquet. He noted that there were many Americans in Paris, including Georges Schlee. He lunched with Alice B. Toklas and photographed the Windsors.*

It was high season in Paris, and even the Duchess of Kent came over to attend the British Hospital ball. Cecil got to bed so late, the sun was already shining. As his week ended, he knew he must make time to visit Schlee. He wrote to Garbo:

*The Duke and Duchess of Windsor were then living in Paul-Louis Weiller's house, 85 Rue de la Faisanderie.

I went to his hotel for a drink & we had a nice talk about you. He was seen at his most sympathetic advantage & talked of you with true understanding & tenderness & appreciation. It all started by my saying "Tell me about the film"* & he talked about the difficulties, his admiration for Josh Logan**—& vague plans. We seemed to get along well & I said "Why not bring Greta over to my house to stay for a bit. It's half an hour by car from Southampton." He took the telephone number & said he'd send a wire when he brings you over. I doubt if he'll bring you here, but he suggested my coming over to see you in Paris—so if you feel like it do get him to send a wire & try & mention my name to him glibly from time to time. It only makes me seem like a ghoul if nothing is ever said. I may be wrong, but I think my visit to him cleared the atmosphere quite a bit—at any rate for the time being—& I'm very glad I went, & thrilled it turned out well. I give you these scraps of information as a guide.[1]

Cecil returned to London to find a letter from Garbo, which he described as a "nice welcome home."[2] She wrote that it was a difficult time and that she was impatient that she had not yet gotten her citizenship papers. She ended by saying she missed Cecil very much, and that she wished she were walking in his woods rather than languishing in her backyard in California.[3]

Cecil replied:

I am sure you can stay on here. I will not go to America until later. You can be here when you want—& it is never too cold here. You like the rooms fresh in any case—& if necessary we can go out & buy you an Union suit. You can be muffled like an esquimo in woollies!! It is impossible to make plans but I am vaguely thinking—more than vaguely thinking—to go to Tangiers in August. 3 weeks—possibly on to Venice—but you must please wire me so that I shan't disappear into the blue without

*Garbo was about to attempt the *Duchesse de Langeais* film opposite James Mason.

**Joshua Logan (1908–88), American stage director who also made such films as *Bus Stop, Sayonara,* and *South Pacific.*

Garbo and Georges Schlee in Paris, 1949.

> being able to contact you. I think George said you would be in Paris about the 20th July, so I shall be standing by in case. . . .
>
> But oh *dear*—I wish you were here now, at this wonderful time of the year. It is England at its peak moment & in its greatest beauty.[4]

News of Garbo's travel plans reached Cecil from Truman Capote, then holidaying in Ischia. He read a report in the *Paris Tribune* that Garbo was expected to arrive in Paris on June 13. This caused Cecil further worries in his role as letter writer: "Respected Sir, What am I to do with my letters when you go away. Write them & keep them until you send me an address? I await your instructions. . . . Any wire to 8 Pelham Place will be forwarded."[5]

The summer continued in all its glory, and Cecil resented having to go to London, this time in his occasional but lucrative role as royal photographer:

> The week in London was horrid. Such a waste to be there in the sunshine. I meant to be there only one day & then they rang up from the Palace that Princess Margaret wanted me to take her photograph on Friday, so that meant waiting three extra days & I had nothing but irritation during that time. The telephone bell never silent & no secretary to answer it, & such tiresome calls. I really only enjoyed myself whenever I got out of the house. I took two young American girls to the National Gallery, & I went to see poor old Gertie Lawrence acting in a *very* cheap novelettish play* & I went to lunch with our Turkish friend** in a huge house she has got in Palace Green. It was like being in Hyderabad again, with a wonderful Indian meal lasting much too long & everything so delayed that the afternoon was almost over before we'd finished the Turkish coffee. The Princess, in European clothes, was

**September Tide,* by Daphne du Maurier, playing at the Aldwych Theatre from December 1948 to August 1949.

**H.I.H. the Princess of Berar (b. 1913), daughter of Abdülmecid II, Caliph of the Faithful, and granddaughter of Sultan Abdülaziz I of Turkey. She lived for many years at Hyderabad House, Kensington Palace Gardens, in London. Cecil photographed her many times.

very shy & giggly but very charming, & interesting when given time & the chance.

The photography at the palace was hard work & didn't give me enough opportunity to talk to the little Princess. She had been out at a nightclub until 5.30 the morning before & got a bit tired after two hours posing. But she is witty & seems quite kindly disposed towards humanity. I had thought she'd just be a little spoilt minx, but she was kind to me & helpful & said she'd try & get her mother to reconsider her verdict about not using those nice pictures I took of her in the black velvet crinoline—the ones in which she looks really quite regal & thin.[6]

Cecil monitored Garbo's movements closely. He noted her departure from New York and then her arrival in France. This was reported in the press. Garbo was wearing "a wool coat, shapeless slacks, and something that looked like bedroom slippers."[7] When a photographer approached them, she seized Schlee's hat. She was too late to escape being photographed. Schlee looked startled.

Garbo and Schlee proceeded to Aix-les-Bains to take the waters. Here too the press were on to them. A journalist named Henriette Pierrot followed Garbo for several days and filed a report to *Elle* magazine about her stay. The whole operation was carried out like a wartime campaign. The journalist used an old *carte d'identité* describing her as an artist and even took her paints to add verisimilitude. She booked into the same hotel and pried from the chambermaid the information that Garbo went to the Thermes each day to take the waters. Her vigil commenced.

At 9:30 A.M. she awaited Garbo's possible arrival in the park. This occurred at 9:46, but she was too afraid to take a photograph. She secured her first one at 11:10—Garbo and Schlee coming out of the Thermes, Garbo with hand in front of face. The journalist then pursued her like a fan and asked permission to take a photo, but Schlee said in English, "It's impossible, impossible."[8] Bravely she attempted some more snaps until a disapproving look from Schlee hastened her retreat.

The next day, differently disguised, the journalist took up her vigil in the garden once more. She even climbed a tree but was spotted by someone. There was no sign of Garbo there or anywhere else. The day passed in vain. On the third day she met another photographer, who had enjoyed some success the previous week and obtained a good pose. They shared the stalking, and two successful snaps were taken soon after ten o'clock.

The journalist then set about trying to find out about Garbo's lifestyle. This did not prove rewarding. The chambermaid said Garbo was very tidy but did not read, smoke, or speak. She always wore the same clothes, never took the lift, and existed on a diet of vegetables with lemon and sugar. The journalist asked about autographs, and the chambermaid replied that Schlee refused to let her sign any: "It is he who decides that. She is basically kind. She always smiles, but she does not understand a word of French. So it is he who translates and gives the orders." The journalist concluded that Schlee was her "impresario, interpreter, secretary, bodyguard, and also probably washer and ironer."[9]

In a letter to Garbo, Cecil remarked on the "great quaffs of evil tasting waters which will restore your Lordship to great well being."[10] Accompanied by David Herbert, he drove to Marseilles on August 4 on his way to Tangiers, regretting only the lost summer that Garbo could have shared with him.

Shortly after he departed, a confused letter from Garbo arrived at Pelham Place. The gist of it was that she and Schlee were not feeling well. The cure was continuing for another week and the doctor had not diagnosed anything specific. She suggested conspiratorially that Cecil and Peter Watson send her a "nice dry invitation" to come see them, and perhaps she could arrange something with her "partner."[11] She thought they might at least see one another in Paris.

Cecil was having a memorable summer in Tangiers. "All types of bad men, all forms of vice are present,"[12] he wrote in a letter to Garbo. So was little Truman Capote, who gave a midnight picnic among the rocks at Cap Spartel and almost succeeded in braining himself against a rock, ending the evening with his hair awry and his glasses knocked off.

Cecil was hoping Garbo might come and see him, either in Tangiers or, better still, in London. His next maneuver was to follow her advice and write her the kind of letter she could show to Schlee. It was written in a much neater hand than usual.

Dearest Greta,
Have sent you a wire today to know if you & George wouldn't like to come here for a bit. We could manage to give you a modicum of comfort. The bathing is the most wonderful in the world & the Arab life would fascinate you.

It is an ugly modern house but cool. We have some comic servants—& I know you wouldn't be molested by people here.

If not perhaps you'll come to England & visit me there. Let me know your plans.

With Blessings from David & myself.

Yrs.
Cecil[13]

Garbo and Schlee did not respond. They could never have come to Tangiers as there was the matter of the Walter Wanger film, *The Duchesse de Langeais,* to resolve. From Aix-les-Bains they went to Rome at the end of August.

As usual Garbo traveled under the pseudonym "Miss Harriet Brown." For a time they stayed at the Hotel Hassler, while negotiating terms for the forthcoming film. Garbo tried to be incognito, but the press soon found out she was there. In the first week of September, she was endlessly caught by paparazzi, leaving her hotel or coming out of St. Peter's Basilica after a sightseeing tour.

The film project failed, as all other similar attempts had failed. The company ran out of money, and Garbo was unimpressed by the suggestion that she should back the project herself. Schlee's interference was certainly a negative factor. As Salka Viertel recorded, it was this fiasco that decided Garbo once and for all to quit the screen. She was lucky to have enough money to remain disdainfully aloof for the rest of her life.

For a time, Garbo and Schlee took refuge in a rented villa outside Rome, and in due course they made their way to Paris. Cecil had arrived there from Tangiers. His first port of call was Garbo's hotel, where he left a note. To his surprise his telephone soon rang:

" 'Is that you Beattie? Well I never,' and I know that Greta is in a good mood," he recorded in his diary.

> Her film troubles are postponed & the relief is great—& she is now full of vitality. I am so pleased at the prospect of seeing her in half an hour—for a walk in the Park—that I dress myself with particular care & I rush along the streets getting very hot in the sun in an attempt to collect my hat from a hotel where I parked it—for I know Greta does not like to see me without a hat (one of the boys—no hat!) & I must not be late.
>
> As I am expecting her descent from her room I am waylaid by a gossip writer—the worst luck—and out of the corner of my eye I motion to Greta to rush past—this she proceeds to do—then returns & we all talk together—& I am once more staggered by her incredible beauty.
>
> I had wondered if her dreadful harassments by press & film gangsters had not left her a nervous wreck, but in spite of her saying "No, I still have eyes to see—& I know how to look" she looked more lovely than I had dared imagine. Her body thinner, her chest quite flat & her waist incredibly small . . .[14]

The pair climbed into a "natty looking" blue De Soto car, and the chauffeur drove them to the Bois de Boulogne. They walked together arm in arm:

> I was more thrilled to be with her than with any other person. I was quite blissful. Only sorry, deeply sorry—& was there a quiet feeling of relief somewhere?—that she was not coming to England—could not come & stay with me if they were leaving on Monday—& then by degrees she told me the awful story of the European trip. 2 months she had been here & she had never seen anything—not been even to a play & the company she was contracted to had told lie after lie. Yes they were ready to begin the film. When by degrees it became known they had no money in the Bank, then they had induced her to go to Rome—& when there had tried to get her to do the business part, to smile at the rich Italians so they would put up the money for her film. But no she would not do that—& the press in Italy had made her life a misery—a dog's life. Night & day a car had been parked outside her hotel & if ever she went anywhere this car followed her with photographers. So she had remained in her hotel with the blinds

> drawn for the room looked onto a courtyard & all the others living opposite stared in at her windows.
>
> "In Italy the press photographers are bandits—bandits—& if I'd had a gun I swear I'd shoot them, as it is one day I had a stick & oh my how I did want to break their cameras, but I knew there'd be such a scandal. But they're just determined to get you under their cameras—or else."
>
> I asked "Why didn't you submit to being photographed when first you arrived on shipboard—you've done it before?"
>
> "I've done it four times, but if you know how much I hated it—it's my character to hate it & I can't alter myself. Then you think maybe you can get away without it—& then when they discover you've eluded them they are after you & they try to make you submit—& then once that happens you just won't submit—& then this happens. I have had no peace. In Rome I only went out twice. Once to a gallery, & once to a church—& I got no peace because a long time ago I used to make films. It's awful to think that you have no private life at all. That an individual can't have any freedom—that if the Press are after you there's nothing to be done!"[15]

Cecil renewed his invitation to England, but Garbo said, "I can't let my partner go back alone—& just say well now I've got a better invitation & am staying."[16]

Later, by arrangement, Cecil went to see her and Schlee together. Schlee launched into a story of how clever he had been in dealing with the film crooks, how his legal mind had saved them from some awful troubles. Cecil was less than convinced:

> As he tried to justify himself I was convinced that he is partly responsible for the fiasco of the film not coming off, for he is an amateur dealing with clever professionals—& the way he has managed to take control of Greta's interests is quite alarming & I see no possibility of her getting free of him—for although they are no longer stimulated by each other's company, & they are apt to sit in silence—she gives a feeling of importance to his dreary existence—& he is not likely to let her slip from his clutches. She,

> meanwhile, is touched by his loyal devotion & his efforts on her part, & thus they are bound to each other . . .[17]

When Cecil told Diana Cooper of his walk in the woods with Garbo, she put her house at Chantilly at his disposal, saying, "But the servants will like it. They love the notables."[18] There was talk of Garbo, Schlee, and Cecil dining on Saturday evening, but because of the trip to Chantilly on Sunday, this did not happen.

Sunday dawned sunny and fresh. Cecil was on his best behavior, as this was the first time Schlee had seen him and Garbo together for any length of time:

> I feel that Schlee was not displeased at the relationship shown to him between Greta & myself. It was the first time he had seen us together for a long while & in the interim there have been so many fusses & I have appeared to him like a ghoulish unknown quantity always to be contended with & never seen. Maybe I am wrong in that he did suffer pangs of anxiety & jealousy but I did my best to keep his ego titillated & especially on the return journey in the car I kept talking to him most of the time—occasionally throughout the day I looked at him with a steely glare of hatred in my eyes, but I do not know whether he detected it or not.[19]

The lunch was a success. Schlee was delighted to be entertained in the house of a former ambassador; Garbo, more sensitive to nature, relished the clean air and presently marched into the long grass of the park. At lunch there was more talk of the iniquities of Walter Wanger and the film crowd. Observing Garbo, Cecil wrote:

> She is still more beautiful than anyone I have ever seen & she has an extraordinary aura & magnetism about her, but unless she soon starts to work hard again & takes on a new life as an actress she is living a long death.
>
> Today was one of her highlit days. Certainly the best she has spent since she came to Europe & the walk to the Château of Chantilly was idyllic. She adored the green avenues of formally planted trees—the clear bathing water—the thick grass—the ani-

mals (she gave half a cigarette to a goat!). Mercifully ignored by the populace at the Château she appreciated its great beauties & criticised its ugliness—very Germanic & heavy she thought the castle—& certain statues & planting of untidy looking plants she resented. She has naturally good taste & an uncanny instinct. . . .

Greta became like a person possessed. She wanted to lie & roll & bask in the golden corn. She was in fact like a child as we knelt down & gathered a bouquet of wheat sheaves.

It was a very fantastic & lovely experience—& I only wished I had been alone with her. But the watchdog never left us together except when he went to the lavatory prior to our departure. Then Greta whispered "Can't you come to America now? I know of 2 people who would lend us their house in the desert—they're in Europe now." But before we had had time to whisper more than a few urgent sentences, the ghoul was back & I rustled some thousand franc notes pretending that we were discussing how much to tip Jean. On the way home in the car Greta kept whispering "Won't you take me to Montmartre" but I knew she was only saying this because she knew I was going to the theatre with Lilia [Ralli] . . .[20]

Later that evening Cecil received an unwelcome shock:

I must admit that I felt slightly rattled when coming back late at night from dropping Lilia home after the theatre, through my taxi window I suddenly saw Greta & Schlee driving home in the blue car. They seemed so very much interested in one another & Greta looking at him with a smile of affection & his head quite close to hers. It made me realise that Greta is really by no means an invalid & that she likes to think that she is tired but in fact goes for an 18 hour stretch without an interest for sleep & feeling much stronger than I could.

I had returned exhausted from Chantilly & half an hour later had been woken from the deepest sleep by Greta on the telephone as chipper & spry as if she had just surfaced to consciousness.[21]

Garbo was causing nervousness on other fronts. Poppy Kirk, away in New York, was worried about Garbo's effect on Mercedes. She knew how depressed Mercedes could become when she was around Garbo, and she wrote encouraging letters about staying calm and not getting upset.[22] Mercedes recorded that she always saw Garbo when she visited Paris during these years. She would drive her round the Place de la Concorde, saying, "No getting out to pick flowers here."[23]

Soon after his day in the country, Cecil returned to London, while Garbo and Schlee sailed to New York on the *Île de France,* arriving home on October 10. At the end of November, Cecil wrote her:

> Dearest Sir or Madam,
> Desperately sorry to hear you haven't been on the crest since you got back. I saw Black and White in Paris about a month ago & she told me of your homecoming. I am more than ever sorry you didn't stay here, after we met, as things would have been very different for you. You would have regained your equilibrium & health. You are in a bad patch & I am going to try my utmost to get you out of it. It is really quite simple—a question of breaking out into a life that is good for you—& not an escape. I don't want to be a bore—but I know you agree with me in your heart. . . .
>
> Now I am coming to New York in January. I have to be there six weeks. Will you still be there—or can you come back from California—or shall I have to come to California? Please try & let me have your vague plans as if I am to be in California I would have to try & arrange this in advance with *Vogue.* It is all very difficult I know but do let us try not to miss each other. Life is whizzing by at such a pace.[24]

To this letter Garbo replied that she would remain in New York until he came, and that he must not contemplate Hollywood unless he had work there. She welcomed him back to Manhattan, warned him to be careful on his trips to Paris, and called him "Honeychild Beatie."[25]

Cecil sailed to New York on the *Queen Mary,* arriving there early in January 1950. Garbo had come unexpectedly from California, and they spent their first night in the city together. Thereafter they met from time to time. He took snapshots of her smiling over a coffeepot, and several articles appeared in gossip columns about their romance. Cecil was annoyed when Ed Sullivan printed a piece stating that he had not been cleared by the Anti-Defamation League of B'nai B'rith, another brief resurrection of the *Vogue* row of 1938. One day during lunch, Cecil sketched Garbo on the menu, and in turn she did a sketch of Mercedes's sister. She scribbled across his drawing.*

Cecil also undertook the designs for a play, *Cry of the Peacock,* and worked with Lincoln Kirstein on the Ashton ballet *Les Illuminations.* On March 26 he returned to Britain. He resumed his correspondence with Garbo:

> Darling Sir,
> A week ago, at this time, we were walking towards the Park on our way to see Katie.** It was such a nice sunny day & we had such a nice walk in the Park, & Katie was very sweet with her sack, & we had a nice lunch together & everything was fine—though overshadowed by our imminent separation. The champagne helped & I didn't even mind that group of autograph nuisances at the door—not as much as usual. . . .
>
> I wonder what your week in between has been? Unborn chickens on your face? massage? the osteopath? I rather hope you have decided to leave for the back alley in California, as the present arrangement of being indispensable & available can't go on any more & should be altered by gentle degrees . . .[26]

Cecil referred to the publicity that had dogged them on his recent visit:

> After New York life is comparatively easy. Not entirely without its setbacks. I was sent from New York a disgusting clipping about us from some column. I don't know if it would be Louella Parsons. But it was like something from the divorce court—& so horrid for you—I only trust that George did not see it (but fear he will have) as it would be very distressing for him. How swinish these gossip spies are in the US, & the vulgarity of it makes me have little relish for the mass of human beings who thrive on it.

*The drawing was done on March 19, 1950. Cecil managed to keep it, and it is now housed in his papers at Cambridge.

**A much-loved orangutan in the Central Park Zoo.

> Do please try & mention my name as lightly & rarely as possible to George as I don't want him to think of me as a bogey. It doesn't do any of us any good.[27]

Garbo replied promptly, thanking him for his wires and assuring him that she missed him and often looked at his tower. She would leave for California on April 10, not for England, however heavenly that might be. She said that she wanted him to have a look at Katie so that he would remember her too.[28]

This was the period in which Mercedes had temporarily deserted Poppy Kirk and was living in New York again. She and Garbo were both preoccupied with their ill health and busily visiting Dr. Max Wolf, whose methods were somewhat dubious. Poppy suggested that Mercedes should accompany Garbo to California, but this scheme held no attraction for Garbo. Meanwhile Cecil put forward the idea that Mercedes should accompany Garbo on her next visit to Europe. He knew he could easily pry Garbo away from Mercedes, whereas Schlee was more of a problem:

> Please let me know (you can ask Crocker) when you are to become an American citizen. When would you possibly come to Europe? Must it be under the same auspices? Please please no. You must try to extricate yourself out of your present trap with great care & delicacy but slowly & surely, & once you have made a move out don't please go right back. It would be like doing that if you were to go abroad again with the same chaperone. You know it would then be impossible for you to come & stay with me here and I do long for that for your own happiness & contentment as well as for my own.
>
> On to other subjects, next time you come over the Atlantic you should have Black and White as chaperone. She could be given relief from her duties once you had arrived . . .[29]

Along with his oft-repeated urgings that Garbo should come to England and not fail to see the spring, he was occasionally quite light-hearted in his approach:

My Darling Sugar plum,
I am ravished by the gay thought of you. I wish you were here so that we could have some good laughs—some girlish giggles & what not. The snapshot I took of you at our last luncheon (not last supper!) is so delightful that just having had a quiz at it I am now in a very good mood. Darling Mmumm! . . . Have you been to the desert? I would like to know what you've been cooking in your double boiler. Is the ulcer reacting to your strict regime? Please bung us a line.

Suddenly you seem so very far away. It is time I telephoned, or got a postcard or some sort of news from you. A friend wrote me an extraordinary account of how he had seen you walking with S. in the uptown streets of New York, & it brought you so vividly to my mind that I felt I was seeing the incident myself.

Has Black & White been in touch? Do get her to bring a "new American citizen" over with her sometime this summer. It would be so nice for me.[30]

Meanwhile, Cecil went to Buckingham Palace to photograph Queen Elizabeth for her forthcoming fiftieth birthday. He went to Wales, and at the end of May he took the boat to Le Havre and stayed with a friend near Deauville before going to see Diana Cooper at Chantilly and picking his mother up in Paris. He paid two further visits to Paris in June. On his second visit, he ran into Schlee:

I saw George (unexpectedly) in Paris & he told me news of you. That you had been together to the desert, that you had *not* got an ulcer, & that you were feeling fine! Fine! I am so glad!! It is thrilling news: I wish you had sent me a wire saying "Ulcer vanished" & I should have had no more mental pictures of you eating blue grey cauliflower.[31]

The presence of Schlee in Paris gave Cecil the curious sensation that Garbo might not be far away. But she did not materialize. In July, Cecil managed a telephone call to her. In his next letter he wrote:

I was working in the library on some drawings when I suddenly realised the time was ripe to telephone to you. It was my bedtime

& at the end of a long week's work here in the country. It was the 7th of the month & 7 is a lucky number. Every other time I'd thought of calling you, it was not a good day or time, & I thought you'd be rushing out for your piano lessons or hurrying off to give away the prizes at the schoolchildren's display when my call came through, & you'd say "Sorry, got to dash." On Friday evening the operator said "no delay" & within a few minutes the message came back "Miss Harriet on the line" & I was suddenly so thrilled & excited that as I waited my heart began to pump & pound so I thought it would burst. It was very alarming. Bang Bang Bang. It made such a reverberation that I thought it would be impossible to hear you on the line & it was practically impossible! a terrible connection. The nice English operator said "It's wicked" & it was. Poor Harriet having to be called back over & over & all the time for a wonky line. However for me it was lovely to talk to you & only sad to think you must be lonely. It is not the best place in the world to be lonely in, & I wish you would let me save you. It is only tantalising for me to try & tell you how much you would like to be here just now, as you have to remain put, for a bit, but afterwards, do think seriously about coming here on your own, you cannot let your existence hang by only one thread. I am sure a change will happen but let it happen, let it happen firmly & by slow degrees. . . . I was most sorry to hear about the wrist, & trust it has not been painful enough to keep you awake at night. When it gets stronger please exercise it on sending me a few snippets. It will be a momentous day when Uncle Sam takes you into the bosom of his family, & I trust from that day forth you will spend much less time on his shores. Will you be coming over here directly? I suppose everything is in the lap of the gods. What a very big lap they must have.[32]

A week later, Cecil was once again in a frivolous mood:

Dear Youth,
Have you yet learnt how to use a razor? Do you strop the blade against a leather prong in the bathroom each morning? Have you got to the age when you wear long pants & a dinner jacket in the evening? Has your voice started to break yet? Have you reached the age of puberty?

Garbo as Marguerite in *Camille*, with Robert Taylor, 1937.

Garbo in *Queen Christina*, 1933.

Garbo played Anna Karenina to Fredric March's Vronsky (above) in 1935. Her last film was *Two-Faced Woman*, with Melvyn Douglas (below), in 1941. It was attacked by the National Legion of Decency and the critics.

Cecil Beaton and Marlene Dietrich were both in Munich in the summer of 1933, after his first brush with Garbo and her affair with Mercedes.

Beaton had his first sexual experience with a woman in 1929, when his friend Marjorie Oelrichs (left), later the wife of Eddy Duchin, offered to initiate him. Adele Astaire (right), Fred's sister and dancing partner, pitched in a few days later.

From 1930 to 1945, Beaton lived in Ashcombe, a magical house in a valley in the Wiltshires. He's posing here with his sisters and his dog.

Mercedes de Acosta specialized in glamorous and interesting women. One of her earliest romantic attachments was the Russian actress Alla Nazimova (above left). During the 1920s, after she had married the painter Abram Poole, Mercedes became involved with Eva Le Gallienne (above right, in Florentine costume). Mercedes met Ona Munson in 1932, when Munson was having a romance with Ernst Lubitsch and Mercedes was with Garbo. Munson played Belle Watling with Clark Gable in *Gone With the Wind* (below).

Reddish House, Broadchalke, Beaton's Wiltshire home from 1948 to 1980.

Valentina Schlee and Garbo were part of a complicated ménage à trois for over twenty years.

Garbo and Georges Schlee in New York in 1946. He was Beaton's nemesis.

In the spring of 1948, Beaton spent two weeks with Garbo at her house in Beverly Hills, where they were "sympathetic companions" and "besotted lovers."

Beaton and Garbo on a London street in 1951. She was staying with him at Broadchalke.

During Garbo's long visit to Beaton's home in 1951, they attended a party with Noël Coward (behind Garbo).

Villa Le Roc, Cap d'Ail, the house in the south of France where Schlee and Garbo spent their summers in the late 1950s and early 1960s.

Garbo in August 1965, the summer after Schlee's death. She and Beaton were the guests of Cecile de Rothschild on a yacht trip around the Greek islands.

During the trip around Greece in 1965, Garbo swam naked and liked to go for walks without her top on. This inevitably led to fooling around with the camera.

Garbo and Beaton on the yacht in 1965, at dusk.

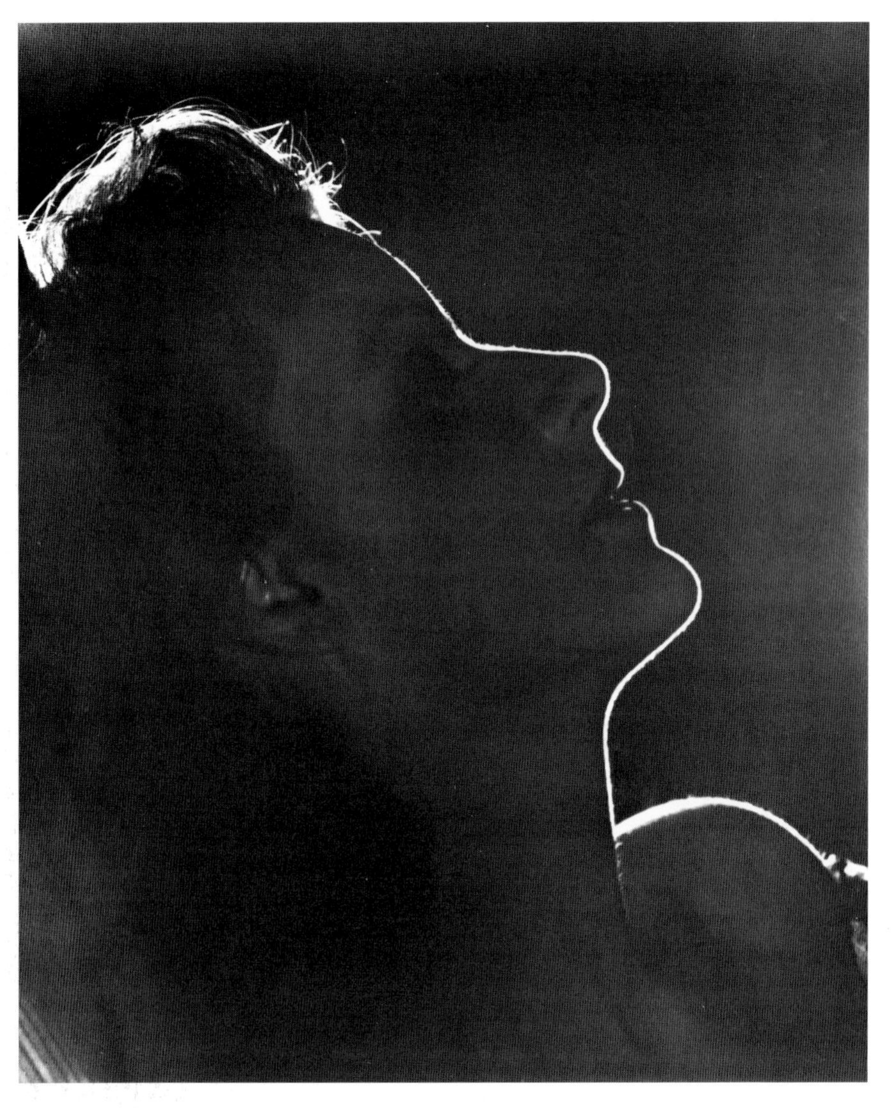

The photograph of Garbo that Beaton kept in his bedroom until the day he died.

I expect you are nearing the stage when you will be thinking quite a bit about lovemaking. If so, & you feel like it, let me know if I can give you any pointers.

Dear heart. I trust you are not too lonely in the alley. Oh dear . . .[33]

But the summer of 1950 did not produce a visit from Garbo any more than the previous two summers had. Cecil felt in need of a change, so he decided to set off to Taormina in Sicily. He went to Truman Capote's pink house on the hill above the town, covered with olive groves. Suddenly one of Garbo's rare letters arrived. She was in a state again. Still undergoing the lengthy process of becoming an American citizen, she had muddled the date and would now have to reapply. She was fed up with her housekeeper, she missed Cecil, and, she told him, she had sent him a present from Bliss Brothers in New York: a ham, which, she added, he might have to track down. She had no other news. She sent greetings to Daisy Fellowes and planted an imaginary kiss on Cecil's brow.[34]

Cecil received this letter in Taormina shortly before his return to London. He replied:

Beloved,
The person I was trying to think of in my last letter, the person you know, was Daisy Fellowes. Her yacht arrived here one morning while we were bathing & that evening we went on board for dinner. It was quite an adventure to get out into the bay where the *Sister Anne* was anchored. First into a rowing boat—then into a motor boat. All this in a choppy sea & in the dark. It was interesting once we had got on board to find such an English atmosphere. All the crew English, the food very English in its worst sense. I don't think Daisy was enjoying her cruise very much & rather bored by her family party & when we suggested it was bed time, she was simply delighted to get rid of us.

Although we had made plans to meet next day she sent up an indecent plate of a pansy sailor as a parting present & the yacht was gone.

Your sweet & delightful letter arrived here last evening & I read it sitting under an oleander tree in the market square. It is a bore about it taking so long to be called but I trust you will have good time in which to learn your lines.

In no uncertain terms will I write to the Bliss Brothers.[35]

Weeks passed, and Cecil became impatient:

My dear boy,

I am getting fidgety that so much time passes while we are on opposite sides of the ocean. It is all wrong & damn silly since we seem to get on nicely with each other. The life in New York isn't all that it should be, & it's sad to let another year pass before you can meet me on my home ground, & discover if you like it. However I suppose these are rare benefits—& joys & pleasures which we must not be greedy to drink to the full. In the meantime I think a great deal about you, & I have your face photographed before my eyes on all sorts of varied occasions.[36]

Cecil continued to campaign for Broadchalke:

I really like to have some congenial neighbour over to dinner & a long talk afterwards, I have told you about some of them. I would like you to know the David Cecils as you would like them—also the wild beast Augustus John who is of heroic stature. Thus you have an example of my quiet life here.

We have not yet heard from the blissful brothers but oh boy I am determined to get that ham from them.[37]

He sought news of Garbo, but in vain. It came neither from her nor from the newspapers.

He went to Clarence House to photograph the infant Princess Anne:

Babies are difficult at the best of times, & this was one of the worst times because the baby only wanted to be allowed to sleep. Who's to blame her. I was not allowed to take a jack along with me to keep her eyes open so we had to make bird noises, rattle keys, clap our hands, jump up & down. The more idiotic the performance, the more bored the baby. Only a drop of glycerine on the tongue seemed to bring any favourable reaction. But I got one lovely picture which I expect you saw in your local paper though you would not guess it was by me. It was of Prince Charles, the fair haired little boy kissing the baby—a pretty picture.[38]

In October, Cecil succeeded in reaching Garbo on the telephone. He found her suffering from a cold. He was due for another American stint, leaving England on November 30 and arriving on December 5. He hoped to celebrate Christmas with her: "I am longing to be with you in the most intimate manner possible,"[39] he wrote. Cecil thought Garbo might be interested to hear that the king of Sweden had died:

> Flags at half mast. Bring out the mourning. Trumpeters play the Last Post for King Gustav is dead. That nice old man who looked like a Tintoretto Archbishop whether he played tennis in a panama hat or sat at home doing his embroidery. It is a sad loss & it was nice to think people said he liked boys too![40]

Before leaving for America, Cecil paid a quick visit to Paris. He went to the forest of Fontainebleau, finding the woods at their autumnal best. He sat by Diana Cooper's bedside. And he went out to lunch with Mercedes, warning Garbo that they would surely "do a bit of confabulating about you."[41] He reported to Garbo what Mercedes said:

> Lunch party great success. Black & white hatless in a mauve shirt underneath her highwayman's coat. She seemed perky & full of confidence & plans. Rather dislikes not being in New York at this time of the year but seems to be poor. It seems it's cheaper here. We *did* confabulate about you, & I was rather surprised when she volunteered the opinion that she once hoped that you & I would be married, & then intimated that it was now too late. Is it? It is very extraordinary to think of that enormous blonde whom Gentlemen Prefer being in possession of her bed.*[42]

*Carol Channing was renting Mercedes's New York apartment. In December 1949 she had scored a great hit at the Ziegfeld Theatre as Lorelei Lee in the musical version of Anita Loos's *Gentlemen Prefer Blondes.*

Cecil was delighted that a letter from Garbo awaited him in London. She was still stuck in California, waiting for her citizenship papers, and hoped to be free by the end of the month. The gist of her message was that she longed to see Cecil again.[43] Cecil recorded his meeting with Mercedes in his diary. Over the years, Cecil and Mercedes had enjoyed many conversations about Garbo. At first it was Mercedes who was the better informed; later Cecil stole a march on her. There were times when he felt he should not talk to her about Garbo, but this was not one of them.

Mercedes told Cecil, "It would be a bad thing for her to play the part of anyone who is even slightly mad—or melancholic or kills someone, for she identifies herself with the part too much & is medium-istic." Mercedes had consulted a handwriting expert, who said Garbo was "a truly great & remarkable person—a superior character. It could be the writing of an actress but it is not possible for such a person to do so small a job as that of an actress. She is a complex mixture of greatness & pettiness." Mercedes described her as "an elemental." And she told Cecil that when the two of them went to the Sierra Nevada "G. was like a maniac—like a fawn—like a little animal running up & down the rocks, holding on to them, hanging by the arms & screaming with joy." Mercedes disapproved deeply of Garbo's present life. Garbo had told her, "I'm just a mass of fears—I'm frightened of everything—even in trains, at night, in taxis, etc." Mercedes concluded, "In these towns she leads such an unnatural life."[44]

Cecil urged Garbo to press Harry Crocker to expedite the American citizenship papers so that she could be in New York to greet him. Then he thought of a better idea: "Do become an English citizen. Make that your good intention for 1951. Then you will be the Festival of Britain. Dearest Heart of a lettuce, I send you my tenderest love."[45]

Cecil arrived at his tower in the Sherry Netherland Hotel in New York on December 5 and found Garbo in town. She was in a nervous state. One day at her doctor's, she broke down and cried. The doctor asked about her private life: "Have you got a boy friend or a girl friend?" Garbo was so surprised that she stopped weeping. The next time she saw him, she asked, "Did you think I was a lesbian?" "Good Heavens no," he replied. "I meant any sort of friend. You're too much alone."[46]

Cecil and Garbo resumed their walks together, visiting Katie the orangutan in Central Park. At the end of his stay, as he returned to Britain, Cecil summed up his progress:*

> Sadly short but very pleasant happy associations this year. G. was unexpectedly in N.Y. when I arrived. She had flown from Hollywood three days earlier to see Laszlo** about a rash that had broken out on her chin. Everything seemed under control by the time I saw her. We spent my first evening in New York together—& were happy. Soon she had to fly back to await her naturalisation papers.
>
> Then began a long dreary wait. "Why did I come back? Why didn't I wait in New York for Christmas?" The waiting continued. She had a bad cold—couldn't get rid of it. Went to the agent—still no summons. At last it arrived. Photographs in all the papers† wearing this winter's discovery—a veil. This spotted veil was a great protection against people spotting her in the street she found—hence a new appearance—very "Flâneur."
>
> Then more sinus trouble & a delay returning to New York. If I had not postponed my departure I would never have seen her—But due to play disappointments I was able to see her twice. On each occasion we got along very well & on the night of my departure I felt I had made great strides forward & that, at last, she had shown emancipation & a real desire to make a life for herself in England.
>
> One evening we went to the 1st night of a new version of my ballet *Camille.*‡ When I went backstage before the performance the dancers said they would be very hurt if I didn't take a call with them. When after the performance the applause warranted my

*This is the full, unexpurgated account of those days and differs from that in *The Strenuous Years: Diaries, 1948–1955* (London: Weidenfeld & Nicolson, 1973), pp. 75–76.

**Dr. Erno Laszlo.

†Photographs of Garbo signing her certificate in the Federal Court of Los Angeles appeared in the newspapers of February 10, 1951. After signing the papers, she took her final oath of citizenship.

‡*Camille,* first staged in 1946 with Anton Dolin and Alicia Markova.

going backstage I asked G. if she would mind. "Oh, no. Don't do that!" She was appalled. But I went. When I returned to my stall she was quite shocked. "Why did you have to do that? You had made your contribution up there and why show yourself to everybody? Really you shouldn't associate with the Ingenues." I realised how vulgar my self display had been and how once again all G's instincts are the right ones— There is just never a particle of vulgarity in anything she has ever felt or done. She is an innately distinguished person.

Quite recently she has been bombarded with offers to do radio & television. She never even answers the requests. But one telegram she showed to George who said "Well I'm sorry, but this is one thing you can't turn down—it'll only entail a half hour's appearance & just look what they're going to pay you—You can't afford to turn it down." "Oh, yes I can. I don't need the money—nothing on earth would make me do a thing like that for an advertisement. Why? Why??"

She talked again a lot about her acting. She moaned "If only one could do one's work when one feels like it, by oneself. If only one could soar—if only one could fly! But it is all so dependent on the mechanical. With the cameras there have to be dozens of retakes—if you don't like audiences it is so humiliating to have to show off in front of people. I don't even like to act in front of the electricians but they've asked me to do a film which takes place in Venice. But that I could never do—not in Italy where people stare so much."

Again and again I realised how dreadful it was for her not being able to avoid recognition. Continuously a mood would be broken by some stranger butting into a conversation—& often now they are insulting without meaning to be. A woman of Greta's age comes up & says "Oh Miss Garbo I used to worship you when I was a little girl." G. laughed: "But she was just as old as I am!"

On our last evening together G. came to the apartment at 6 o'clock. She looked so well, apricot skinned—a beret on her head—the usual nondescript clothes. This year she *would* come to England—alone. She couldn't give up all her life to one human being. But it was hard to break a habit. It had been quite a fight to get here this evening. Later we dined downstairs in the Russian atmosphere of the Carnival Room. We ate Schslaslic, drank vodka & joked in the highest spirits about the prospects of our marriage. "I probably will" became a tag line.

G. hurried back to her hotel to telephone farewell. Shall we do our favourite trick of waving to each other? It was night. So I waved a sheet out of my turret window on the 37th floor across to her at the Hampshire House & there a new star was born as in the clear night air a moving light sparkled at her window. It was a lovely farewell gesture & I feel that with the years our friendship has been cemented even firmer. She said "With me that generally happens. I have few friends but they always stick."[47]

Garbo in Beaton's drawing room at Reddish House during her two-month stay in the fall of 1951.

CHAPTER 10

"SHALL I HANG UP MY HAT WITH MR. BEATON?"

In 1951, Cecil achieved two long-held ambitions. One was to have his play, *The Gainsborough Girls,* staged; the other was to lure Garbo to Broadchalke. Few people have fought two such long and potentially hopeless battles with such tenacity. As it turned out, Cecil was doomed to suffer the disappointment that befalls many whose prayers are answered.

When he returned to England from New York, he resumed his correspondence with Garbo, but now his letters were less regular and much shorter. It became almost a balanced correspondence, with Garbo writing back more frequently.

Cecil went to Spain, which he described as "someone else's idea of Heaven."[1] He disliked the first-class hotel and, most of all, the Americans abroad. In May, he went to a preview of the Festival of Britain in London:

> I am glad the effort has been made to show what this country can produce—& certainly the old things shown at the Victoria & Albert Museum are absolutely marvellous, & give one a warm whiff of childhood. One realises what a rich & secure period the Victorians lived in with their wonderful Turkish towels warmed in front of a fire, safes & jewel caskets that even a bomb couldn't hurt, & a Sheffield knife with ninety different blades which looks like a Picasso sculpture. Well all this is the sort of thing you have to read if you're a friend of Beattie.[2]

In America, Garbo sold her Beverly Hills home after a long period of waiting. She wrote to Cecil, telling him that she had been going through a sad time. Georges Schlee had been hospitalized, and she had been obliged to spend several hours a day with him. He had been discharged the day before, she wrote, but was already back in the hospital.

She herself still had a cold, now into its sixth month. She urged Cecil not to get overtired, told him that she thought of him often, and invited him to send her a list of any pains from which he was suffering, so that they could compare notes.[3]

Cecil saw the wisdom of Garbo's disposing of her large California property, and he hoped this would liberate her to come to England:

> I'm not complaining, because a lot of progress has been made, but I know once you come here & breathe in the country air you will wonder what you have been doing all this time. It will be like going back to your natural element. No more cement side walks, & scrub for you, but springy grass, & moss, & a carpet of leaves & twigs.
>
> Hurry! Hurry![4]

Referring to Garbo's letter, Cecil wrote:

I am sorry to hear that George has not been well. He doesn't look very spry, & I fear, his illness cannot have made things easier for you. I am sad about that.

Remember! I am banking on your showing a little independence in September. It is time you allowed yourself the luxury of doing what you would like to do. It will be good for you, & will prevent a lot of unhappiness, while creating new happiness. Here endeth the fourth lesson.[5]

Cecil telephoned Garbo, and then he wrote again, from the train to London:

Dear Boy,
Jolly nice talking to you. But that call was a bloody nuisance to you I'm afraid. For three days I'd had it "in"—& whenever I expected I might be talking they said there was no connection owing to atmospherics—or later the "Party don't answer" or else it would be the middle of the night for you.

When, at last, it did come through my Mother walked into my bedroom to tell me she'd bought three silver toast racks for me as a present, so I couldn't turf her out, & I felt rather self conscious talking to you in front of her. Hence my rather brusque manner. I'm sorry to think you'd been kept on the hop too.

I am very sorry for you in your present predicament. I wonder what can be wrong with the poor man. You certainly have bad luck in getting so inextricably involved, but maybe things will right themselves. I am making no plans for August (late part) & September so am banking on you giving yourself up entirely to me.[6]

Garbo sent a brief line to Cecil from Beverly Hills, telling him that she could be reached care of Harry Crocker until about July 1. Georges Schlee was still in his bed, and she might go and stay with him at 450 East Fifty-second Street. She told Cecil that she was dead tired from all her packing, and she wished him good luck with his play.[7]

Cecil was increasingly preoccupied with the opening of *The Gainsborough Girls* in Brighton. In London he saw Harry Crocker, who told him that Garbo had moved to New York and was now visiting Bermuda. Subsequently she wrote to Cecil, announcing that she was on British ground, traveling with Schlee, and that he had scared her by taking to his bed, yet again, for two days. The only impression she had of Bermuda was the view from her terrace. It was humid, she complained, there was no shortage of rain, and her trousers clung to her legs.

Garbo wrote that she would return to New York around July 20 and that Cecil could write to her there. She inquired after the play and said she hoped to get together with him soon.[8]

The Gainsborough Girls opened to disastrous notices. After the performance on opening night, Diana Cooper rushed about, urging everyone to give Cecil a huge ovation when he arrived at the post-theatre party. Cecil was not taken in:

> Dearest G,
> I don't know how I've survived the last week. I'm sure it has given me stomach ulcers. I've woken up every morning very early with the most awful sick feeling as if I'd committed some terrible indiscretion—as if I'd given birth to a monster. The play got very poor notices & everyone says the critics were unnecessarily harsh. Maybe they were. The play was much too long. It was a pity we'd had no time for secret performances in front of an audience. The work that has been done since the first night has made a considerable improvement. It is now quite a nice little play but it has come as a shock to me & to the audiences to find how very unsophisticated a play it is—& how simple & heartfelt. I secretly don't feel very optimistic about its prospects & I feel very dunched as it has been such a terrific lot of work & it has taken me so long to do, & I don't feel that at the moment I should be able to write a better play. However we go on a 4 weeks tour after another week here & maybe we can get a bit more depth into it. It needs solidifying. One should be deeply moved at the end. As it is one is just slightly touched. C. [Constance] Collier & Kate Hepburn came down to see it last night & were enthusiastic & helpful. We'll see. We'll see.[9]

The play ran for two weeks and the local audiences liked it, but the backers grew cautious and postponed its move to New York, stored the scenery, and cut their losses. Cecil concluded that his life was "a hell of a mess." In a letter dated July 31, he poured out his heart to Garbo:

> I've been so busy doing all sorts of work that doesn't amount to much—& all the main & essential problems seem to have gone by the board while I've been so busy chasing my tail. I feel my life very empty & lonely. I really want very much to get married, & make all sorts of radical changes. I feel hemmed in by my secretary,* & don't feel my life is at all as I would wish it. I daresay this is all part of an anti-climax after the excitement of the past weeks, but it certainly shows up a lot of things in perspective.[10]

Cecil went to Venice at the beginning of September, when, in a rare and successful collaboration, he and Oliver Messel dressed Diana Cooper as Cleopatra for the Beistegui Ball. Two letters arrived from Garbo. The first announced her plan to travel. She was flying to Europe with John and Jane Gunther on September 17, despite being near to breakdown. She hoped to spend ten days in Paris with them; then, after they left, she might at last be able to come to England, if Cecil still wanted her. She told Cecil that Georges Schlee was hovering between illness and health, and that all hell had broken loose when she had told him she was planning to travel. Her plans, she said, would remain up in the air until the last minute.[11]

Then, late in September, Cecil received a second sweet letter in response to his recent letters, especially to the depressed one of July 31. Garbo sympathized about the play, suggesting that he take consolation in remembering that such disappointments had happened to others, too. She was still busy, she reported, trying to talk Schlee out of any thought of traveling to Europe, and the entire situation was very disturbing for her soul; she was as morbid and tired as ever. But in this, of all her letters, she concentrated more on the need to boost Cecil in his lonely moment.[12]

It looked at last as though Garbo might really come. From Reddish, Cecil sent her two letters, one for her eyes and one for the eyes of the Russian sturgeon:

*The increasingly awful Maud Nelson.

Dearest Greta,
Very glad to hear you're coming to Europe. Don't go back without coming to England. If you want a quiet rest in the country my manor would be here to welcome you—I only trust you'll be able to make it soon as autumn is so fast giving way to winter—at the moment everything looks wonderful & I've had some lovely walks—But oh how wet it can be! Writing not too good—I cut the top of my finger (first on right hand) opening a tin of Spanish nougat. This [is] slightly irritating as I'm here very busily re-writing my play.

Do trust George is feeling better—He sounds to have had a rotten time—give him my best wishes,

In haste
Love Cecil[13]

Then there was the second letter:

Darling—have just written formal letter for you to show to George (oh how I hate these deceptions!). You *must* fight to come over—otherwise you'll lose your only chance! Life's too short. You've got to live it yourself.

Hurry up & turn over a new leaf![14]

Garbo arrived in Paris on October 8, and, proving anything was possible if she so wished it, she appeared at Southampton a few days later. Despite her attempts to leave Schlee behind in New York, he too was on board. But Cecil seized the opportunity of the moment. He whisked Garbo away from Schlee before either of them really knew what was happening.

Garbo now began a stay of two months. Cecil watched with pride as she regained her self-assurance, health, and happiness. "The months in the country were quite idyllic,"[15] he wrote. In the mornings Cecil worked on his play, and in the afternoons he devoted himself to Garbo's whims. They visited Bath and Oxford and took his nephew, John Smiley, out to tea from Eton. They went to the great houses of Wilton, Crichel, and Hatfield.

At this time Hal Burton was staying with Cecil, helping with technical aspects of *The Gainsborough Girls*. Hal did not meet Garbo for some time, though he was aware of her presence in the house. When they did meet, they became friends because his quiet, unthreatening personality appealed to her at once. He recalled her great happiness at Broadchalke, despite the reporters who jumped out of hedges with monotonous regularity. He was also able to help her through a difficult evening when all Cecil's family gathered to help celebrate Mrs. Beaton's seventy-ninth birthday. Cecil's mother felt she was an exile during Garbo's stay and referred to her as "that woman."[16] Cecil's sisters were disapproving and made little effort to be friendly. Nor, of course, did Garbo make any such effort. Maud Nelson, ever the troublemaker, exercised her habitual jealousy and sided with Mrs. Beaton.

Bravely, Cecil introduced Garbo to Peter Watson, the earlier great love of his life. She was jealous of Peter, but he was at ease with her and almost mockingly amused that Cecil should be pursuing this course. Alastair Forbes was at Broadchalke one day when Garbo inquired casually, "Shall I hang up my hat with Mr. Beaton?"[17]

Cecil's reclusive neighbor at Wilsford Manor, Stephen Tennant, had been a Garbo fan for years. He was delighted when Cecil brought her over, and even more so when she admired his new blue venetian blind on the upper landing. Determined to see her again, he took his guests, Julian and Juliette Huxley, over to Reddish for dinner. Garbo questioned Sir Julian closely about the male-eating courtship of the praying mantis, while Stephen admired the star's "lovely hands, long, petal-like fingers."[18]

Clarissa Churchill, Cecil's Wiltshire neighbor, then hovering on the brink of marrying Anthony Eden, immediately fell under Garbo's spell. "Who can resist the fascination of Greta when the allure is turned on," wrote Cecil, "and it was certainly turned on for Clarissa's benefit."[19]

The Marquess of Bath failed to recognize the glamorous lady Cecil brought to Sturford Mead, and when he asked Cecil who she was, Cecil explained, "It's Garbo, you clot!"[20] Augustus John, long since selected by Cecil to be one of the few privileged to meet her, was wholly captivated. He wrote to Cecil:

> I fell for her of course and hoped to see her again in these parts but I hear she's gone to America. Quel oiseau! Will you send for her? I really must try to capture that divine smile but to follow it

> to the USA would kill me. I wouldn't mind so much dying *afterwards.*[21]

Lady Pamela Berry invited Cecil and Garbo to her *Daily Telegraph* election party. The Marquess of Salisbury, Anthony Head, and other distinguished politicians were also there. The ladies were upstairs after dinner, and Lady Pamela said, "I do wish they'd hurry up." Garbo said, "I'll go and get them." Downstairs she went, surprising the gentlemen by throwing open the dining room door and announcing, "It's time to go now!" Lady Pamela was taken aback when Lord David Cecil declared excitedly, "I touched her!"[22] For once Garbo was the life and soul of the party, throwing back her head in happy laughter.

James Pope-Hennessy became so infatuated that he could do no work for five weeks:

> She has the most inexplicable powers of fascination which she used freely on all and sundry; but whether it is deliberate or not nobody knows. . . . I think, in fact, she is the Troll King's daughter from *Peer Gynt*—some strange remote being from a haunted northern forest who has got loose in modern life—she is only explicable as a mythological figure. And then it gradually dawns on one that she is entirely uneducated, interested in theosophy, dieting and all other cranky subjects, has conversation so dull that you could scream. . . . Cecil Beaton guarded her like an eagle, and nobody was ever allowed alone with her; she lunched here with John [his brother, the art historian] and me, and I saw her altogether nine or ten times; once I contrived to be alone with her for one and seven-eighths minutes, during which she asked me if I could explain why she had a cold in her head ever since she had been in London. She is now in Paris, looking for fresh worlds to conquer.[23]

Diana Cooper had pressed Cecil to bring Garbo to France, but he did not enjoy being with Garbo on turf that was not his own, despite what he called their "great intimacy and happiness."[24] Staying in an expensive hotel was irksome, and they went out for every meal. Cecil had too much to do in life to fall easily into the role of escort, and he tired, albeit reluctantly, of the endless question "Where shall we go today?"[25]

Mercedes was in Paris, living with Poppy Kirk, and was often with Cecil and Garbo. One evening they went to call on Alice B. Toklas. Alice had lately remet Mercedes on a bus. She had observed a lady opposite her wearing beautiful canary-yellow gloves, and Mercedes had introduced herself. Alice was surprised: "She has become so bourgeois looking and comfortably middle-aged."[26] Mercedes, Cecil, and Garbo knocked on the door of 5 Rue Christine one evening, but Alice did not hear them. Mercedes later phoned and made an appointment. Alice reported on the visit to Carl Van Vechten:

> Cecil very tousled exhausted and worshipful—she a bit shy—quite Vassarish—unpretentious but very criminal. She asked me with simplicity and frankness—Did you know Monsieur Vollard* was he a fascinating person—a great *charmeur*—was he seductive. She was disappointed like a young girl who dreams of an assignation. Do explain her to me. She was not mysterious but I hadn't the answer. The French papers say they [Cecil and Garbo] are to marry—but she doesn't look as if she would do anything as crassly innocent as that.[27]

Cecil had intended to extend Garbo's British entertainment by taking her to Vaynol for Christmas with his friend Michael Duff. But she suddenly decided she had to return home. Reluctantly, Cecil left her in Paris with Mercedes as chaperone.

Unbeknownst to Cecil, Mercedes's care of Garbo was not a straightforward matter. According to Ram Gopal, there was a dramatic scene in Mercedes's flat during which Garbo and Poppy Kirk fought. In a longer letter written to Mercedes in 1955, after she and Poppy had gone their separate ways, Ram wrote:

> Remember the way you and I roared with laughter when you told me how she banged your head against the walls and floor and tried

*Ambrose Vollard, Paris gallery owner who dealt in the works of Rodin, Renoir, Picasso, and others. Gertrude Stein had been one of his clients.

> locking you up or out of something in the Savoy, all because you stayed with me here in London for a few days!!!!! And the way she and Greta fought at your flat at the Bisson hotel—Thank GOD that is all over now . . .[28]

Garbo flew home to New York on a Pan Am Clipper on December 15. Mercedes accompanied her to Orly Airport, and they took refuge in the bar. Garbo lit an "Americaine" cigarette. They were left in peace until Garbo set forth to the customs barrier. At this point the press surged forward and Mercedes shouted at them, "Vous faîtes un métier honteux. Allez au diable!"[29] Garbo's four cases were marked "Harriet Brown, c/o George Schlee, New York."

Arriving home before Garbo had left Paris, Cecil sent off a letter from frosty Broadchalke. He reported that his housekeeper, Mrs. Murdock, bemoaned Garbo's absence. "I missed her more than anyone we've ever had to stay," she told Cecil. "For three days after you came back without her I felt quite lost. She's so easy & without any effort. She's got what it takes."[30] Cecil was sad:

> No good saying how lovely it was having you here. You know how we all adored you & only wait for your coming back to your true home. Love Cecil.[31]

During their stay together, the subject of marriage had again arisen, and Cecil had been pleased when he asked a direct question: "When I asked her if she thought she ever would marry me she said she probably would."[32]

Cecil knew, as far as anything was certain, that he would see Garbo again in New York in three weeks' time. Later, he would describe Garbo's visit to him as "a long and emotional autumn," which, with the work on his play, "had reduced me to a jellied pulp."[33]

News soon came from his departed guest. Garbo wrote to thank him for all the Christmas telegrams she had received. She was touched to have heard from Clarissa, James Pope-Hennessy, Hal Burton, and even Mrs. Murdock, who had amused her by saying she was welcome back anytime. She asked Cecil to bring over some of his red paper for two lampshades, and in turn sent her fondest regards to Juliet Duff, Simon Fleet, Clarissa, Hal Burton, Mr. Bundy, Mrs. Murdock, and all the other inhabitants of Reddish House and of Pelham Place.[34]

Not unnaturally, Cecil telephoned Garbo the moment he arrived in New York in January 1952. His attempts to reach her were in vain, the switchboard announcing, "Miss Garbo don't answer."[35]

Cecil was devastated: "This is the old treatment. I can hardly believe it possible."[36] Cecil was further angered by a crazy letter that he received from Garbo, accompanied by a pink azalea "banked by common ferns in a pot." Garbo told him she would not be calling for several days, said he would think she was mad, hoped that time would fly, and hinted darkly that there were various reasons for her silence.[37]

Cecil thought this was monstrous since they had "been three months together as man and wife."[38] He felt he had been honest with her, never pretended to be anything that he was not, and he felt he deserved more respect.*

Back in England, Cecil's friends were anxious for news of their visitor from America. Cecil's accounts were far from positive. To Lady Juliet Duff he wrote, "Michael and I are supposed to have dinner tomorrow with Greta but she has been in such a silly state ever since she came back here, with a bad cold. She was much happier at Broadchalke . . ."[39] Hal Burton wanted to send Garbo a book. To him Cecil wrote, "I'm afraid it's no use your trying to do anything about Greta. She is in a better mood now but so negative—& I don't think she ever reads anything. She is once more tied down to the loyalties of this rather sinister little Road Company Rasputin & I don't know how she will break clear. She moans 'C'est la vie!' but it isn't—it's her!"[40]

Hal sent his book, and Cecil reported slightly more positive news:

> Greta asks me to send you her tenderest love—& to thank you for her lovely book. She always says such nice things about you. You were more of a success with her than anybody—& I think you could help her a lot. I see much less of her than before as her

*Garbo was by no means reclusive at this time. On February 6, 1952, the day King George VI died, she attended Valentina's cocktail party for Noël Coward.

> friend is so jealous & so very predatory. She is like something mesmerised. It is sad—& when we do meet we get on like houses on fire. But any chance of her breaking away again seems very remote. Meanwhile life goes on.[41]

When Cecil finally saw Garbo, she complained that she had had a bad cold ever since her return and that Schlee was so depressed that he was going into the hospital. After dinner with Michael Duff, Cecil walked her home to Hampshire House. But Garbo still would not make definite plans, and Cecil became irritated. Recalling the advice of Mona Harrison Williams, he became distant, pecked her on the cheek, and walked away without a backward glance.

A fortnight passed, and Michael Duff was due to leave for England. Cecil suggested that all three should lunch, and Garbo agreed. But Cecil did not invite Michael. He converted the lunch into a twosome at the Colony Club, and he questioned her about the reasons why she had not wished to see him. "Oh I couldn't tell you those now, I'm tipsy," she said. But Cecil persevered:

> "Well I don't think I could return home as I shall be doing soon, and tell my friends and your friends that I haven't seen you at all. Besides you see I feel I deserve some explanation. It seemed to me that we were both very happy with each other in Europe. We didn't have any cloud on our horizon. When we left each other it was with great tenderness. I have a completely clear conscience about the way I behaved to you. I've never pretended to be anything I'm not, and have given you my complete confidence and unless you have some good reason I feel that the fact that you would not speak to me on the telephone and gave the operator instructions 'She don't answer' was very shoddy behaviour."
>
> "I daresay I am a very bad mannered wretch."
>
> "Not only that but you must be a very unhappy person."
>
> "I am."
>
> "You must have such a bad conscience. It must make you feel very badly that you have behaved so badly to me."
>
> "It does, and yet I feel you wouldn't mind very much."
>
> "You thought I wouldn't say I'd jump out of a window."

"If you said it, I wouldn't believe it."

"Admittedly I'm not the sort to bring my life to an end. I have interests. I have my work and friends and activities, but you have the power to hurt me very deeply, and I have been very hurt. Do you like hurting people and making them suffer?"

"No, but I don't think you would suffer so very much."

"Why? Is it not rather peculiar after all our intimacy and mutual devotion that you should abruptly bring everything to a halt?"

"I don't think you loved me very much by the time we left one another in Paris?"

"Admittedly I wasn't as happy with you in Paris as in the country in England, but that is because I loathe the café society way of life. It seemed so pointless. But you really think I didn't love you?"

"I don't think you've ever really loved me."

"Then what have I been doing for the past five years—using up my emotions, my tenderest feelings?"

"Oh I daresay you have enjoyed fooling around. It's been quite a change."

"I can't believe you feel that. You know me too well to feel that. You must have a terrible remorse when you behave as you do to your nearest and dearest." I had meant to allude to her bad treatment of her mother and brother, from whom she has completely cut herself off. To me she pretends her mother is dead—but her mother happens to be living in Connecticut.

I admonished Greta for drinking aquavit in the middle of the day & promptly ordered myself another whisky sour. I became quite drunk. After a bit another aquavit was drunk. We were both tipsy & Greta did not understand my allusions to "nearest and dearest" and thought I was referring to Schlee—that he had influenced her against me.

"That is quite untrue," she said. "He has nothing to do with this. I had made up my mind before you came. It has nothing to do with him what I decided to do, but you see you have such vitality—you can't keep quiet and relaxed. One has to be on the run with you all the time—& I'm going through a bad period in my life (the change) and I didn't feel up to seeing you. Everything is erratic. I'm feeling anxious and uneasy and low and I can't face up to the pace you set."

"Do you mean you can't relax completely when you're with me?"

"No. I just don't feel up to it. You don't know me. You pronounce such strict verdicts. Someone sent me your scrapbook on Valentine's Day and in it you wrote I have no heart—I am not capable of friendship.* That is not true."

"But that was written twenty years ago—when I didn't know you & I didn't know anything about life but just blowed my top. In any case I think it most unfair to hold something against me that I wrote twenty years ago before I knew you & have forgotten completely."

Suddenly I realised where the quote came from that was used in a horrid article about would we get married?** The words had seemed familiar but I couldn't imagine how I had used them—how anyone had discovered them. In an indiscreet letter maybe? Now here was the truth—& I realised she had been wounded to read these words, but it had not made all that difference to her attitude to me.

"So then what? We are at the end?"

"Well." She looked at me askance. "You're looking very pretty," she said. "You're thinner."

I passed her no compliment. I said "I know exactly how your hair should be" . . .

She liked it when I took hold of her hair and I emulated her by saying "Nicht machen."

"Do you remember how violently you took hold of my hair in that Paris restaurant?"

"Oh you were furious."

And now I realised she had loved it. Well by now we were

*Cecil had written, "She is not interested in anything or anybody in particular, and she has become as difficult as an invalid and as selfish, quite unprepared to put herself out for anyone: she would be a trying companion, continuously sighing and full of tragic regrets; she is superstitious, suspicious and does not know the meaning of friendship; she is incapable of love" (*Cecil Beaton's Scrapbook* [London: Batsford, 1937], p. 55).

**Garbo employed a clipping service and thus knew what was written about her in the press.

> back where we used to be. The strain had gone. No bitterness left . . .[42]

Cecil took Garbo back to his hotel so she could powder her nose. Waiting for the elevator, he sensed she wanted him to kiss her. He did so.

> Next morning I telephoned. We were old pals again. It was as if nothing had happened to part us—or interrupt our intimacy. We talked of Truman [Capote] and when I eulogised him she said she'd be right over any time we were drinking martinis together. She'd be right over to see clothes, to go on all sorts of expeditions.
>
> The meeting with T. went well,* but she had to dine with Schlee. Later she was unable to come to the ballet on account of possible persecution of the press, so I paid her out by refusing her favours and dating up someone who happened to ring while she was in the room.
>
> A strange unaccountable person who should not be given a free rein to make her own disastrous mistakes.[43]

The root of the cooling down between Garbo and Cecil was, of course, Georges Schlee. He had been seriously worried by Garbo's two-month stay with Cecil and for the first time considered him a serious threat. Pressure from Schlee had made Garbo suddenly flee back to New York before Christmas.

In the middle of April, Cecil returned to England. A letter from Garbo soon followed.In it she came as near as she could allow herself to apologize for her aloof behavior. She blamed it on the difference between them: her nervous state as opposed to his zest for life. She asked after Cecil's mother and sent her love to him and to England.[44]

*Truman Capote said soon after, "I stopped by the apartment of a friend who previously that afternoon had entertained Garbo at tea. As I entered the room and started to sit down in an especially comfortable chair piled with pillows, my friend, a very sane fellow, suddenly asked would I mind not using that particular chair. 'You see,' he said solemnly. 'She sat there. The dent in the little red pillow, that's where her hand rested—I should like to keep it a while longer.' I understood him completely" (unidentified press cutting, April 14, 1952).

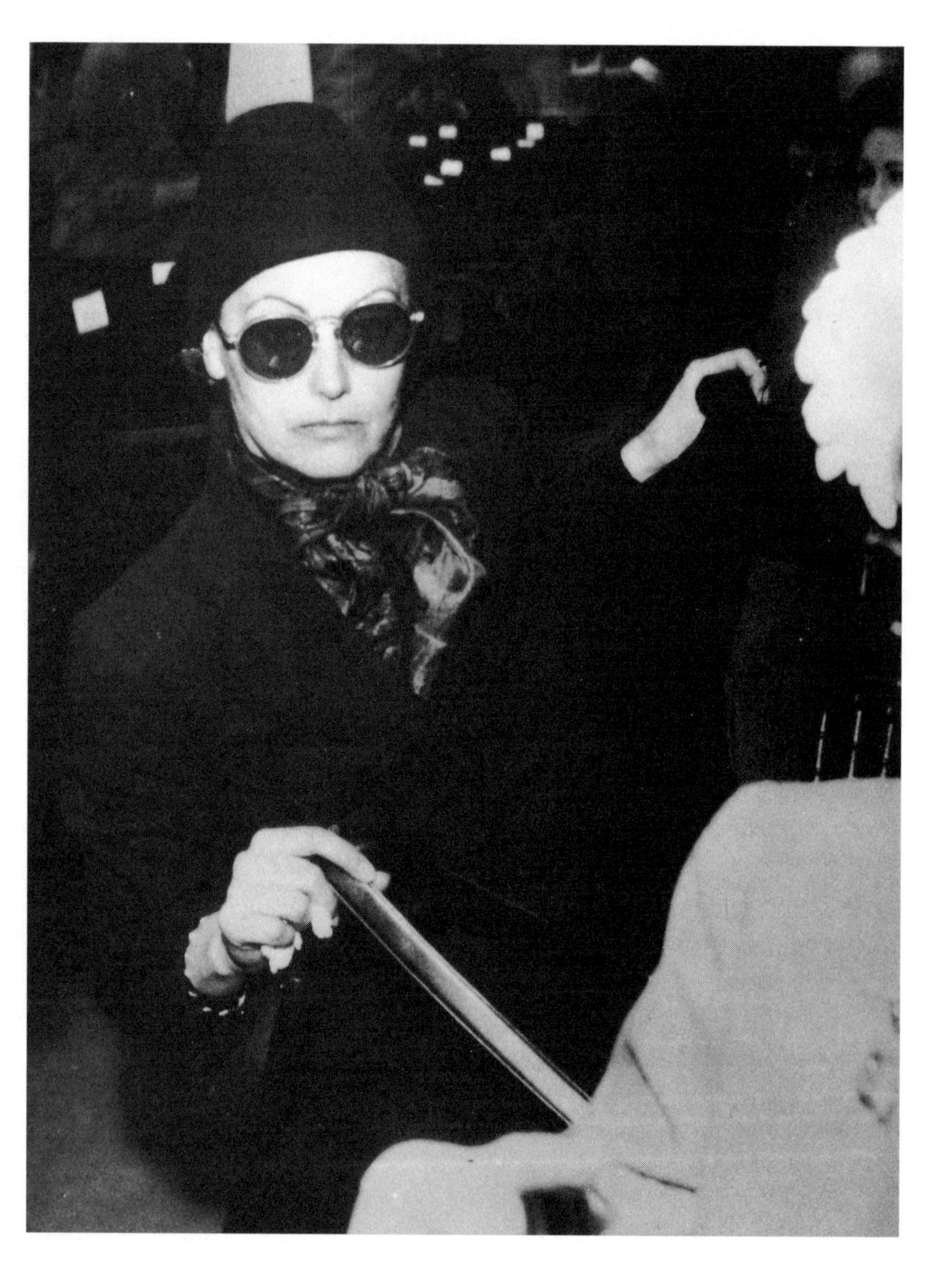

Garbo in Paris in the early fifties at the sale of an art collection.

CHAPTER 11

"THE GODDESS HAS GONE."

Cecil sailed home to London in early April and threw himself into his work. Garbo went on her travels once more. In a letter to Cecil, she told him that despite her recent silence he was not forgotten. She had been to Austria unexpectedly with Eric Rothschild* to see his wife, Bina, and her mother. It had been a strange time, but Garbo wondered if Cecil

*Baron Eric Goldschmidt-Rothschild (1894–1984), one of the Viennese Rothschilds, was easing himself into the role of Garbo's new admirer. His wife was Bina Henckel von Donnersmarck, who played the Queen of Transylvania in the film of *My Fair Lady.* They had one son. The Baron, who lived partly in Rome and partly in New York, shared his latter days with his stylish Belgian cousin Baronne Renée de Becker, who predeceased him.

would have liked to go there with her. She thought Austria a "sweet" country. But it was overshadowed by the imminent arrival of "Schleisky." As for Garbo herself, she felt increasingly lost and thought Cecil would perhaps be glad that she was making no plans. She wondered what he was up to and again told him to send any letters to her to Morgan's Bank in Paris.[1]

Cecil went to Scotland to put the finishing touches to the Lunts' tour with *Quadrille,* a romantic comedy by Noël Coward. It was a triumphant success for them and for once a happy collaboration for Cecil. His mother had a heart attack, which worried him, but there was better news to report:

> No doubt by this time you will have heard of Clarissa's marriage to Mr. Eden.* She "turned him down" a year ago, then 6 months later decided to accept. I am very happy about it, as she is a remarkable person & her new role will give her opportunities to use her very great qualities. She has been at her best all this summer, looking radiant & being sweet & forthcoming. All the troubles of last autumn sprang from her sense of uneasiness & frustration.[2]

Garbo was equally excited at Cecil's news of Clarissa. She took some credit for the alliance, pointing out that it might never have happened had they rented a house as suggested. Instead, she wrote, Cecil would have been chasing Clarissa round the beach advising her to marry Mr. Eden. She wondered if the foreign secretary was aware of how much he owed Cecil. As for her, Cecil was lucky not to be involved. However, she might go to Paris around September 5. The Morgan Bank was again the place for letters; her neck hurt her. She sent her best to the new Mrs. Eden.[3]

In September, Cecil replied:

*Clarissa Churchill married Anthony Eden on August 14, 1952. A reception was held at 10 Downing Street, where her uncle Sir Winston Churchill was hanging on as prime minister until the bitter end. Eden was then foreign secretary. He became a Knight of the Garter in 1954 and succeeded Churchill as prime minister in 1955. He resigned due to ill health in 1957. He was created Earl of Avon in 1961 and died in 1977.

Dearest G
I'm still here but my nice long uninterrupted sojourn here ends this Sunday when I have to go to London for a few days. Then back here for snatches. The London house is slowly being redecorated. I might come over to Paris if there's a chance of seeing you under favourable conditions & perhaps you'd like to come back here with me? I shouldn't have thought there was much need for you to hurry back to New York & that hairy Mrs. Bates.* But maybe there is? The other Clarissa is coming down to her cottage for a spell on the 14th. It would be nice if we could all have pickled herring & slivovitz together again.

Blessings from B

Garbo and Cecil did not meet that summer. Nor do his letters evince the same driving enthusiasm for a meeting as those of 1951. In October Cecil came down with a bad cold, and on October 13 Garbo returned from her travels, docking at Manhattan. Cecil wrote:

Thank you for your nice letter. I am sad to think we are both going through such a static, frustrating period & I feel Nella Webb** must be wrong with her dates. However she did tell us not to worry & that all would come out well. & remember you have as big a future in front of you as you could possibly wish. I am certain everything will soon turn out well, as you have behaved so well while waiting—& you will be rewarded.

I wish I could come out & join you, as it seems so difficult to get you here, which would really be so much more sensible.

There are two white roses in a long glass on the fireplace opposite. I wish that I could give them to you just as they are. I think a lot about you. I think a lot of you.[4]

Soon it was November and time for Cecil to return to the United States. He left with a warning from Truman Capote:

*Mrs. Clarissa Bates, a chiropractor.

**Garbo and Beaton's New York fortune-teller.

> Darling, I hope you can have an easier, at any rate less neurotic rapport with Greta G. But I'm afraid she will never be a satisfactory person, because she is so dissatisfied with herself, and dissatisfied people can never be emotionally serious. They simply don't believe in anything—except their own limitations.[5]

Cecil arrived in New York and reported to Hal Burton, "Have talked to Greta but not seen her yet. She seems full of sorrows & can't get rid of a cold. The same old story . . ."[6]

Cecil also relied heavily on Mercedes, with whom, throughout the 1950s, he kept up a regular correspondence on the state of Garbo's health and mind, her peregrinations and mood changes. In a sense they were caught in the same web. Garbo had become a fixation. They both knew her intimately and felt they had earned her friendship and trust. They were protective of her and frequently depressed by her lack of initiative. Mercedes suffered, and Cecil suffered too. In times of rejection, it was natural that they would turn to each other for succor within the magic circle. On November 19 Cecil wrote to Mercedes:

> Greta still complains of sinus—& not being able to get rid of an interminable cold. I think the real trouble is she can't get rid of an interminable bore—but she is resigned—& more than ever is content to wait for "orders." The trouble is such a lot of time is being wasted—& the influence has gone so far that she now begins to talk in those well known ungrammatical Schleeisms—a mixture of Slav, Brooklynese & Baby Talk! A dreadful bathos for a noble creature to squander life away in such a way.[7]

Cecil had delayed calling Garbo lest she fail to answer. But he made sure she knew he was in New York. Finally he called, and they shared a listless conversation. They met a few times, but rather unsatisfactorily. They lunched together: "G. looks very different, more conventionalised with short hair permanently waved, less eye make-up, a pale, thin face very secretive, tightly drawn, a grey woollen dress, a Napoleonic coat of sow's ear material."[8] Having been rather nervous, he felt relaxed in her company. They walked away hand in hand: "A tenderness springs up.

I am confident & in a kind way take advantage of my domination. So much that can appear complicated, her elusiveness, her secrecy, is easily understood when we meet."[9] Yet he was worried about her. "Ten years ago she was so beautiful. Those ten years have not been kind. The next ten years are not likely to be less cruel."[10]

Cecil was annoyed that Garbo would not spend New Year's Eve 1952–53 with him. She dined with Schlee, returned to her bed, and lay in solitude listening to the car horns until 4:00 A.M. At the beginning of that year Cecil set out for a prolonged lecture tour of the United States. Garbo came to bid him farewell. During their lunch, Cecil read out an article about her in *The New Statesman* in which she was simply described as "Incognita." She was delighted: "How sweet life can be if people behave like that to make it so."[11] Cecil found her "affectionate & vulnerable, deeply pathetic."[12]

During this visit, they met but intermittently, and Cecil became resigned to an unpleasant truth: "She showed me that Schlee was the most important consideration in her life, & that she herself was too indefinite a person to bank on."[13]

In March 1953 Cecil returned to Britain and was soon absorbed in photographing the Queen and all the Royal Family for the coronation. From Broadchalke, on March 14, 1953, Cecil wrote Garbo, "Just a note to keep in touch,"[14] passing on the local news of the adornment of the London streets, his luck at getting a seat in Westminster Abbey, and the various improvements to his garden. There seemed no chance of Garbo's coming to Europe in the near future. On Easter Monday, Cecil wrote to Mercedes:

> I'm sorry about Greta not coming over to Europe & hanging on the last minute orders of that little Jerk—but there isn't anything for her other friends to do if she feels her life is over & nothing is of any use. I must say I don't like the American slang expression "so what?" It seems to convey a rather smug acceptance of ignorance . . .[15]

In the summer, though, Garbo did make her way to Italy, where she joined her friends Rex Harrison and Lilli Palmer. Harrison had a villa (called San Genesio after the patron saint of actors), and here Garbo and Schlee came to visit while living aboard a yacht, moored uncomfortably in the farthest and dirtiest end of the harbor in order to escape press attention. The locals were used to celebrities and tended to rush forward for autographs, but with Garbo they stood to applaud. "She would hurry across the piazza," wrote Harrison, "trying to hide herself, and they would stand and clap, which I've never seen before nor since. . . . She loved to walk, undisturbed, up the tracks to the farms beyond our house, and sometimes I went with her. I loved talking to her. She had great moments of gaiety—in an evening she could be scintillating for hours on end and then she'd go back into a deep depression."[16]

Harrison took Garbo on board Daisy Fellowes's yacht to meet the Windsors. Conversation did not flow easily, and Harrison reported that whenever there was a sticky moment, the duchess's friend Jimmy Donahue would throw himself, fully clothed, into the harbor.

Lilli Palmer is a more informative source on this adventure, noting that Donahue was drunk and threw himself overboard only twice. She was particularly fascinated to observe the duchess and Garbo together: "Looking at them, I thought that life casts people in roles that a good scenario would never assign them. The woman for whom a man would be willing to give up his throne should obviously have been Greta Garbo, forever the world's most beautiful woman, unique and unattainable."[17] Lilli noted that when Garbo swam, "she would dive and reappear on the surface with drops of water clinging separately to eyelashes that looked as if they had been bought in a shop."[18]

Garbo once asked Lilli, "Why haven't I got a husband and children?" and Lilli replied, "Are you serious? A million men would have been happy to crawl on all fours to the marriage licence bureau." "No," replied Garbo. "I never met a man I could marry."[19] The Harrisons went on board the Schlee yacht, and Lilli was duly appalled at the way the press kept it under constant surveillance. She strayed into what she thought was Garbo's bathroom and found an array of colognes and perfumes, bath salts and oils beside the bath. This proved to be Schlee's bathroom. Garbo's was opposite, sporting only a toothbrush, a comb missing several teeth, and half a bar of Lux soap.

Lilli noted that when they went ashore with Garbo, she was physically afraid. There was a huge crush of photographers, causing the ever-pugnacious Harrison to punch "anyone within reach."[20] At their villa, protected from the hordes by a high fence, she was safer.

The press attention found its outlet in many headlines and articles. On August 16 *The New York Times* published a photograph of Garbo wearing a bandanna and dark glasses and stepping onto a motor launch at Portofino. The caption read "Fugitive Celebrity."[21] There was a mass of other publicity, not all of it kind. *Epoca* wrote, "She has a sad face, a bitter mouth, and her legs are skinny." *Tempo* began well but ended badly: "The face of the actress that has thrilled two generations has now lost all its freshness." *L'Europeo* observed, "She's still more or less slim, maybe a little large at the hips," conceding that this might have been an effect of her slacks.

Nor did Georges Schlee escape press scrutiny. *L'Europeo* christened him "the Blue Pirate" and deemed him "tall, straight, robust, and without a shadow of fat." The French papers thought him "old and ugly," adding that they had studied him on a swim with Garbo. "His body was flabby-fleshed, showing the wear of living with the 'cream' of New York society. When he finished bathing, a sailor had to help him up on the platform."[22]

From Italy, Garbo wrote to Cecil, saying she had no plans but would probably go to Paris soon. Cecil himself was in Portofino that summer, staying with Truman Capote, but not at the same time as Garbo. He went on to Venice and then home to London to begin an art course at the Slade.

Mercedes was back at 471 Park Avenue. She wrote to Cecil in October:

> Greta is back but I have not seen her. The night before she left for Europe in July she made a remark about you which I defended (too complicated to tell you about in a letter).* We got into a row and I told her one or two truths. She was angry and left without calling me the next morning or saying good-bye. So, now, on her

*This concerned references to Garbo in Cecil's 1937 *Scrapbook*. Mercedes was accused, not without reason, of having furnished Cecil with some of the details he used about Garbo.

return, she has not called me. She has taken a flat in the same building with George Schlee and will move into it soon. It is really so idiotic and unnatural that after years of friendship, one has to still go on handling her with absurd "kid gloves," or else suffer a falling out of some kind. Naturally I miss her and not seeing her makes me unhappy. Life is rushing by so quickly it is a pity to miss any moments with people one loves![23]

Cecil replied:

Dearest Mercedes,
Very pleased to hear from you though sad to think you have had a falling out with Greta especially as it was on my account. It is very sad when people who love one another should see less of each other than those on more casual terms, & I feel very sad for Greta who is far from happy, & making her life all the time much more difficult. I don't know why she should turn against either of us as we have always been honest & have wanted to do the right thing for her. I trust she will have got in touch with you, as I'm sure she needs you—& I've always thought that the two of you would end your days together. I wish I genuinely thought that Schlee was a good person for her, but apart from any feelings that might be personal, I don't consider he is able to give her any of the things she *needs,* & she sacrifices all to a comfortable "safety first" policy.[24]

Cecil did not go to America that Christmas, on account of his Slade course. This provoked a letter from Garbo asking where Cecil was, wishing him a happy Christmas, and inquiring as to his plans. She was in bed with a cold and regretting the beastly weather. She sent greetings to Juliet Duff, Simon Fleet, Clarissa, and Cecil's family, singling out Hal Burton for special mention.[25]

By January 1954, Cecil was at the Ambassador Hotel briefly. Then he repeated his lecture tour of the previous year. He began at the Beverly Hills Hotel. His thoughts turned to Garbo, and he felt nostalgic and sad:

Everything was as it was—but everything was missing—& Greta was the missing element.

Ever since I first came to this place twenty years ago she has been, in my mind, the one person to elevate it into a completely [*sic*] above all its vulgarity. Because she lived somewhere—three hills—even before I knew her, the suburban road, the gas stations & fruit stalls had a certain magic. They were part of the place that she dominated. When I was here with Anita Loos in the 20s she was [the] ghost that haunted me. . . . Later when I came here alone, she was the lure—& at last I met her—an extraordinary wonderful meeting that was not to be developed until an interval of the war & so many long years had passed.

Then as lovers we were here together for many very happy days. It was as if I were married to the goddess of the place & for weeks on end I saw nobody but her—spent all the days & nights with her—walking back to my . . . bungalow in a cloud of love at dawn. We had gone to the Farmers' Market, driven along N. Bedford Drive until we knew every palm tree—& I felt so Olympian that I had a certain pity for the other people who were going about their funny little lives.

And now I am here, she is far removed. She is ill, she is sad, infinitely pathetic with this small girlish voice sounding very plaintive on the other end of the wire in New York where it is cold, & she is in bed for many days & still suffering from a cold that had taken control of her for many months. It is as if a death had taken place. I talk to people who know her & admire her, but I am conscious that we are the older generation. A new crowd of would be stars with eager eyes & in willingness to sell all in order to succeed are filling the hotel lobbies. . . . The film industry still thrives, but this place is without interest as a community. The goddess has gone & I feel that my memories are so worthless for she will never come back. She can never come back. Hollywood wouldn't really want her now—she is ten years older—& that is the unforgivable. . . . The sun still shines, & the orange trees have blossoms on them, & the air is clear & wonderful, but somehow it is all pointless—& I shall not be sorry to leave.[26]

Hal Burton, ever faithful, sent Garbo another book. From Chicago, Cecil wrote to him:

Greta was delighted with yr. letter & the book—& sent nice messages. I expect you'll be receiving a tie from her when I

> return.* She seems aimless & doesn't have any interests—but very busy getting into an apartment. It is better for her than an hotel, but why live in NY? It is quite antipathetic to her.[27]

On his return to New York, after his tour, Cecil had the chance to inspect this apartment, four floors below that of the Schlees' at 450 East Fifty-second Street. He was pleased that she was putting down some roots after years in impersonal hotels, but all was not well, as he recorded in his diary:

> Alas the event is not cloaked in smiles. She is not thrilled to have her own rooms. She calls it "a bloody bore" (her language has deteriorated!). She is anxious, & overtired rather than content. She will trust no decorator to guide her—so had done the whole place on her own, & the result is a horrible mess. She has not learnt, what she knows instinctively so well in her acting, that the most effective results are achieved through boldness & simplicity & contrast. She says she likes "gaudy colours"—& instead of having a background in which they will appear even more brilliant, she has not chosen one piece of material in the drawing room that is negative in tone. The result is a dreadful hotchpotch of colours that clash & do not produce an effect of colour. The walls are of a piggy beige, the curtains have pink in them, the cushions are every colour of squashed strawberry, dirty crimson to dirty rose. Some chairs are upholstered in striped rose & buff, there is a horrible Savonnerie pink carpet on the floor—& even her wonderful paintings, the Renoirs, Bonnards, Rouaults, Soutines & Modiglianis do not come to her rescue. It is a hopeless muddle which results from her [not] being able to make a definite stand about anything. When she asked me my advice about her bedroom with its lavender walls, pink carpet, appalling Italian woodcarving on wall (put in by her—I said "How can we get rid of that?") it was difficult to know what to keep. I discovered that by dying the carpet very dark grenadine colour the walls came to life & she could successfully employ the dirty mauvy pink striped

*Cecil brought several ties over from Garbo, given to Hal with her love. These he sent to him on March 26.

material that she wanted for the curtains. But she never realises that one thing reacts on another & she never remains firm about anything for more than a couple of days. Later I heard her discuss the possibility of having a flowered Aubusson in her room. Everywhere are flower pots turned into lamps, pink, dirty pink, rose & red. The effect much the same as she created in Hollywood—as she has done in Schlee's apartment. But this is more heterogeneous & inhomogeneous than anything she has ever done. It is strange to think of this wonderful person living in such ordinary surroundings. It is likewise strange that this poor girl from a slum quarter of Stockholm—who was sent away for the holidays to the country as a charity child (where she first tasted chocolates) to be living—on her earnings—in such expensive surroundings.

She has in many respects come a long way—the apartment is one of the most expensive in New York, the pictures on the walls are by the most renowned Impressionist and modern painters, & the cigarette boxes, the lampshades are the most fashionable—as is the placing of the furniture in the manner of the moment. It is all quite wrong for it in no way expresses her life. She does not sit around on sofas with a cigarette table in use nearby. The apartment should express someone completely unconventional, with wonderful simplicity & an understanding of quality & restraint.

I made a few random criticisms—though it was hard to know where to start or to stop. "Please get rid of those cupids—the quality is not good enough. They don't come up to scratch." But the expression of sadness & pain was too hard to bear. I hated myself for being so brutal.

I do not think she is proud of her home. She is not pleased with any of it—& that is sad too. But saddest of all is the fact that she is leading here such a futile life of frustration—& that all this comes from her own character which seeks to destroy herself—& which in spite of her miraculous beauty, sensitivity & talent she has almost succeeded in doing successfully & completely in spite of the world still clambering for the effects of her genius.[28]

Cecil was less caustic in his next letter to Garbo, written on his return to Broadchalke:

Dearest G,
I wonder if you are enjoying a little more the amenities of your "luxury East River apartment." Whether the ice cream kitchen is still your favourite room, or if your affections have switched to the dining room—or maybe the guest room with its red carpet? I wonder if you have been bold about making alterations or whether you are dithering. I trust, now that spring is here, that you'll have time to look out across the River towards the Sunshine Biscuits & to think of me . . .[29]

Cecil returned to the theme of another visit from Garbo, this time more out of despair for her present existence than from his wish to capture her:

When will you come? I fear your life has taken on a pattern that can't be entirely satisfactory. I wish you'd make a sign of friendship to Mercedes & get her to fly over here with you, & let me have you deposited on some lovely green turf & clear air. We would pamper you in our rustic way.[30]

This needed to be discussed with Mercedes:

It's sad Greta wouldn't come over & get out of her rut—but I have no influence in the face of the Valentinas.

I'm really sad she hasn't come along to see you. It *will* happen sooner or later that she puts an end to this ridiculous situation but it's awful that she doesn't have the same feeling that others have that *time* is important. To her it hardly exists & it means that although she is never living for the minute, she doesn't realise how soon life passes by. In my last letter I certainly recommended that she should become friends with you again with the unaltruistic suggestion that she should come with you to Europe where I, selfishly, would like to share the pleasure of her companionship. Apropos the Crocker story, it makes me annoyed that he, who is such a good friend of Greta's, should have repeated the adventure to anybody. Greta told me that she had been out with him, that they had had a bottle of red wine on top of cocktails, & as a result—wasn't it awful!!—she'd gone to sleep at the play.

> It is something that happens to all of us—& I can't think what with the heat of the theatre & the boredom of the plays—how any audience remains upright. It is a ridiculous exaggeration to use the story as an indication that she is seriously drinking so whoever told *you* should be contradicted. G. occasionally takes a nip to keep warm or to brighten her spirits, but she's not dependent on it as a regular habit though God knows with that Schlee as intellectual mentor one might have recourse to *anything*!! I have of course torn up yr. letter* & wouldn't even dream of remembering yr. version of the story which in itself was harmless. To hell with the gossips—& Harry Crocker should know better![31]

Garbo wrote to Cecil to tell him, not for the first time, that it was lucky for him that she had not gone with him. She had been very down. At present she was still in New York, wondering daily if she should head off to California. She wondered what chance there was of seeing Cecil's face on the streets of Manhattan. She begged him not to think her too strange for having been so silent.[32]

To this Cecil replied:

> Honey,
> Was glad & sad to get your letter from N.Y. yesterday. Glad to have news of you & sad that you should be feeling a bit hopeless. I trust the mood has passed. I too have been having lots of soul searchings of late, & wondering what life is going to produce in the way of future surprises, & it's just about at this age** when one has to take stock.[33]

Cecil went to America that fall to design *The Chalk Garden* for Irene Selznick. Before he left, he reported to Mercedes that he had not heard from Garbo for six weeks. He soon discovered what had happened. Garbo had not made her annual trip to Europe with Schlee, largely because she could not make up her mind. Finally Schlee had set off on his own as he had business commitments. He left New York in a pique.

*Unfortunately, he really had.

**Cecil was now fifty.

Garbo went to California in order to escape the heat of New York and consigned herself into the care of Harry Crocker. After a week she could not abide him a day longer and departed for New Mexico. But at the beginning of August she was in Los Angeles, where she was questioned by a reporter from *Time* magazine. "Are you in love—Are you going to be married?" he asked. "Please," she replied with distaste. "I do not want to talk about that. I'm so tired—so very tired."[34]

In New Mexico she joined her family—her mother and her brother, who suffered from a weak heart. After two days there was evidently nothing left to say on either side. Garbo became ill and returned to New York to see her doctor. She had planned a six-week break but somehow succeeded in remaining away from her apartment for four months.

Garbo was back in New York in mid-November, as Cecil reported to Mercedes:

> Greta returned 3 weeks ago from New Mexico where I suppose she stayed with her brother but as you know she never gives out any information one has to surmise. She has been ill for 4 months—has got very thin—but I don't know what's wrong & I don't really think there's anything physically wrong. But she sighs & is incapable of snapping out of a mood of lethargy—except when she comes out & then she enjoys life. The usual nonsense of hanging about on Schlee's word—so no plans are made in advance & she sees very few people. It is a sad story—but still she looks well & beautiful in the face, is as appealing and childlike as ever. But from ordinary standards she wastes rather a lot of ephemeral time.[35]

One Sunday in December, Garbo came to lunch with Cecil in his apartment. She wore her hair in Directoire rat's tails, with a few fronds for a fringe. Cecil was delighted by her beauty. He recorded this meeting and a subsequent meeting in his diary. A blazing row was about to ensue between them, which was an important turning point in their relationship:

> I was enchanted to be looking at such beauty. I felt very near to her although she never gave me any personal information—as

usual I never asked her many questions—nevertheless, as always, it is possible to pick up all that one wishes to know by instinct & by the clues that she sets. We were very happy together. I was somewhat appalled by the thinness of her body. She seemed half the size of the person I had known ten (?) years ago. She complained that she was far from well—that nothing could be done about it. She sighed "C'est la vie." I thought, that considering the intimacy of our relationship she left somewhat abruptly—I was almost hurt that she seemed determined to visit—of all people—the Gunthers whom she pretends to be bored by. But the times when I am deeply hurt by her offhand or elusive behaviour, are happily over. I no longer have the capacity to suffer the pangs of an insensate lover.

Every day, or every other day, telephone calls—I keep the tone light. I feel that is my role with her. I do not sympathise too deeply with her sighs—"How are you?"—"Won't tell you. It's not a very agreeable subject"—deep sighs—"C'est la vie!" Plans to go shopping or meet for a meal are put off from day to day. Can't be helped. I am busy & G. says always "If you get anything better don't hesitate to put me off at the last moment." She means it & is generous. I make a double date, with a certain feeling of guilt—but her date always falls through. . . .

Instead of asking her to come & have a drink with me today I suggested going to her—She was a little surprised but said "What shall we have, Martinis?"

I arrived late—the doorman had been warned that a visitor was expected. G. said he must have died of the surprise. The flat looked much more homogeneous & complete than when I last saw it. It was less garish & I was impressed by the huge shelves of beautiful bound books, the pictures in the sitting room are of a good quality—Renoir, Soutine, Bonnard—& there were lots of pink roses and carnations in the vases. Greta in grey, jersey, a short jacket and grey tweedy trousers with straps round the calf—red bedroom slippers. In the pink brothel lights of the hideous lamp shades her face looked somewhat colourless. We sat on a sofa drinking vodka martinis, & eating slithers of a gruyere cheese that she had provided. We talked of Christmas & she said somewhat surprisingly that she thought I would be here for the holidays—

that I couldn't go home as intended & that possibly we might celebrate it together. She was determined not to go upstairs to the Schlees: "Last year it was torment, nothing will make me do it again. In any case it's so different from what it used to be at home when I was a child. In our country we celebrate Christmas Eve—not Christmas Day."

I talked about the importance of family ties, how the bond of relationship held one to reality—she agreed but added how short a time it was before we had little to say to the family—that joy of reunion lasts perhaps two days: "How sad it is! This time I'm going to take home the papers on which I have written down all my New York engagements . . . & yet how uninterested they will be in these unknown people. Oh how sad it is. But no," Greta said. "It's not sad for them—They don't feel the lack, the gulf—they don't mind the silences. It is only we creative people that know it could be so much more intimate." "But," I said, "it can exist—take the Stacey family—Stacey the gardener who lives in the cottage next to Clarissa—one night Clarissa arrived from London unexpectedly at midnight—& went timidly to wake them up for the key. She, Mr. & Mrs. Stacey & the daughter happily & enthusiastically arguing about the manner in which spiders make the initial move from one side of a lane to another. After this they can crawl along the thread of web they have created—but do they make the initial journey flying in the air." Greta said "But you see Stacey has been working all day in the garden, Mrs. S. has been working alone & her daughter too—then they get together & talk for the first time in the day & it's not to be wondered at that they have so much to say to each other." I was somewhat surprised at G's imagination—at knowing what the lives of these remote people would be—but nevertheless I said "Yet how sad when it isn't like that—My Father never knew what to say to my Mother or to us—We would have dreadful silent dinners & he would always be taking out his gold watch & chain to see if time had progressed a little quicker than he knew it had."

"I'm always looking at my watch too," said Greta & she was torn between cutting short our meeting (for Schlee was intermittently telephoning from above) & continuing our gossips. We had more martinis & talked about film making—Her agent Minna

Wallis (whom I met in London) had wired her to play some unsuitable role—Greta said "How could I face those cameras after a sleepless night—& I'd never sleep through worrying & films are a messy form of work—you're dependent on so many things—you have to perform in front of people, electricians & lights."

I fear I do not give an adequate picture of the clarity & precision of G's mind. When she philosophises she is on sure ground—her instincts are very strong & she speaks with a conviction that she lacks in everyday life. She manages, in a way that I am incapable of conveying, to couch her phrases with a complete modesty. Her criticisms are veiled—(I said I had spent an evening with Irene Selznick & had become completely exhausted because she talked so much—that she was a most intelligent person but that my voice had left me through sheer fatigue by three o'clock in the morning. G. said "How can a person be intelligent if they do not notice what others are feeling—if you don't notice they are exhausted").

She has the feminine charm of obliqueness. I was impressed by her in this vein—It is when I like her the best. It takes a long time to get her in this mood—& I thought we were very much in harmony.

However, out of the blue, or so it seems to me—for I cannot remember the context—she said that I would not be able to understand her point of view on a certain subject because I was a flippant person. Flippant? The fat was in the fire! I suddenly felt myself roused to fury.

"May I ask in what way? For what reason you consider me flippant." She then cited the Book of Satirical Memoirs I had written, *My Royal Past*—"That was flippant & only a flippant person would write about me as you did—without knowing me—in that Scrapbook (published in fact in 1935*) that someone gave me."

My eyes blazed. This was the book that had come between us after she had left my house in England almost on the verge of marriage. When I had arrived later in N.Y. she treated me as a

*In fact, in 1937.

stranger. When we met a few weeks later for lunch she had challenged me for writing about her in this way ("She does not possess the gift of friendship"). We had had a row. I felt it unfair that she should bring up something written in the early thirties before we had become lovers.

Later she had reviled Mercedes & they had not been on speaking terms for many months—accusing her of having told me all these intimate facts about her.* Again the twenty year old book was brought up. I was now furious beyond imagination.

"May I talk to you for 4 minutes without you interrupting me—May I tell you that I think it outrageous of you to judge me today, a man of 50 by something I wrote when I was half that age." She interrupted "A person is always the same—only a flippant person would write that I smell like a baby." I pointed out, though not as clearly as I would have wished, for my fury somewhat clouded the clarity of my brain, that Greta had once admitted to me the intimacy of the film medium, when she had seen some little negro boys dancing among themselves, that an unforgettable moment was caught for ever. When she was in pictures she fired the imagination of artists & creative people that's why she was the success she was & that it was only natural that I should surmise a good deal about her from the intimacy of the screen & from her legend. She was in the public domain as a muse. I felt I knew her. My writing about her was a natural thing to do. It was no breach of intimacy—I didn't know her but for a short meeting, & was under no moral obligations to her. I had not in fact broken any code of intimacy by saying that she smelt like a baby—that it was my imagination that prompted me to thus surmise.

I lashed out at her pettiness in quoting something so long forgotten. "Have you no feeling for the way I have protected you from the world since I've known you? Have you no feeling of loyalty, gratitude or fondness for my devotion—Have I ever let you down by ever saying anything indiscreet? disloyal—Have I ever exploited you like your intimate friends?"

She defended her friends—she knew their faults, their weak-

*Garbo had struck the truth here.

nesses. We shouted at one another. I felt completely sure of my self righteousness. I yelled "The sooner you forget old grievances the better." It did not matter if she was going through change of life ("Many women go mad," she said).

I was far too riled to pull my punches. I got up & put on my coat. She said we had both drunk too many cocktails—in vino veritas—she'd still got this chip on her shoulder. Why didn't she read what I had written lately. If she wasn't so damned lazy she could read my latest book* that I'd given her—she could read this & see if I was the same person that she used to call a "cut-up." Would I have succeeded in the way I had all these years if I had been flippant. My work would not have gone on being appreciated if I was a flippant person.

"You have many talents but you are a flippant person." "I have no talents. I merely have character—& it's the seriousness & determination of my character that has made me continue—not my flippancy. Yes, I used to be glib & facile. I was a late developer & fighting to assert myself in life & I was a very wild erratic person when young."

Admittedly I was flippant at 25—but in my behavior to her I had been everything but flippant. In fact no flippant person would have been so deeply emotionally hurt as I had been when after a long silence—after some misunderstanding—after a year or more of suffering the torture of unrequited love, she had come to see me & without any word had gone to the bedroom, pulled the curtain cords—had turned down the bed. I had fulfilled what was expected of me—but my feelings had not been those of a flippant person. I had been deeply shocked—deeply wounded. I think this was a blow that struck home. None of my other ripostes had convinced her of anything but of her certainty that she was right & I was wrong.

Now she tried to kiss me. I turned my face away. "No I don't want to kiss you." A moment later she said something about "Don't you want to come and live in this apartment when we're married?" No, I didn't want to live in this apartment—& I looked with horror at the pink lamp shades, the evidence of Schlee taste.

* *The Glass of Fashion,* published in 1954.

I was now in charge of the situation. I was angry—disenchanted—wanting to leave. I called for the elevator & the old man who answered my summons caught Greta in the act of hanging on to my coat collar. I was pleased to go—but too strung up to be able to relax.

I came back to my hotel rooms & walked about like a caged lion fuming with fury. I was full of righteous indignation. I was so convinced I was in the right—that her attack on me was quite indefensible. I thought of all the things I should have said to her but nevertheless I hadn't done too badly. Greta is impossible to worst in any argument. Some time ago I would have been deeply sad that such a scene had taken place, but I felt tonight that it had had a salutary affect on both of us—& certainly I do not feel any bitterness—only anger & sadness that I am not capable of bringing out the best in her.[36]

In January 1955, Cecil was back in London, from which he sent her a stiff letter:

Dearest G
Was sorry we didn't have an opportunity to talk again before I left. I expect you were extremely busy & I had rather a lot to do. I was sorry because I think, maybe, we both drank too many vodka martinis when last we met, and parted from one another's company without certain explanations. While at the same time perhaps we both said a few things that had been better left unsaid. However "in Vino Veritas" & I think I should explain that my high state of emotion was caused less from anger than from the decisive acceptance of failure that I felt for myself; a failure, that, after all these years, I am incapable of bringing out in you your qualities of trust, intimacy & unselfishness.

I'm afraid I had always only half admitted this to myself, but had gone on hoping that one day you might be somewhat touched by my continued loyalty.

Alas! by harping back to the fact that I, among a thousand other writers, saw fit to print something about you over 20 years ago & that this somehow has more importance to you than anything I have done or felt for you in the years since we got to know one another. It was a cruel revelation.

> I realise, of course, that you were not, at this time, feeling your best—& again I believe I have made allowances on that score for you on account of your ill health as on so many other scores, I hope I shall hear that you are soon feeling so much better that you are able to take up some interest, possibly like Madame de Becker & working in a hospital or doing any little job for other people that will also have the benefit of taking you "out of yourself." If this sounds impertinent it is because I feel that only those who haven't your future interest at heart could encourage you to continue to lead the listless & ingrained sort of life you do in New York. Only your real friends are willing to risk causing you displeasure by trying to adopt a more charitable attitude towards life.
>
> In spite of realising how little you think of me I cannot but still consider myself to be one of that number . . .[37]

This was not the sort of letter to which Garbo would have considered replying.

Some of Cecil's bitterness poured out in his next letter to Mercedes, written to her at the time of Ona Munson's suicide:

> I'm also terribly sad about Greta not seeing you. I'm afraid she has very little gratitude in her disposition, takes everything as her due—& gives mighty little to others. I'm afraid nothing will alter her, it's no good scolding. The only thing is to protect oneself against useless suffering. Life must go on, & there is much to interest & stimulate one each day. One cannot regret, too much, the past. I'm afraid Greta isn't going to have a happy old age—but then who is? It's difficult. I quite agree that unless one does kindnesses to others that one becomes paid out for one's selfishness.[38]

Meanwhile, in February, Truman Capote spotted Garbo at a cocktail party and told Cecil that she looked "extremely well—though her hair seemed a peculiar color: sort of blondish lavender. I think she must have dyed it."[39] And in May, Noël Coward saw her at Valentina's Russian Easter party and found her "in unusually merry mood."[40]

Garbo with Aristotle Onassis in Monte Carlo in the summer of 1956.

CHAPTER 12

"SHE LEAVES—SHE DOESN'T LEAVE."

Garbo turned fifty in September 1955. John Bainbridge's biography of her had been published a few months earlier, in March. It was not a work of genius, but it remained the only mildly serious work on her life for nearly forty years. Bainbridge pointed out that Garbo's Hollywood career had been by no means conventional. She had refused to allow herself to be molded into a standardized Hollywood product. Nor would she tolerate the second-rate. He was the first to give a plausible account of her love for John Gilbert, her strange European tour with Leopold Stokowski, and her later attachments to Gayelord Hauser, Eric Goldschmidt-Rothschild, and Schlee. In *The New York Times,* the critic Gilbert Millstein assessed Garbo's character as portrayed by Bainbridge:

> She has always been what she is today, a woman with a child's tragic innocence. She is shrewd, selfish, willful, instinctive, completely self-absorbed. From her intimates she demands total attention and devotion; otherwise she sulks. She is secretive ("Garbo would make a secret of whether she had an egg for breakfast," a friend* said), and she has a child-like indifference to all desires but her own.[1]

Mercedes reported to Cecil that Schlee had bought a villa at Cap d'Ail in the south of France near Monte Carlo and that Eric Goldschmidt-Rothschild was now Garbo's most faithful companion. Cecil replied:

> I was very *bored* by the book on Greta, but no doubt it is a best seller. I think Rothschild is a good companion for her. He has infinite leisure—in fact nothing to do—is quite a delightful person with knowledge of objects d'arts & cultivated tastes. She might learn from him & if she applies herself, become a connoisseur of porcelain. It's monstrous of her not to go & see you. I fear she takes friendship for granted. I suppose having such a success wherever she goes makes her feel that it is her due to have people to do her bidding. I trust it may always be her lot to find people who are willing to do what she wants without anything from her in return. I think Schlee will find a 1900 villa built for the winter sun** will be a flop in summer. I'd like to see the decorations he whips up—with signed pieces of auction room furniture & brothel lamps. What a giddy lot they are![2]

Garbo did not read the Bainbridge biography. Sailing to Europe with Schlee in the summer of 1955, she tossed it overboard. "She never even opened it,"[3] said Schlee.

There was little contact between Cecil and Garbo at this time. His career changed direction again. In February 1955 he lost his contract

*Jane Gunther.

**Georges Schlee and Garbo would now spend part of each summer at Villa Le Roc, while Valentina spent her summers in Venice, as she had done for many years.

with *Vogue* once more. He undertook a lot of photographic assignments, gathering material for his book *Face of the World.* Much of the year was taken up helping Enid Bagnold with her play *The Chalk Garden.* This proved deeply frustrating, particularly since Irene Selznick, the play's producer, finally altered the sets without informing him. Cecil was not employed on the London production of *The Chalk Garden,* as a result of which he would not speak to Enid Bagnold or its London producer, John Gielgud, for many years. Later in 1955, Cecil began work on the costumes for *My Fair Lady,* his greatest stage triumph and perhaps the high point of his career.

In July, Garbo and Schlee were spotted boarding Aristotle Onassis's yacht, the *Christina,* bound for Capri. Mercedes, still out of favor with Garbo, sent Cecil one of the press photographs. He replied:

> Thanks for the photograph of Greta. The papers have been full of her & this week's *Paris Match* has a spread in which Schlee has been promoted to banker & a director of De Soto Motors. There is one picture of Greta which breaks my heart & is too dreadful to send to you. I'm sorry she didn't call you. It's difficult to understand her at times . . .[4]

Mercedes was now beginning a phase of being unwell and relying heavily on doctors. This was a situation that would deteriorate steadily over the years that followed, involving her in the ministrations of dubious doctors, in whom she placed her ever-childlike trust. The Indian dancer Ram Gopal, a longtime Garbo fan and Mercedes's friend since the thirties, commiserated with her:

> I hope [Garbo] has come to see you since we've last met here and since her return to New York. Is she annoyed with you that she does not come to see you, when MOST you need her, or what? It mystifies, puzzles me. So sensitive (on the screen) a woman surely cannot just neglect YOU of all people when you're ill and need visits from those you love—and she's No. 1 Goddess in your life. She surely has seen you by this time. How restless she must be, and how lonely, and how utterly *cut off* from her mediumistic

> screen work where Higher Forces than she knows possessed her—ONCE. And now to CUT OFF while still so young and beautiful and able, this must cause her to erupt within herself.[5]

A few weeks later, Ram returned to the theme, this time giving his views on Poppy Kirk, who was now no longer Mercedes's girlfriend. Ram wrote:

> There will NOT be any need to be careful of what I say about Maria. . . . I shall, if I say anything, talk about how good she's been to you as you alone know. In the past, I was only upset and annoyed and disliked her ONLY from the first hand news of her bad treatment she meted out to YOU, which I got from YOU. . . . so naturally I disliked her, and I knew instinctively she disliked me and didn't like me—then . . .[6]

There was little more news of Garbo that year. But shortly after *The Chalk Garden* opened in New York, Noël Coward attended a small cocktail party given by Valentina at 450 East Fifty-second Street. Garbo looked in for a while, appearing, to the "Master," "lovely but grubby."[7] Cecil was still in New York, but his bitterness had by no means worn off. He wrote to Hal Burton, "I've seen Greta at intervals only because I've been so busy & too busy to put up with her continued nonsense of saying no to everything including Life . . ."[8]

In March 1956, *My Fair Lady* opened in New York to a blaze of critical glory, and Cecil was also busy photographing Marilyn Monroe and Joan Crawford, as well as undertaking a considerable amount of fashion photography for *Harper's Bazaar.* But when he returned to London, he heard news that caused him lasting sorrow, as he reported to Garbo:

> But now I must tell you of something that has made me feel so upset, so abysmally sad that I have been crying like a hysterical child most of the day & night. My lifelong friend Peter—died yesterday.* He had been ill this winter with anaemia & low blood

*Peter Watson died suddenly on May 3. There was much speculation as to whether his death was from natural causes or whether he might have been mur-

pressure—so went to Gottfried.* After a few treatments he improved enormously, became a better colour & was in good spirits when we had lunch together on my return. Unfortunately he caught a bad cold a week ago—went to the country for some fresh air to get rid of it—motored home & very tired late at night took a bath. The water went on running—& when the Police broke open the door Peter was dead—his nose & mouth under water. We don't know yet whether he fainted & was drowned—or slipped—but Gottfried says his heart was in good condition.

Anyhow it is a terrible accident to have happen to anyone but that it should have been Peter who is no longer with us, is very hard to bear. He had been through so many vicissitudes & at last had come through as such a fulfilled & integrated person, on terms with everyone—& his own terms. He had developed enormously as a person & had become a sort of queer saint. For me no man has ever had equal charm & for 25 years I have been equally overcome each time I've been with him. That he is irrevocably out of my life makes me feel terribly terribly forlorn. Everywhere I go in this house I see things that remind me of him & of times we have spent together all over the world. No-one has really made quite such an impression on me. I can't bear to think there's no further link. I don't even have the consolation that other bereaved people have that there is an afterlife. The void is utter.

Of course I shall continue tomorrow morning with my active life . . .[9]

Garbo replied to Cecil without referring to Peter Watson. She began at once, as so often, with her own problems. She had been out of order, was cramming "poison" down her throat, and thus would not be traveling. She wished she could have come to England and wondered if he might come to the States in August. She hinted she might be in Paris that October; as usual, however, nothing was settled. Meanwhile she

---

dered by his sinister friend Norman Fowler. He almost certainly died of a heart attack in too hot a bath.

*Cecil's doctor.

might accompany Schlee to the south of France. These were her uncertain plans. What a mess she had made of her life, she concluded.[10]

Cecil wrote back at once:

> Dearest Mrs. Rokeby,
> Very sad to think you're not well enough to come over here. Don't take too much poison. It can't be good for you in such long doses. I'm sure fresh summer zephyrs & long walks on green grass would do you much more good. Anyhow I'll let you know my plans which seem to change all the time. . . .[11]

Later in the summer, Garbo was once more in touch about her plans, proposing vaguely that they meet in Paris after her trip to the south of France and then go to England and back to the United States together.

Ram Gopal kept an eagle eye on Garbo's moves, reporting to Mercedes:

> I see from the papers that the Divine One, your Greta, is in the South of France hobnobbing with Onassus [*sic*]. She has bought a sprawling villa on the sea not far from Somerset Maugham's place. London has had a Garbo revival month of her best pictures. My God, there will never be her like on the Screen again. She was and is Divinity.[12]

Garbo traveled with Schlee to Villa Le Roc at Cap d'Ail. At the end of August the paparazzi caught her attending a party at the Sporting Club of Monte Carlo, seated next to Aristotle Onassis, a key figure in her south of France life during the mid-fifties. Cecil was also in Europe. He went to Capri, then to Venice, dashed to New York on September 9, then returned to London. He had received a letter heralding a visit from Garbo. As ever on such occasions, it provided specific information. Garbo would be at the Crillon on September 20, by which time Schlee would be heading back to the States. The Gunthers would be in attendance and would accompany her to London. Maybe Cecile de Rothschild would come too.* Being without a coat, joked Garbo, she might have

*Cecile de Rothschild (b. 1913). Like other members of the Rothschild family, she became a friend of Garbo's through Eric Goldschmidt-Rothschild.

to make a copy of Cecil's. All this might happen sooner than he realized.[13]

From New York, Cecil wired Garbo in Paris and was told that she had a cold and he must come later. He telephoned her and she sounded "very groggy." After more unhelpful exchanges, Cecil arrived in Paris and found her at the Crillon, sitting in her small sitting room with Cecile de Rothschild, Garbo looking "pretty battered," adorned with a frown plaster, her hair untidy, her face wrinkled, and the room full of half-dead flowers and fruit.

After Cecile left, Cecil and Garbo sat talking. He learned nothing of her summer holiday, only that she had been ill and coughing. Later Cecile, Garbo, and Cecil went to the theatre to see Julien Green's *L'Ombre*—which bored them and which they left after the second act—then they dined at Cecile's apartment. The next day, Garbo told Cecil that his arrival had cheered her up and she was feeling better. They set off on a round of exhibitions, lunched at the Mediterranée, and spent a long afternoon antiquing. Cecil noted wryly, "For an invalid she has the most tireless energy."[14] Wherever Garbo went she created a trail of interest in her wake:

> In the Rue Bonaparte a Greek student came up to her after dogging her for half an hour to declare his passion & ask her to sign a cross—a line—anything in his notebook—& I have never seen anyone quake with emotion as he did—his voice came out in quivers. I must say that I have known Greta for 25 years now, & although time has touched her in many of its usual unkind ways the magic is still there—the incredible mystery of beauty, the alive sparkle—the laugh—the sensitivity—the receptivity, the utter fragrance of beauty— There is something innately theatrical about her effects but they are just the natural ones of life—the natural streak of drama cannot but come out in her, so that whenever she comes into a room it can be remarkable.[15]

At the end of Cecil's Paris day, Garbo was put out that no taxi came and began to complain, threatening that she would be too tired to travel to England the next day. As the hapless Cecil continued to try to hail a taxi, Garbo commented; "You see I'm too tired for this any more—that's why it's so necessary to have Mademoiselle Cecile—she always has her car & chauffeur."[16]

Cecil was left to worry about the next day's trip, and his worst fears were almost realized. Garbo was tired and irritable, she announced that she had to wash her hair, she struggled with the packing. Getting her out of the hotel was an elaborate nightmare, and a crowd of onlookers gathered on the pavement as he waited endlessly for his suitcases. They headed for the airport and, rather than risk photographers, went for an autumnal stroll in some nearby tulip and gladiolus fields. The sun and fresh air worked wonders on Garbo, and she seemed to Cecil as "young and lithe" as when he first knew her. At the airport all was well:

> She was not spotted by strangers even—& there was no photographer. My feelings throughout the journey were mixed—hopeful that all would go well & smoothly for her—& that she would not be made unhappy & yet enjoying secretly the excitement of the press onslaught—I felt very clever at arranging the whole thing so discreetly. At this hour of the Saturday evening there were few Press people about—we ducked out of sight when there were spectators. The whole experience of smuggling Garbo into London without being noticed was just as exciting as a mystery play. I arrived at my house with her for a cup of tea without a word to say. I looked at myself in the glass & my deep set eyes told of my exhaustion.
>
> She is like a man in many ways. She telephoned to say "I thought we might try a little experiment this evening at 6:30." But she spoke in French & it was difficult to understand at first what she meant—but soon I discovered although I pretended not to—she was embarrassed—& a certain prudence on my part made me resent her frankness & straight forwardness—something I should have respected.[17]

The story had not changed. Even after so many years, Cecil was still dancing attendance on Garbo, while she treated him partly as an escort, to be criticized if the tiniest detail of their plans was at fault, and partly as the lover he had once been.

The press may have been absent at the airport, but they were soon on Garbo's trail. She was sighted at 10 Downing Street on October 17, her presence at Claridge's was recorded on October 18. She went to the ballet of *Romeo and Juliet* and dined at Cecil's London house. According to the *News Chronicle*, the ballerina Ulanova* went to be photographed at Cecil's house and there unexpectedly met her heroine, Garbo. That evening there were two rival dinner parties, Oliver Messel entertaining Ulanova on one side of Pelham Street and Cecil entertaining Garbo, Cecile de Rothschild, and Hal Burton on the other side.

Cecil reported the visit in detail to Mercedes in a letter which he urged her to tear up but which she faithfully kept:

> I've been busy keeping horrid newspaper stories about Greta out of her ken. Not that she's interested in newspapers. Newspapers criticise her for not being co-operative—& pretend that she's not news any more. But she will always be a remarkable fascinating person who will have people in trances of exstasy any time she wishes to beguile them. This weekend she has been like a child—very happy & funny, full of tricks & wit. Of course she is a genius at making things difficult for herself & everyone around her but the difficulties this weekend have been of the most superficial character & more in the nature of a tease.
>
> She has gone off to Oxford today in the company of Cecile de Rothschild whom I think is a very good companion for her—a person of complete integrity & lack of vulgarity—a person who has quality & knows values. Certainly an improvement on all that cheap Russian baby talk & 2nd Avenue junkshop level—and she has nothing to do but make things easier for Greta—who needs more & more someone to protect her.
>
> What an enchanting person she is. Really the great enchantress of our time & it's wonderful to have known her—but again how sad it is that her very nature makes it impossible for her to lead an easy life like less remarkable human beings. I don't know at all, how long she plans to stay here—or if she intends to go back to France . . .[18]

*Galina Ulanova (b. 1910), Russian *prima ballerina assoluta.* This was the Bolshoi's first tour of the West.

In his diary, Cecil described Garbo's every word and move. He found her as indecisive as ever, wishing to stay in alone, urging Cecil to see his own friends and forget about her, musing on the deliciousness of the food and then complaining that Cecil made her eat too much. One day she looked sadly in the mirror and was displeased with the sight that greeted her:

> "Poor little Garbo—I look so awful. These wrinkles (wrrinckels) are worse than they've ever been—& the neck sags—too late—too late—It's lucky I'm out of the business—Can you imagine the horror of having to face the cameras looking like that? It was so awful when Barrymore he had to have his chins strapped up & he could be photographed only from one side—But it's so cruel that we have to go on getting worse each year. It's so dreadful for a woman—a man doesn't matter—women like a man to be a bit battered. It makes him rugged—& virile—But I look so awful—That's why I don't want the photographers to see me. And there's nothing to be done—can't put on powder, that would only show up these wrrinckells worse—they're so sad these lines—& they come from being so tense."[19]

Like Gayelord Hauser before him, Cecil resented the boredom of life with Garbo; moreover, she wouldn't let him draw or photograph her. And she was not a sympathetic companion. She would take an intense interest in the fate of strangers, a man having his suitcase opened at customs, yet make no inquiries about Cecil's well-being. When they drove in the car together, she first complained that it was too hot and airless, then minutes later that she was about to catch a cold. Then she found the contradiction amusing. Every autumn she caught a cold; every winter further exhausted her and undermined her health. But she liked her drink, telling Cecil: "I'd just love to have a schlug of whisky—I just think of the time when I can indulge in my first drink. It's bad for me I know—but I *love* it—it makes you feel so goody."[20]

Cecil liked to record her curious use of English:

> She is modest in her phraseology: "Excuse me but may I remind you that I'm not deaf"—"Cleverer people than me would know." *But* she has great sense of her own importance. She puts

herself high among the Goddesses. She is critical of other people's manners & crudeness—although of humble origin: "One does not do that." She smiles widely: "I couldn't bring myself to do that. Once that is gone nothing remains."[21]

On this visit, Cecil took Garbo to visit Sir Anthony and Lady Eden at 10 Downing Street. Garbo had remained interested in Clarissa's life since she met her at Broadchalke in the autumn of 1951, and when Cecil phoned to suggest a call, the idea was greeted with enthusiasm. Clarissa said, "I hate not to be more hospitable, but come for a drink on Wednesday." She called back to ask if Garbo would prefer to come in by the garden entrance. On their way to No. 10, Cecil showed Garbo the guards at Buckingham Palace, in those days in sentry boxes outside the gates. Garbo was fascinated by them and imitated their walk with childlike elation.

Garbo was excited and nervous at the prospect of seeing Clarissa in her new role as wife of the prime minister. They entered, unobserved, by the front door, walked along the corridors adorned with images of former prime ministers, saw secretaries tidying up papers in the Cabinet Room and the reception rooms filled with flowers by Constance Spry for the dinner for the president of Costa Rica that night. Cecil reported in full:

> Clarissa very thin—in tweed with untidy hair—full of vitality—Greta appeared—Kisses—"Well well well. Fancy being at No. 10." Greta was éblouiée. "How strange life is—well hay ho." Clarissa hiccupped with laughter. "But it's charming (by the drink table) & a bucket of ice on the floor. Why a bucket on the floor it's like home!" We sat drinking vodka & ice. Clarissa beguiled & delighted by Greta's fantasy & imagination—For Greta was suddenly making merry of her many complaints. She elaborated upon the noises at Claridge's during the night: "Have you ever listened to garbage grinding? They grind garbage all night." Clarissa being a light sleeper was sympathetic & talked about ear pads: "Anthony is suffering from insomnia & he is kept awake here by the Vespas*—one Vespa & his night's rest is ruined. . . ."
>
> Greta saw Anthony coming towards her at the end of a long emplade—"Oh Heavens!" she cried. Clarissa murmured "He

*Small motorcycles.

> can't keep away." The Prime Minister looking utterly boyish & young, gangled in like a colt—eyelashes flickering, eyes flashing, teeth discreetly hidden: "This is a wonderful moment. I've always wanted to meet you. I've admired you ever since I first saw you in a silent movie of *Anna Karenina*—I think it was called *Love.*" Greta with cigarette holder between her teeth smiled broadly, nervously. "Does that take you back into another world? Does it make you think how strange it was that you should have been that person?" Greta grinned silently. "You do remember it don't you? Did you enjoy being a great movie star?" Greta said "I'm afraid I don't think about those days of moving pictures any more—they don't mean anything to me any more & I don't generally talk about it." "Then I'm afraid I haven't been very diplomatic in talking on that subject." The P.M. went on to talk about Sweden which is another topic that Greta doesn't enjoy talking about. However, the little gathering was a great success. Anthony lying back with legs stretched out told the people who needed him that they must wait. . . .[22]

Garbo was shown around the prime minister's residence and later introduced to some cabinet ministers, including Lord Kilmuir, the lord chancellor, and Harold Macmillan, the chancellor of the exchequer. Unfortunately, on their way out, a photographer snapped them, and Garbo became upset. The press in London was very persistent, constantly hounding Garbo and making her life difficult. The night she was rumored to be dining with Ulanova, a crowd of photographers gathered in the street, and Garbo's companions speculated about her escaping by climbing over the garden wall at the back of the house. Hal Burton called a taxi in the hope that the reporters would give up, but no ruses worked. Finally Garbo and Cecile de Rothschild rushed out. Cecil wrote:

> The effect was like a storm of atomic explosions. About twenty flashes went off again and again. It seems strange, now, that I should have been so upset. But my stomach was completely upside down—I was unable to sleep—Greta was very firm—& if not suspicious that I had in some way been directly responsible for such a scene said "The boys do too much talking—maybe it's

> normal—they do talk—I don't. Probably I'm not normal, but I shouldn't probably see so much of Mr. Beaton for a few days." This horrified me—& I wondered whether or not the visit to the country would be ruined by the presence of a loitering photographer. I rang her & said that I couldn't guarantee that there wouldn't be inquisitive press around, and if she didn't feel like taking the risk I would understand though be very unhappy. She was willing to take the risk & I was relieved beyond belief to find that whenever I looked out of the window fearing to see a flash bulb reflector I only saw a bundled up old yokel trundling off to get a can of milk.[23]

The weekend in the country was idyllic, Garbo in black slacks and sweater with a pink scarf, in good health and good spirits. She imitated everyone and made ribald jokes as they watched the Bolshoi Ballet on television: "Much of the time the jokes were of a sexual nature & directed against me," wrote Cecil. "But they were innocuous and done with great charm."[24] They explored the countryside, Ashcombe, and Salisbury Cathedral.

Cecile de Rothschild was with them, and Cecil examined his feelings about Garbo's new companion: "The three of us got along well together—though I find Cecile—like myself, like everyone, wants to purloin Greta & make her give up her independence to them."[25]

They dined with Juliet Duff, who announced, "It doesn't seem possible that four years has passed since Miss Garbo was last here!" Nevertheless, Garbo restricted her socializing and turned down an invitation from the Edens to visit Chequers. One day Garbo and Cecile went to visit Victor Rothschild at Cambridge. That evening Garbo had a headache but was talkative. Cecil, on the other hand, had a gnawing worry to face. At the beginning of the evening Garbo had planted the idea that she might "rush away." Later that night she confirmed her plan:

> She would go back to Paris with Cecile & then on to America. She didn't feel well—she was "topsy turvey"—she didn't feel able to cope with anything but a quiet life—of going to bed at 7

o'clock—I was terribly dejected. I had hoped she would come & stay in the country for quite a long time—that perhaps, even, we might get married. I told her that she had recently blamed me for not taking her by the scruff of her neck & marrying her—How could I now prevent her from making another mistake? "Oh I always make mistakes." She took the matches out of a box & went through them as a lover pulls at the petals of a daisy. "She leaves—she doesn't leave"—I was convinced that they would come out that she wouldn't leave—but with a gay laugh of triumph she said they came out that she should leave—& leave tomorrow. I felt sick—I'd had very little time with her alone—first the Gunthers—then Cecile—Now she is being delivered into the hands of the Rothschild set—Back to the rut of her ridiculous life in N.Y.—a life so unsuited to someone so near to the earth as she is.

We were both tired & somewhat fractious so argument would only become petulant—I took her back to Claridge's then sank depressed into my bed. The next day we met for last minute shopping & packing—& then a lull before departure. She explained that she'd thought this out carefully—if she stayed on Cecile wouldn't be here to take her into a shop—I was too busy to go with her—she couldn't go alone—"But I've nothing to do for a month—I've kept this month clear for you—you should come to the country—& go for long walks—you'd feel better there & give yourself a chance to feel well—There's always Doctor Gottfried in case of need." . . . No she had panicked—had taken fright & rushed back to her habits—& now at the 13th hour she was uncertain. "Perhaps I've made a mistake—what if I unpack—Oh God I always make such mistakes," & full of regrets we parted outside the hotel—I was very near to tears & she looked very forlorn, a white pinched face with dark eyes peering out of the windows & waving as the car with all its luggage on the roof drove out of sight.

There went my chances of marriage for another 4 years perhaps—but perhaps it was ridiculous to think ever of marriage—of her binding herself to anyone—and it was very sad for although she is difficult she is the person I most feel at ease with & attracted to—I feel completely natural with her—& everything we do together is simple, inevitable and delightful.[26]

Garbo was back in New York by the end of November, and Cecil was attending to practical matters.

He wrote:

> The only pale blue woollen underpants at Lillywhite's are ankle-length. The knee length ones are in Royal blue, bright scarlet or canary yellow. What to do? Let me know.[27]

To which Garbo responded promptly: she had given him the wrong address for the woollies, she said; he must go to Harrods. He would find that she was the same size as Lady Elizabeth von Hofmannsthal (she made a gallant, unsuccessful stab at getting that name right). Garbo's waist, alas, was now twenty-nine inches.

Meanwhile, she had no Manhattan news.[28]

Garbo and Georges Schlee on the Riviera in the summer of 1958.

CHAPTER 13

DRUGS AND DIET DOCTORS

Cecil was appointed a Companion of the Order of the British Empire in the New Year's Honours List of 1957, a parting gift from Clarissa following Anthony Eden's departure from 10 Downing Street. In the New Year he undertook a trip to Japan and the Far East with Truman Capote. He was busy with books, photographs, and his work on the film musical *Gigi* in the early and middle months of the year. In March his mother, then aged eighty-four, fell ill, and he rushed to be with her. Mercedes wrote a note of concern, but "Of course no word from my dear friend Greta."[1]

Garbo being Garbo, most of Cecil's news of her came from Mercedes. There was a misleading snippet in one of the London papers causing Garbo's distant fan, Ram Gopal, to believe that she was again staying with Cecil in the country. Ram beseeched Mercedes to arrange for him to meet his heroine:

> I only wish you were here to arrange this meeting, but since the elusive one is here staying with Beaton, and since there has not been much publicity about her visit this time in England—except for one small, insignificant paragraph in a paper announcing that she was staying at his country home in Salisbury—I thought that maybe as you had always said before that Mr. Beaton—who has become as regal as the Queen of England, as elusive as Garbo and as prissy as the fussiest Edwardian! said upon your suggestion that he would condescend to arrange for Ram to have the great honour and privilege of meeting Miss Garbo, he might do this. . . . If it is at all possible, I would like to meet the great one. But if there is any trouble, or if she wants to be left alone allowing Beaton to wear her cloak of mystery, please do not bother, and forget about it . . .[2]

Nothing came of this, since Garbo was not even in London at the time. She was in New York, suffering from a bad foot. In the summer of 1957, Garbo and Schlee were at Cap d'Ail. In July, Noël Coward spent an evening with her, which he much enjoyed. He wrote that he collected her from her "beautifully situated but hideous" villa, and took her to a restaurant in the nearby port of Villefranche. Coward found Garbo "bright as a button, and, of course, fabulously beautiful." They inspected the little chapel, rather overadorned by Jean Cocteau, causing the waspish Coward to note, "I had no idea that all the apostles looked so like Jean Marais."[3]

The relationship between Mercedes and Garbo remained as fraught as ever, as Cecil recorded in his diary that winter:

> [Greta] really has been feeling ill, & altho' she does not say what the matter is her kidneys are out of order & she has painful inflammation of the feminine organs.
>
> She has gone from one doctor to another. Suddenly she started to feel better when she was given Insulin injections by a quack. "I can't come to you everyday & take my turn in the queue" she

said. "I have (with a laugh) too much to do." (She has nothing whatsoever to do!) The Doctor said "You come in by the side door here & I'll always let you in—Don't miss a day though, not even Sundays."

So on the Sunday Greta went, found the Doctor in his dressing gown. "Excuse me not being dressed & unshaven like this. It's so wonderful not to have to shave & to be dirty for one day in the week." Greta sympathised, got her shot & left.

Next day on arrival she told the liftman she wanted to see the Doctor. "The Doctor ain't no more. He died last night." Greta felt faint: "Would you mind if I sat down for a moment." She was stunned for several days afterwards & lost.

The Doctor's death may have been a blessing in disguise because friends later told me that he reduced his clients to such a nervous state with these shots that they all got to the condition known as the "shakes." However, Greta did not know which way to turn. She suddenly recontinued her friendship with her friend Mercedes—for a year or more she cut her. If she met Mercedes while walking with Eric [Rothschild], she would nod only in the most cursory manner. Then suddenly Greta telephones, comes round to Mercedes—bursts into floods of tears. "I have no one to look after me." "You don't *want* anyone to look after you." "I'm frightened. I'm so *lost*!"

Mercedes is her very best friend & for 30 years has stood by her, willing to devote her life to her. Once again she rallied. She prevailed upon a little Italian doctor to break his rule of not having private clients to come to New York from Rochester each day to look after Greta.

"How do I know what you're doing to me? How do I know you're not killing me?"

The little man, very Italian & gallant, kissed her on the cheek—& said "I think you're the sweetest person I ever knew." But when he asked her for her telephone number she refused to give it. "Very well then I shall not continue to look after you. I've never heard such nonsense in my life. If your doctor can't telephone to know how you are responding to his treatment, there's no point in his continuing."

"Very well, but you're not to give that number to Mercedes."

"Do you mean to say you haven't given your number to the person who begged me to look after you?" "I'll give it to her later." The doctor rang Mercedes: "Would you mind if I ask you a very personal question. Have you or not Miss Garbo's telephone number?" "No." "I'm shocked. That is the most selfish thing I've ever heard in my life. It's absolutely inhuman."*

In spite of everything Mercedes continues to do all she can for Greta.

G. arrived unexpected at her flat, very upset. She had been to the Health Food store & the woman owner had said "Oh Miss Garbo you don't look at all well." G. was in tears. "Do I look so changed? Do I look so old?" Mercedes secretly ran to the Health Food Store & shaking a finger instructed the woman "Don't you ever tell Miss Garbo she doesn't look well again! However badly you think she looks, tell her she looks fine." The woman was dreadfully apologetic & upset.[4]

In failing health, Mercedes had become deeply depressed. Following a serious infection in her right eye in 1957, she had taken to wearing an eye patch, which added considerably to her piratical appearance. She became even more depressed when she was forced to move from her Park Avenue apartment to a new place on East Sixty-eighth Street. Wilder Luke Burnap, a loyal friend, recalled that on many occasions he was sent away by Mercedes just before Garbo loomed around the corner. He often saw her approach but never met her. When Mercedes was on cortisone and feeling particularly low, she threatened suicide, assuring him she had a gun to do the deed. She asked him to take a note round to Garbo on East Fifty-second Street. Soon a reassuring telegram arrived, which began, "Darling Boy . . ." Mercedes put her gun away.[5]

Mercedes wrote to Ram Gopal telling him how ill she felt, adding that Garbo was disillusioned with her New York doctors. Ram wrote back:

YOU'VE simply got to pull yourself out of the RUT of ILL health and nerves, and the disastrous effects of that ghastly killer drug

*Mercedes certainly had Garbo's last telephone number in her address book, so this story may be muddled.

you took and I KNOW that the only way to recover mentally and physically is this cellular Therapy. You've GOT to have it, and stop listening to those idiotic New York and anti-Niehans* quacks who swindle you and Greta out of small fortunes.[6]

There was talk of Garbo's going to Switzerland to see doctors there and the possibility of Mercedes's going with her. Cecil also wrote to Garbo:

Try & put on a bit of weight. We don't want you to become a Fakir however much your religious thoughts might turn towards the Orient. . . .

I was sorry that you have had such a wretched time with the doctors & only trust now you are feeling fitter & that when I come back to New York you will be in a more playful mood. It would be nice if we could go off on a slight jaunt somewhere together. There are such remarkable, romantic places within flying distance—& it's silly not to explore the less obvious places.

Keep chipper—be brave & be patient. I love you very much & rely upon you to feel the same way about your old friend

Beet[7]

Cecil had the chance to inspect Garbo again during a visit to New York at the end of 1957. Again he found that the story was of doctors on the one hand and cruelty to Mercedes on the other:

The Italian Doctor is superseded by a diet doctor in California. Greta has taken the plane to stay with some woman & her husband in Santa Monica for 3 days. Then she does not know where she will go to stay or what new alias to use, possibly to a 16th century monastery. But with the rush of leaving she did not telephone to say goodbye to me, but told Mercedes to say au revoir, but not until after I've left. "Beaton may go out to dinner & tell someone that I'm on that plane & then the photographers will be after me with the carm-rahs." Mercedes said "Never mind

*Dr. Paul Niehans (d. 1971), the famous monkey-gland doctor.

the minute you've gone I'll ring up Louella Parsons." G. rejoined "This is no laughing matter."

Mercedes suffers dreadfully at Greta's cruelty—& after all these years has not adopted an invulnerable attitude. Yet she can be funny about Greta's extraordinary behaviour—& instead of getting angry (as I am apt to do) she giggles: "Well we really must admit she's a character—if not a real eccentric. . . ."

She goes on hiding, and it is only because of her elusiveness that there is any chance of her being chased. I suppose that the damage done to her privacy & pride in her youth will last a life time. . . .

She has not been to a theatre for a year—& done very little shopping with Eric [Rothschild] & Schlee has seen much less of her than usual.

On arrival I telephoned & she seemed delighted that her solace had been broken in upon—she came around that afternoon & stood looking like a terrified urchin at my doorway—her eyes wide open & mouth agape as if ready for any torture. We laughed, we drank a little vodka, although she should absteem, & she would have stayed for dinner if I had not already made another engagement.

"That is the usual story—If you hadn't been doing something much more exciting." "But if I had left the evening free I would have found myself let down & alone—at the last moment." I had no anguish, no heartbreak—no shattering disappointment. Everything on a much more even keel, yet I felt a great tenderness for her most of the time—& very little exasperation. My heart was touched by her, & I enjoyed telephoning to her many times a day to find out how she fared, to keep in touch, to clock in, even if I knew there was nothing much to discuss.

Sometimes she would be depressed & sigh—sometimes say nothing but "Yaish Yaish." Once when she was not feeling well I only got birdlike peeps & nos out of her.

We went at her suggestion, to tea with Mercedes—& there she sat against a window—was in a draught & caught a cold which lasted a month. "You're too thin. You're undernourished. You have no stamina to fight germs. Your spine sticks out of your back like a python." "How do you know?" "I saw it when your sweater rode up as you bent down to do up your shoelace." . . .

One evening I suggested our taking Mercedes out to dinner. The miracle happened & she not only decided to come—but everything went well. The Colony provided a quiet sympathetic background & the dinner was excellent & Greta enthused "Never in my life have I eaten such goody lamb chops." She even admitted she had enjoyed the evening & on returning home telephoned me to say what a success it had been. She was as gay as a cricket & looked like a wild ragged but beautiful gipsy with straggly hair & in a high necked black jersey.

In the taxi going home she took my face in a fist & squeezed it tight. I put my tongue through her fingers. The gesture was repeated.

One day she came early for a drink. She found me asleep. She was discomforted that I hadn't prepared a biscuit & a drink & was not ready for her. "I expected a little charm." I ragged her about this later when her displeasure had worn off.

One day she said "Oh bother what I wouldn't give to have back the last 10 years! I'd behave so differently. If only I hadn't missed the bus." Several times she alluded to what I can only assume to be our "marriage manqué."

I knew that at the present moment it was inadvisable to try & discuss the situation again. I would always take on what would probably be an appallingly difficult life task—but no decision would be possible now. She was too ill & disorganised, too abject—too much embedded in her frigid rut—to lose her head enough to make any affirmative gesture. It is not the time for anything but treading water, for enjoying minor pleasures—& seeing if the future may bring about a better change.[8]

Cecil won his first Oscar, for *Gigi,* in 1958 and put the final touches on the London *My Fair Lady* at Drury Lane. Garbo spent some time in Los Angeles, caring for her friend Harry Crocker, who was dying. Cecil wrote her there in May:

Things are quieter now. My Mother who has become very old & frail has gone to stay with a sister, & I'm alone for the first time.

> It is at such moments that I wish you were here—instead of there—particularly as I hear you are not well. It is awful that you don't come to this part of the world where everything is green & smells good & where the air—not to mention Dr. Gottfried, would do you such benefit. Anyhow you always make your own plans but if you feel like it, & don't wish to spend all your summer on a Riviera rock, then you are more than welcome to all that I can offer you here . . .[9]

Cecil's recent Hollywood work and success with *My Fair Lady* having won him some rare financial security, he was able to resume work in earnest on his own ill-fated play, *The Gainsborough Girls.*

Garbo went to the south of France during the summer, and for once she was rather social. Toward the end of August it was reported that Sir Winston Churchill, then aged eighty-three and in failing health, had stayed up past midnight dining with Garbo and Onassis at a famous Riviera restaurant, almost certainly the Château de Madrid. "The three have been seen together with increasing frequency," wrote the *New York Times* stringer.[10] Sir Winston, who was recovering from a two-month bout of pneumonia, was staying with Lord Beaverbrook at his villa, also on Cap d'Ail. He invited Garbo and Onassis to be his guests at his golden wedding celebration on September 12. A dinner was given by the local prefect, greetings arrived from the Queen, President Eisenhower, Harold Macmillan, President Coty of France, and General de Gaulle. A five-liter bottle of Cognac more than 119 years old came from the Château de Madrid, as well as a multitude of flowers, and Sir Winston himself stood on the terrace in a white summer suit, puffing his cigar, while his eight-year-old granddaughter, Arabella, gave a faultless rendition of a poem about roses.

When Garbo herself celebrated her birthday a few days later on September 18, she invited her famous Riviera neighbors but ended spending the evening in the sole company of Georges Schlee. She was reported to be existing on a diet of fresh fruit, yogurt, and iced tea. Presently they went on to Athens and then to Rome, where Garbo was spotted walking hatless and casually attired on the Via Veneto early in October. Without seeing Cecil, Garbo returned to New York. In November he wrote to Mercedes:

Am glad you took Greta to the movies. I suppose being bedridden is the next step. . . . It's terribly sad—& I have the awful example of Stephen Tennant* in the neighborhood. He is really dotty by now, & so self centered that the doctors are in despair. It fills me with gloom & horror. There was much conversation in Paris about Schlee's behavior on board the Onassis yacht this year. It seems he is not likely to be invited again. It's a wonder to me that they were able to put up with him as long as this. But they're not great masters in the art of discrimination . . .[11]

Early in 1959, Cecil was in New York, working on Noël Coward's production of *Look After Lulu.* He phoned Garbo shortly after his arrival, and she came around for a drink.

I watched Greta with love & compassion. She had aged so much in the twelve years that I've known her well that it's cruel & unbelievable. I've never seen anything so dazzling as her periwinkle blue eyes when I first walked with her on Fifth Avenue. Her face was flawless. Now the crevices are deep. Yet it is still a beautiful sensitive face & the play of expression that runs over it while she tells a story is an enchantment to watch—The lips move over the teeth in the most perfect delicacy of meaning. . . .

My birthday. She took me to lunch, at the Passy—since there were, to quote Art Buchwald—too many people "we love & admire" at the new successful restaurant La Côte Basque. Here today there were even more friends & acquaintances than at the other. We were completely surrounded by Fairbanks, Mellons & Berlins. The same badinage: "Shall we talk about something serious today?" I asked. "Nothing wrong I hope?"—"No I trust not." But I would like to have cracked below the surface of our superficial badinage. We talked a little about Hollywood & her last visit—how she looked after Harry Crocker until he died [on May 23, 1958], how the head of MGM had been the only one to pay attention to her; he sends flowers & wants her to go back to films. "I'm quite realistic about it. It would be worth them

*Stephen Tennant had retreated to bed as an invalid in the late 1920s and remained there—except for certain memorable excursions into the outside world—for more than fifty-five years.

risking just one film. They say they can still photograph me well on the screen—& I believe it—although now in news pictures I look so terrible—I was shocked to see all those lines above my mouth show—I know I have them & I asked Laszlo if he couldn't get rid of them (he can't). But now they show in the photographs!" "But what part would they give me? They haven't found anything. There was one crackpot with an idea—& he kept badgering me—but why should I go through all that suffering—for what?"

Occasionally we talk about things of the past that are interesting but so much time is spent in childish make believe which soon makes me feel somewhat self conscious. So much time is spent in conjecture: "Let's go—Let's go to Mexico, or Florida or Spain & to the Cha Cha competition." But I know we'll never go anywhere.

I want to ask her what is her link with Schlee. I want to know why at the last minute she always reverts to him. I wanted to tell her that I had seriously been considering getting married,* & quite suddenly I did.

I must say she coped with the situation very delightfully: "I'll be right over to stop it. I'll come over to cut her head off. Well, well, well. So you've got a girl, have you?" She looked quizzically at me: "There's only one objection," I said. She forestalled me: "You don't love her?"—"I'm not in love with her. She's an angel. I know I'd be terrifically lucky if ever she would marry me. She's adorable—everything that's good & brave & noble & attractive. But I just don't feel that *coup de foudre.*"

It is desperately sad when one is given the brush off. I was miserable when Greta paid no attention to me. But it is sad in a much more negative, depressing way when one feels less strongly about someone who has meant so much to one—when one has to feel that one must be kind in brushing them off. I realise, at last,

*Cecil was preoccupied with the idea of marrying June Osborn, the attractive widow of the pianist Franz Osborn. Lady Diana Cooper urged him to do so, and to have a child. There were some nervous meetings, dinners, and a weekend together in the country with friends. Then in December 1959 Cecil proposed and was gently turned down.

> it is too late for Greta & me ever to marry now. The first interest has gone—& there is nothing left to talk about.[12]

At the end of January there was an awkward episode with Garbo and Victor Rothschild at Cecil's hotel:

> Victor & his wife came in—delighted to see me—after a long interval. They then discovered the presence of Greta. Huge delight & surprise. Victor, coarse as he is, spoke in a robust somewhat challenging vein to Greta: "Why did you go on Onassis' yacht? What do you get out of it?" Greta was a little nonplussed. She is generally witty & quick of answer but the bull-like Victor was too strong a breath of air for her. Victor addressed himself to me. He joked & laughed with me—& we had a good time—conversation being more or less general. Then Greta got up & left.
>
> No regrets from the R's at her departure—& on to more jolly jokes. I wondered why Greta left so early. Immediately after the R's had left to catch the elevator G. telephoned. "Don't let them know who you're speaking to—if they're still there—But what happened? I didn't enjoy myself. The Lord never even looked at me. He paid no attention to me whatsoever. It wasn't at all a nice atmosphere & I was numb & I've come home very depressed. I was very sad in the taxi." It made me very sad that she was sad & apologised. I told her that all Rothschilds are coarse. "Well when you're as sensitive as I am it isn't very pleasant, especially when you go out as little as I do you expect it to be an exception & very gay." Then I said "Well please forget it & I'm sorry" & she said "Give me another chance. Good night Beattie." My heart broke.[13]

Cecil saw little of Garbo for the rest of the year. The only news of her came from Mercedes:

> Greta has just this second telephoned and we have had one of those "zesch" conversations!!
>
> We went shopping this afternoon and it is remarkable the

sensation she always causes. Every block someone remarked her and some girls followed us and tried to photograph her. God knows how they recognize her for she had a muffler tied round her head, that old tired seal-skin coat down to the ground and great snow boots. Hardly the conventional movie star but the little face is always beautiful and they probably just see that.

The "Baron" [Eric Goldschmidt-Rothschild] is back here in New York but Greta does not see him. I wonder what happened between them after so many walks together. I'll bet he will never be so well exercised in his life again![14]

CHAPTER 14

RESENTMENT AND REGRETS

One day in the winter of 1960, Garbo was in New York, perusing the wares on the lower shelves of her favorite health food store on the corner of East Fifty-seventh Street and Lexington Avenue. Suddenly, on the floor in front of her, she saw a long-toed, silver-buckled shoe come into view. Out of the corner of her eye, she observed the corner of a black highwayman's cape.

"Aren't we on speaking terms today?" asked Mercedes. Garbo neither looked up nor spoke. Presently the toe withdrew.[1] It was Garbo's only encounter with Mercedes that winter.

Garbo felt she had many reasons to be annoyed with Mercedes. She had suffered a dislocated hip from the ministrations of Mercedes's doctor.* Then Mercedes committed the crime of publishing her memoir, *Here Lies the Heart.* Mercedes had been busy writing this memoir for some years, and in March 1960 she sent Cecil a copy. Cecil responded:

> Many thanks for sending the book which has appeared at long last!! It must be a great thrill to you. It seems to be very well produced & I trust you are pleased with the look of it. Did you ever have it published in a magazine? I imagine this would be the only way to make any money out of it. I shall be most interested to hear about the reactions. There is so much good stuff in it & I have enjoyed it a lot, especially as I was lucky to know quite a lot of the people you write about. I lent the book to Juliet Duff, my neighbour, who was *fascinated.*[2]

Alice B. Toklas was another reader: "Your book has left me breathless—excited and very happy. . . . I curtsy before your tremendous accomplishment. It is your heart that keeps you so modest. Pardon all my surprise. For example your story of Garbo is a classic—at the end you have made her one of the heroines of all time—just as you have left Marlene Dietrich a warm but ordinary woman."[3]

Here Lies the Heart was one of those books that came out at the wrong time. The fascination for Garbo and Dietrich was not as strong in the early 1960s as it subsequently became. And Mercedes herself was so difficult to deal with that she did not inspire confidence. Many did not believe her stories, one friend dubbing the book "Here lies the Heart, and lies and lies and lies." However, the stories have stood the test of time, and if some of the details were muddled, some of the dates haphazard, and some of the mysterious coincidences benefited from hindsight, the essence of her story was true. One reviewer wrote of "the mind and heart of a woman whose life was both a courageous search for spiritual truths and a gallantly, frequently extravagant adventure" (Mercedes retained this press cutting in her papers). But, despite considerable publicity, Mercedes earned not a penny in royalties. And soon after the

*Dr. Max Wolf.

Mercedes published her memoirs in 1960, and Garbo never forgave her. The jacket photograph is by Marlene Dietrich.

publication of the book, on New Year's Day, Garbo hung up on her when she telephoned, saying, "I don't want to talk to you."[4] Mercedes reported this to Cecil, who replied, "How childish of Greta to ring off like that—simply maddening."[5]

Garbo remained in New York "wasting away in that ghastly flat" and "traipsing along those oven streets to get a package from the Health Food Stores"[6] until her annual peregrination to the south of France, followed this year by a month in Klosters, Switzerland, with Salka Viertel to help get over the dislocated hip. The south of France was not stimulating: "I saw nobody," Garbo told Cecil.[7]

At the end of November, Cecil was favored with a visit from her. She came to London, accompanied by Sydney Guilaroff, the celebrated Hollywood hairdresser. Cecil recorded the occasion in his diary:

> Guilaroff, the hairdresser from MGM & the only person with whom I had difficulty at the studio when working on *Gigi,* rang to say Miss Harriet Brown was staying with him in his small flat in Shepherd's Market. This seemed very odd & unsuitable for this is hardly the best auspices under which to see London again after 7 (?) years. Indeed it turned out to be a flop. Guilaroff—third rate—his apartment much too small & uncomfortable. However, Greta arranged to come down to the country for the weekend. The visit was curtailed for a dinner appointment that, of course, did not take place, & almost contrary to expectations, she arrived, under Simon Fleet's care, on the Sunday morning.
>
> She did not look as "downtrodden" to use her word, as I had expected—after an interval of nine months. As she got out of the train accompanied by a self important Simon, she was torn between making a demonstration of joy & affection, & of not drawing attention to herself. She laughed with lowered eyelids. Then, when she saw there were no spies she abandoned herself to friendliness & gaiety kissing Juliet [Duff] (who was meeting Simon) & me—which is something she never does in public. She was wearing ski clothes & a terrible pixie woollen hat that children wear in the Tyrol. Hair maroon colour—long & trilby fringed. "Well, Well, Well—Fancy that."
>
> She was in the best spirits as we drove through the autumn

tunnels towards Broadchalke. The only anxiety was would my mother still be hostile to her. Last time my mother had thought Greta was taking me from her—& there was quite a situation. I comforted Greta that my Mama was now beyond any such feelings, but Greta got a terrible fright when, mistaking it for her own room, she went into my mother's room. My mother was asleep & not disturbed. But this upset was followed by another when Greta could not find her handbag. Had she left it in the train. Why had Simon been talking as they came to arrive at Salisbury (really!). Just as I had visions of telephoning the police & this would have meant publicity, Greta discovered that she had left it in the lavatory. But these two incidents on top of her arrival, unnerved me somewhat. There is always a jinx around her. What next would go wrong?

Fortunately the rest of the day was without setback. The sun continued to shine. After an enormous lunch which we both enjoyed we went for a walk of great duration & variety. A few complaints about my being mad to take her where there was so much mud, but then she wanted to see her friends the pigs & the calves—& there was mud where animals tread—particularly at this flooded time in England. However we walked high over the downs—in an empty pure landscape & the air went into one's lungs & made one feel so well. We climbed gates with much protestation & when it was becoming dark returned by a hedged path to visit the Bundys' Farm. Then fifty young pigs, then week old calves. We had crab apple jelly, scented with sweet geranium for tea.

Little of import was said. . . . In the drawing room Greta made herself at home in that wonderful way that she has. When she is settled in a sofa with cigarettes by her side she gives you the impression that nothing in life exists outside the present moment. It is one of her great assets & I'm certain this is the reason why George Schlee has been able to put up with her so willingly in spite of all difficulties. . . .

I wanted to play some comic records to her—& the Nichols & May highbrow couple listening to Bach amused her tremendously, but I have never seen her laugh as she did at Peter Sellers's Indian. She said that she wasn't accustomed to laughing nowadays, & this gave her a pain—so that she had to lean forward as she screwed up her face in helpless amusement.

Dinner at Juliet's was sympathetic as old friends were there—Sidney [the Earl of Pembroke], Michael [Sir Michael Duff]—& Greta was at her most demonstrative. She looked quite remarkably transfigured from the somewhat drab visitor arriving on the platform. She still wore her black ski pants & maroon sweater, but added a mauve chiffon scarf which was just the colour of her hair. Her face was animated & her smile is enough to disarm all criticism. And there was a certain amount of criticism from her—of myself. "Mr. Beat is always so busy in New York that he can only spare a minute for me. He's so much on the run that I never catch more than a glimpse of him. Of course Mr. Beatty has changed a little—now he's running around in cuicklurles [circles]."

The others were amused & I suppose once I would have been proud to think that Greta was in fact running after me. But I was vaguely out of sorts at the implied criticism being made so public. And really it is long past the time when she should call me Mr. Beaton in front of our mutual friends. It is a habit that should have been dropped, because it is now merely idiotic, & a sad example of her not wishing to commit herself. She will run up to no friend. Although she was very discreet about him, one knew she had realised her mistake in coming to stay in London with this *pas sortable* hairdresser.

Enough. Back home. Kisses & sweetness in the warm drawing room—& then to our separate rooms. "Oh I'm such a sad little man. I've been out of life for so long!!" . . .

I found the journey back to London rather over-tiring. Greta never reads, & in any case had not brought her glasses so could only glance at the headlines of the newspaper I gave her. She felt somewhat put out that there were other people in the compartment (the train being very full). She kept up an incessant battery of questions. "Where could I get a carpet that is pink? If only I could get some painted furniture." Each suggestion I make is hopeless for I know that she will never go to these shops, or if she does she will never buy anything, or if she does she will not know where to put it. I felt jaded, gruff & depressed when, at last, we

> arrived in London. When I dropped her at Shepherd's Market I saw this dark, eccentric figure doddering towards her lodgings; my heart cracked. It was so pathetic a sight to see her disappearing in the fog & yet nothing could be done about her—her case is so hopeless. Moreover she does not ask for help—she is independent & will not put out her arms towards a helping hand.[8]

Garbo and Guilaroff came to dinner with Hal Burton that evening at Cecil's place in London, and Cecil found it all "too sad":

> Hal's wisdom as we held a little post mortem was the only good thing of the evening. He said it was sad but inevitable that the scales should one day fall, & that when they did there should be a little resentment. For Greta had never really played an honest game. She was always pretending, & she would never have committed herself. Moreover, Hal said that he had noticed a certain hardness in her. That she now no longer seemed the helpless hopeless waif, but knew perfectly well that she was heading to perdition, but that she damn well would go without any interference from others.[9]

Cecil's tolerance of Garbo was waning. In 1961 he was in New York undertaking his first work for the Metropolitan Opera. While in America he turned to contemplation of the Mercedes-Garbo situation:

> I have always thought that Greta would end her days with Mercedes—a sort of desperation solution for two lonely people. But it seems Greta is really "through" with Mercedes—not for the reason that Mercedes imagines—that Greta has not forgiven her for writing about her in her book (Greta never bothered to read the book—& in any case the indiscretion has come twenty years too late!). But the real reason is that apart from being irritated & bored, Greta feels that Mercedes brings her bad luck. This conviction was culminated in the awful experience that Greta had when recommended to some sort of chiropractor—not really that—who she said made her bones float about her body, put her hip out, & caused her mouth to go lopsided.

> Mercedes, the last of the loyal fans, is desperate to get back into favour even though she knows how badly Greta treats her friends. She makes sporadic attempts to make a gesture at a suitable time of the year. . . .
>
> This Christmas time Mercedes arranged for a very beautiful spruce Christmas tree to be sent to Greta. The messenger denoted the delight of Greta on receiving it—even though she discovered the name of its sender. Greta did not acknowledge the gift. However when Mercedes, encouraged, sent a basket full of jokes & toys, mistletoe, & a specially good bottle of vodka that she had brought back from Paris, Greta returned by a frightened child-messenger—the entire basket full except that she had taken from it the bottle of vodka.
>
> Greta continues in her nihilist ways. Her selfishness is beyond endurance—an old friend from Sweden arrived here—to be cheered up on the recent loss of his wife. Greta asked him & a Princess Bernadotte to go out to dinner. At 6.30 she put the old man off—she did not feel like going out—would the Princess just come & eat dinner alone with her—they'd have some vegetables. The outraged Princess refused.
>
> I have been here nearly two weeks & though I've made very few halfhearted attempts to meet her, have not yet set eyes upon her. We have had long idiotic conversations on the telephone.
>
> However yesterday she committed herself enough to say she would lunch at the Caravelle. She arrived distraught at being late. She should never have come out. "Do you know this is the first time I've lunched out in I don't know how long?" ("What of it?" I felt like saying).[10]

In June 1961, Garbo attended a farewell party that Valentina gave for her husband in their apartment on East Fifty-second Street. Soon afterward, according to custom, Schlee and Garbo retreated to the south of France for the summer and Valentina went to Venice. Cecil was in Venice attending a Volpi ball and ran into Valentina, as he reported to Mercedes:

> I saw Valentina in Venice (to which I am returning tomorrow after a very quiet spell on the Isle of Spetsai) & she told me that

> La Divina was, as usual, at Cap d'Ail, where she [Valentina] would be joining George & Greta. I do wish you would try not to be hurt by Greta's ruthlessness—but if one suffers then there is no point in trying to be offhand. Luckily I am not able to be hurt by her anymore & this too is very sad. I shudder to think of what may happen to any of us in 10 years time but for Greta the prospect must be pretty grim unless suddenly she decides to turn over a new leaf & not be selfish, & this I doubt . . .[11]

Cecil published the first volume of his diaries, *The Wandering Years,* in July 1961 and sent Mercedes a copy. He was delighted that she liked the book:

> I'm very happy to think you like my naïf book & am glad you appreciated its frankness. It was hard to decide to "publish & be damned" but I thought it no good giving a watered-down version of the original diaries. God knows what'll happen if I ever bring them more up to date! Greta will be coming to Paris any day now. The usual window shopping & regrets. Then suddenly the decision to take the next airplane back to the rut. How *does* she keep interested?[12]

In October 1961 Garbo was indeed spotted shopping in Paris with Rita Hayworth. Then she returned to New York, where Cecil caught up with her in the course of a ten-day visit. He was in America to undertake the decor of a charity ball.

When Cecil telephoned her, she greeted him, "Well, well. I was just thinking about you yesterday. I wondered where Beet would be. Have you come over to propose to me again?" Garbo dropped by his hotel, where he was making a portrait of a society friend, Chiquita Astor. Garbo told Cecil that she was even more isolated than hitherto and that she did not even go upstairs at Fifty-second Street to drink a vodka with Schlee. Her hip was still causing trouble, and so was her stomach. But she was still going for walks each day. Cecil found her life depressing, but Chiquita Astor told him she had never seen anyone with such depth of beauty.

During this trip Cecil and Garbo lunched together at the Passy. They met outside; she was as punctual as ever, while he was late. He spotted Garbo in the distance, dressed in navy blue, a dark chiffon kerchief on her head. She was smiling sweetly, and Cecil observed her face in the distance: "It has a quality that no other New York face has."

> I am a swine not to unbend completely, not to dissolve into tears, but I cannot. She has hurt me a lot in the past & I'm resentful. And I'm resentful of the continued waste, the continued regrets, the lost opportunities sighed over & the new ones never faced. It is sad, sad, sad, such sweetness & such strength of cruelty too—though she would never admit to its being cruelty. (When I told her that Mercedes whom she will *never* make up with & see again, might soon die (she is to have another brain operation), Greta was deeply, deeply upset. But she would never relax her judgement.)[13]

Both Cecil and Mercedes were surprised when Garbo suddenly flew to Sweden to spend Christmas with Count Carl Johan Bernadotte and his wife. She arrived there on December 9. Mercedes relayed the news to Cecil:

> I imagine you will be in the country for Christmas and how lovely that will be. Here you know what New York is like, and in this commercial panic I find each year it grows drearier and sadder. I envy you in the country. You, no doubt, know that Greta has gone to Sweden. I learned of this from John Gunther although it was in the newspapers but on reading it I did not believe it until he told me it was true. He said she has gone *just* for Christmas but the newspapers said she had left America "for good and intended selling her flat." I must say, this gave me a *terrific* heart stab because I cannot imagine New York without her. So it was a great relief to me when John said *this* was not true and that she would be back. I imagine she has gone to stay with the Wachtmeisters who have a *lovely* place in the country and are distinguished people. I have not seen them since Greta and I stayed with them in 1937 and I don't believe she has seen them since then either. It may do her good to go back to her roots and at least be in the country and good food.
>
> I remember they had *wonderful* food! But it is strange how

lonely I feel now that I know she is not in New York. Even though I do not see her there was always the possibility of running into her, of hearing some news of her or even of her calling up. I was trying to make up my mind about sending her a tree.

Do let me know if you have any news of her plans. She will probably write to you or may even go to England to see you . . .[14]

To this Cecil replied:

I'm sorry you continue to suffer from her absence. There's nothing that one can say about it—except I do feel she's so peculiar that it would save you a lot of heartbreak if you could take a more remote view of her & just laugh off her peculiarities. She's really a very strong character but she seems determined to do the unwise thing for herself & to accumulate regrets. Maybe she is happy in her present life—& she *says* she's never bored, but heaven knows how she gets anything stimulating into her head. She has shut herself off to almost everything . . .[15]

Cecil underwent a difficult time that Christmas, watching his old mother slowly dying. She died at Broadchalke when he was away in Paris in February 1962. The death of one he had so adored during his life cast a long shadow over him.

News of Garbo and meetings with her became ever more intermittent. "No news of Greta," Cecil wrote to Mercedes in March 1962. "I heard she was in St. Moritz at the Palace of all places. But the snow of Switzerland is better than the slush of Third Avenue."[16] Then, in July, came a letter from Garbo. It was as inconsequential and full of excuses as ever. She was in worse health than before; she saw no one. She had told Schlee she would not go to the Riviera this year and he was upset. He had no one else to see. If she came to Europe, she might see Cecil. She hoped, rather feebly, that he might consider a visit to California, in which case she might come too.[17]

Cecil reported on this letter to Mercedes:

I have had no news of Greta except a *typewritten* letter (!) dated July 17 when her plans were negative—as usual. I s'pose she went

> back to Schlee. We all got up at 9 o'clock in the A.M. to see a festival of *old* films on the Lido Beach. The *Anna Christie* was a great experience not a bit dated—& Greta's performance wonderfully touching. They also showed extracts of a ghastly film called *Inspiration* in which Greta had frizzy hair & vampire's clothing, but even in this she was so much more marvellous in taste, tact, wit & quality of beauty than that cow Dietrich whose *Morocco* etc. were shown *afterwards*!
>
> Bad luck on Dietrich. She looked good in close up with overhead lighting but in all the other shots was a German fat hausfrau with a potato nose . . .[18]

More long silences followed. Cecil went to Hollywood for ten months in February 1963 to design the costumes, scenery, and production of the film of *My Fair Lady,* for which he eventually received two Oscars. This was a constructive period but not a happy one. Cecil disliked being forced to remain in Hollywood, and he quarreled with the director, George Cukor. In July, writing from the Hotel Bel Air in Los Angeles, he reported a disagreeable Garbo experience to Mercedes:

> I am sorry not to have had time to see you in N.Y. but I was only there for a long weekend to photograph most of Saturday a rich lady in New Jersey. I rang Greta—out—a maid answered—& then on the day of leaving a *secretary* rang to know how long I was staying. "You're Miss Garbo's *secretary*?" I asked incredulously. "What on earth does Miss Garbo want with a secretary?" Anyhow, as usual, I missed her & since then not a civil word. What a mess! She *loathes* Valentina & vice-versa & so it's particularly poignant that they should spend so much time in each other's company. Nureyev is here & he told me he got on beautifully with Greta. They are 2 of a pair (Did you see him perform? He really is a genius!).[19]

CHAPTER 15

AFTER SCHLEE

Georges Schlee died in Paris on October 3, 1964. It was a death that has long been the center of conflicting stories and reports.

The summer had found Garbo on her travels around Europe. She accompanied the actor Brian Aherne and his wife to Switzerland, where they saw Noël Coward. He was on the same plane when the Ahernes and Garbo, the latter "quivering with neurosis," flew to Rome on July 4. Garbo traveled economy, Coward supposing this to be for fear of being recognized: "She needn't have worried because no one recognised her at all."[1]

The group set off on a small yacht trip. Later Garbo joined Schlee at Cap d'Ail. They left for Paris at the beginning of October, planning to fly to New York on Sunday the fourth. The following summer Cecile de Rothschild, no fan of Georges Schlee, gave Cecil her version of what occurred:

> She told me of how Fate had ordained that she should come to Paris on a certain day earlier than she intended—to find Greta & Schlee at the Crillon before leaving the next day for New York. They dined together. Greta left with her companion at 11.30* —she to bed—he to walk a little—whereupon he had a heart attack—went to a Bistro—asked the proprietor to telephone Greta—became worse & on the way to the hospital died. Greta meanwhile receives a call from an unknown man who she cannot understand because he speaks French. She tells him to call Cecile—who is given the news.[2]

The stringers for *Time* magazine were hard at work, and they produced a contradictory version in a report for the editors compiling the story:

> Officials at the Crillon Hotel vehemently deny that Schlee died there and claim that he passed away quietly in a right bank Boîte de Nuit. But this song and dance is only to protect that noble name of the Place de la Concorde establishment. We called the American Embassy posing as a distant member of the family and they confirmed that he did, in fact, die at the Crillon. Cause of death: a heart attack.
>
> Valentina arrived in Paris Monday and left for Los Angeles with the body on Tuesday. We were unable to learn whether Garbo left too or is still in town.[3]

The New York Times reported that Schlee died in a Paris hospital, but there were the inevitable rumors that he had died in a brothel, enjoying the favors of a young lady or even, it was said, a young man. The version

*The distance between Cecile de Rothschild's apartment and the side door of the Crillon was minimal.

Garbo photographed by Beaton during a cruise of the Greek islands in 1965.

most likely to be correct is that of Cecile de Rothschild as relayed to Cecil.*

Valentina flew into Paris on Monday, October 5, to collect Schlee's body, and Garbo disappeared. She was around the corner, at Cecile de Rothschild's apartment in the Rue du Faubourg Saint-Honoré.

Schlee's funeral took place in New York, at the Universal Funeral Chapel at Fifty-second Street and Lexington Avenue, with Valentina heading eighty-five mourners. Pushkin's three-line poem "Exegi Monumentum"** was read in Russian and then in English. The Russian Orthodox service was conducted by two priests, who chanted prayers and lit candles.

Though Garbo was conspicuously absent from the funeral service, she continued to live at 450 East Fifty-second Street. Valentina, who had tolerated the ménage with Schlee all these years, now swore that she never wanted to set eyes on Garbo again. Her declared reason for this was Garbo's desertion of her husband at the hour of his death, but in fact it was the culmination of years of bitterness. More reports were sent to their editors by the stringers for *Time,* energetically consulting any source they could to fill in the staff in New York on the activities of the eccentric trio:

> One of our very reliable sources here (a close friend of Garbo) tells us that Valentina was far from frowning on the free living setup. "She was not only one of Garbo's former girlfriends" our source claims "but also has boyfriends in Venice for the summer." Things couldn't have worked out better than the pattern of the last 15 years: George and Greta on the Côte d'Azur, Valentina playing around with her Counts and Dukes in the

*Antoni Gronowicz's book *Garbo: Her Story* (New York: Simon & Schuster, 1990) gave yet another contradictory version of the death, which further serves to discredit the book's overall veracity.

**"I have erected a monument to myself, not built by hands. The track to it shall not be overgrown. It has raised its indomitable head higher than Alexander's column."

> upper lofts of the Royal Daniele Hotel. Was he more than a business partner and companion? Most definitely . . . he did just about everything for Garbo . . . devoted his life to keeping the embers of the living part of the myth alive. He was Mr. Garbo and relished the role. But everyone knew he couldn't do everything for the woman he was protecting. Their relationship was strictly platonic.[4]

Now that Schlee was dead, Valentina gave vent to her rage. She summoned a priest to exorcise her apartment, to remove all traces of Garbo. The priest was bidden to pay particular attention to the refrigerator, into which Garbo had occasionally reached for a can of beer. Valentina seized the villa at Cap d'Ail, which, the following year, she loaned to Diana Vreeland. She told her, "I had it exorcised. There will be no sign of that woman!" But, as Mrs. Vreeland commented, "It was so full of spooks you could hardly move."[5]

Valentina remained on the fourteenth floor of her building, Garbo on the ninth. Their uneasy proximity was to last for the next quarter century.

Cecil and Garbo were not in touch at this time, though he sent her a message at Christmas. She cabled back her love and thanks.[6]

While Cecil was in the United States working on the film of *My Fair Lady,* he had made friends with a young Californian teacher named Kin. The young man flew to London in June 1964 and stayed with Cecil for nearly a year. It was a strange period for both of them. In August 1965, Kin acknowledged that there was no future in the relationship and retreated to San Francisco.

On the very day of Kin's departure, Cecil set off to Athens for a cruise on which Garbo was a passenger. Cecile de Rothschild was the host. She had taken Garbo to Sardinia for two weeks, and they picked Cecil up at Vougliameni, near Athens. With her now-well-tried ability to find someone to tend to her every need, Garbo had adopted Cecile as her gofer. In Cecil's words, "Cecile fills the role of Schlee in Greta's life—Schlee & Mercedes combined, for I cannot think that Greta treated Schlee as badly as she does Cecile."[7] He left an account of the cruise in his diary:

Cecile was serious—heavily Rothschildian & slightly preoccupied lest her guests—Frederick Ledebur* & Princesse de Broglie** would not turn up. But they did—& soon we were settling down to our shipboard life. . . .

Cecile . . . is a good humoured, kind woman who has not let her great wealth ruin her life. She does manage to do interesting unconventional things with it—& shows enthusiasm & imagination. . . .

She is very happy to have Greta on board—for she is besotted. She snickers at everything Greta does—even if it is a slap directed against herself. . . .

Cecile & Greta have recently been for 2 weeks in Sardinia where Greta slept well & behaved beautifully, even socialising with a great group of strangers—but the *Sieta* being a small boat echoes all the sounds of the night & Greta was unable to sleep in her cabin. Moreover she had a stomach upset & my enteroviaform came to her rescue only just in time—for if Greta had not recovered there was talk of Cecile having to take her home. Greta was terribly unkind to Cecile—I was shocked—& Greta at night came to her cabin door & said "I've got a temperature. Isn't that frightening! You see I should never travel!" . . .

Cecile brings the top of a garment to Greta's cabin. "Here is the top of your bathing suit." "I know it is, but how do I know now where I'll find the other part?"

"My shoes—they're all feelthy. I wash 'em."

C.: "Why not put them in fresh water?"

"No. First in the veema (vim?) then in my cabina."

C.: "But let me wash them. It amuses me to do it—but after lunch—because lunch is ready."

"Naaow!"

"C.: "Lunch is ready."

*Count Friedrich Ledebur (1900–87), wild giant of an Austrian aristocrat whose varied career included being a bit actor in various Hollywood films. (He was the bemedaled admiral in Fellini's *Ginger and Fred* in the 1980s.) A keen horseman, he had legs so long that when he rode, they all but touched the ground. He married the poet Iris Tree and later Countess Alice Hoyos.

**Princess Jeanne-Marie de Broglie, for many years director of Christie's in Paris.

"What, you mean lunch is ready now?"

C. (politely): "Well we said we'd have lunch at 1 or 1.15."

"Why don't you give me a straight answer? What is the time now?"

"One o'clock."

"Then I wash them now straight away." . . .

By being so solitary all these years [Garbo] has never learnt to speak grammatical English. The result is that in her beautiful, touching voice she uses the idiosyms [*sic*] of the Hollywood electricians. Sometimes it is almost impossible to understand her, & since I am the only one on board to "kid" her at all have asked "Would you please translate that last sentence into Swedish!"

Cecile, while we were anchoring in a marvellous green bay surrounded by forested hills, remarked how wonderful it was to be woken by the tinkle of sheep bells & the calls of the shepherd. Greta appeared. "I couldn't sleep. Did you hear that bloody shepherd? Fancy being woken by a shepherd!"

In this cruel harsh sunlight on board one sees every crinkle & crevice in the most cruel way. I have hawklike watched her in all lights, without mascara even—this is a severe test & she does not like to be seen without this armour & only ever appears this naked if she is swimming early before the rest of us, or if she has gone to bed & returns to complain about the noise. . . .

Yet at other times—& under stark conditions she can still be extraordinarily beautiful. The angle of nose jutting unhesitantly from the profile is unaltered. The nose is cut with a high deep bridge and the eyes are deeply set—so that there is always a cavernous shadow above the lid. With age the cheekbones have become more modulated & firm & the teeth though they have lost their dazzling whiteness (no doubt partly due to the non-stop smoking of cigarettes) are still big & bold & by slanting inwards complement the perkiness of the nose (& incidentally used to catch in a wonderful way the reflection of the studio lights).

In the apricot coloured light of evening she still looks absolutely marvellous & she could be cleverly photographed to appear as beautiful as ever in films. But it is not just her beauty that is dazzling, it is the air of mysteriousness that makes her so appealing particularly when talking with sympathy & wonder to children or reacting herself to some situation with all the wonder and surprise of childhood itself.

Cecil continued his account as they reached Sciathos:

It is 8 in the morning—the others have gone on shore to buy honey cakes while the ship is refuelled. Greta put her head out of her cabin & said "Wait for me"—so I suppose the others waited—for Cecile would never go without Greta. Stubbornly I have stayed put in my cabin to finish my volume of Proust & now I have left the yellowing trees in the Avenue des Acacias & taken up my pen to try & capture the atmosphere of this holiday trip. It is a changing & strange atmosphere—on the surface & because we all are civilised human beings the atmosphere is light & "sportive"—emotions under control—but I find that I am not the only one to sense the vibrations of rancour, jealousy & criticism that exist beneath the surface.

Last night after our dinner in the Quai when the others had left our disappointing taverna for coffee in a café, Jeanne Marie de Broglie & myself sat eating baklava at a cake shop & we for the first time discussed our fellow travellers. No more unselfish sweet tempered person exists than Jeanne Marie. Looking like an Ingres model of 18 it is incredible to think that she is a mother of grown children with quite a career as an art dealer, so sweet & "open" is she—that it is surprising to find that she does form her impressions—not always favourable—of those she loves.

Less in a spirit of complaint than of analysis she discussed our hostess—with whom she shares a cabin. Therefore there is no question of ever reading more than a page of a book without being interrupted—for Cecile's restlessness has become so neurasthenic that she cannot be alone—for one moment—nor can she stick to any subject for long—except if the subject be Greta—by whom she is obsessed. With Greta she is a kid hypnotised by a snake. She is willing to become Greta's slave—she only wishes to be badly treated by Greta—& she will snigger with glee. But it is not a good way for her to spend these years—now that she is feeling more than ever the lack of a man in her life. . . .

Greta walks along the shore in a petulant mood. Cecile follows ten yards after her. Only when a pile of rocks brings her progress to a halt does Greta turn to welcome Cecile.

Jeanne Marie remarked that she had been fascinated to watch "the Queen," that in a bathing cap she still looked beautiful with the well known line of nose & forehead & neck—that she could be extremely funny—& her clowning was wonderful. But she is always so critical: "Did you notice when Cecile asked if she wanted eggs & bacon, she said: you're not to order them or they'll get cold or I'll have to come when I'm not ready. I'll come when I'm ready & order them then & then they'll be hot." At dinner she remarks: "How beautiful this fruit looks. But it's all rotten—not ripe—hard—uneatable."

Even Frederick Ledebur, the great gentleman that he is—so wise and understanding and forgiving—has remarked upon Greta's being so critical of everything. But no-one is as critical as I am. Not because I have any resentment or prejudice—but just because having loved her so much it is a nightmare for me to see what inevitable paths her negativeness & selfishness have brought her.

Yesterday was not Greta's worst day. She felt quite well—but it was a pique day. While I wrote [my] diary next to her on deck she was restless & bored—When we bathed she rested on shore—when we were about to leave she bathed. At lunch she moved plates, fumbled with cigarette apparatus—always needing something—& remarked in childish or critical terms on the food: "Could I have a half lemon—I can't get anything from these slices—this is goodie—shall I try some coffee?" Otherwise she was out of the conversation & I was determined that the meal should not go by without any topics to be discussed & so worked hard in spite of interruptions from both Cecile & Greta. We talked of movies of today—Greta silent. She did not even know that Jeanne Moreau had made a film of Mata Hari. She had never heard of Antonioni, Fellini, Richardson,* or the like.

She remained stubbornly silent while the pros & cons of Dietrich were discussed. She took no part in an explanation of expressionist painting. When Jeanne Marie asked the date of Augus-

*Tony Richardson (1928–91) had recently directed *Tom Jones.*

> tus, Greta said: "I know 'nuttin.' " One sees that those endless days & evenings doing nothing have resulted in negation. She has never let any new impression or influence come into hand for more than a moment in the last 20 years. The funny stories of Chaplin she tells me are those she told me when I first met her. She bothers not to learn the names of even the people she has perforce got to see. I doubt very much if she has even learnt Jeanne Marie's name & refers to her as "this lady." . . .
>
> The evening sunlight fading to make the colours burn more & more melodiously was a pleasure to us all. Greta did not seem to notice the magical effects—of which she in pink with pink and white striped trousers became a part & in this light she became as beautiful as her legend. But it is a legend that does no longer exist in reality. If she had been a real character she would have left the legend, developed a new life—new interests & knowledge. As it is after 30 years she has not changed except outwardly—& even the manner & personality has dated. Poor old Marlene Dietrich, with her dye & face lift & new career as singer—with all her nonsense—is a live & vital person—cooking for her grandchildren & being on the go*—That is much preferable to this other non giving, non living phantom of the past.[8]

A further incident occurred on this cruise when Cecil, Garbo, and Friedrich Ledebur discovered a deserted cove in which to swim:

> No sooner had we arrived, stripped naked and stepped into the sun than a distant boat roared towards us. It was a funny scene, Greta trying to get to shore in time on her behind; I, bare assed, walked out. Friedrich was marooned with his white patch of skin and huge hanging balls an embarrassment to him and all who would study the unusual sight.**[9]

*Dietrich made her concert singing debut at the Sahara in Las Vegas in 1953. The next year she took London by storm, and thereafter she toured the world, almost invariably accompanied by the composer Burt Bacharach. She continued performing until she fell off a stage in Sydney, Australia, in 1975 and broke her thigh. She died in Paris on May 6, 1992, aged ninety.

**Friedrich Ledebur had endured several adventures with Garbo and was no great admirer of her whims. She used to like to walk naked, but he had to walk in

Garbo toyed with the idea of going to London with Cecil after the cruise but finally opted for returning to New York.

On September 18, Garbo passed her sixtieth birthday. The event was celebrated in the press with a profile by Hollis Alpert, author of *The Barrymores.* He penned his piece while Garbo was traveling in Europe but noted that "hundreds of New Yorkers have been granted a glimpse of her still haunting face" as she advanced on her walks through the Fifties and Sixties, sometimes going as far west as Sixth Avenue. But to write with any authority of her life was no easy matter:

> She becomes so alarmed and disturbed by the slightest breach of her inner security by her friends that they now flutter off like frightened pigeons at my suggestion they say anything about her, no matter how complimentary."[10]

Alpert did succeed in gleaning some information, though. He learned that a trust fund that had matured in 1952 was giving her an annual income of $100,000, that she was often entertained by Countess Bernadotte, and that Richard Griffith, who worked at the Museum of Modern Art, was a friend and often screened her films for her. She had given up visiting exhibitions since she was spotted at an exhibition of Mexican Indian art and ended up crouched in a dimly lit replica of an Indian cave. She sometimes weekended with Eustace Seligman* in Greenwich, Connecticut; she stayed in Barbados with Goddard Lieber-

---

front and if a peasant approached, he warned her and she dressed. After two such incidents he got bored. The next creature he saw was a mule. He gave the same warning. She was furious, but he said, "Oh, I thought perhaps you didn't want a mule to see you."

Another time he accompanied Garbo, Salka Viertel, and one other person on a camel trip. Garbo refused to pay her share or to sign the photo their guides produced: "I'm invited. I don't pay." Ledebur was furious: "You're invited? By someone with a tenth of your money." He made it clear that if she didn't do both things, she would be left in the desert. She did both (Count Ledebur to author, August 22, 1982).

*Eustace Seligman, a partner of the law firm of Sullivan and Cromwell, described as "a social registerite known for his fondness for celebrities." He attended Schlee's funeral.

son and indulged a taste for rum cocktails. Jane Gunther was persuaded to reveal, "She has a poetic magic, so difficult to describe, and all one knows is that one wants this in one's life," before retreating into the customary silence of discretion.[11]

On the day of her sixtieth birthday, Garbo was not to be found in any of her regular New York haunts. Allan Elsner, the proprietor of the Swedish Book Nook on Eighty-first Street, was asked for news of her. He said he had not seen her in months, adding: "But the last time I saw her she looked fine." "Does she seem happy?"—"As happy as ever."—"Is she lonely?"—"I don't know."[12] There were no parties, but the Swedish consul general sent her flowers. On such unenlightening snippets were the American public fed.

Cecil returned to England in order to try to paint more seriously. In December he received a typed letter from Garbo, saying she was back in Manhattan, apologizing for not having come to England, wishing him a happy Christmas, and saying she would write again.[13]

But Garbo did not write again. Their friendship had dwindled away.

CHAPTER 16

MERCEDES: "I'M SITTING HERE ALL ALONE."

Mercedes suffered considerably in her later years. In the spring of 1961, she had undergone serious brain surgery, leaving her feeling "anything but well."[1] She sold her diamonds to pay her medical expenses. Her last home was a two-room flat at 315 East Sixty-eighth Street, with the kitchen in an alcove at the end of the living room. She shared it with Poppy Kirk's cat, Linda.

During this time Mercedes made friends with William McCarthy, the curator of the Rosenbach Museum in Philadelphia, consigning her collection of papers to his care. At one time a dealer offered her ten thousand dollars for her Garbo letters, but, despite her financial difficulties, she declined and stipulated that they would be sealed at the Rosenbach until ten years after Garbo's death. When Abram Poole died at Old

Lyme, Connecticut, in April 1961, her allowance from his estate was frozen for a while, and she asked McCarthy for a small advance on the papers she was sending. But when McCarthy was ill, she returned his check, feeling he needed it more than she did.

At that time, September 1961, she took up with a young actress suffering from tuberculosis, who could not get work because she was British and who had been reduced to working in a Chock Full o'Nuts coffee shop for thirty-eight dollars a week. This girl was considered somewhat unworthy by Mercedes's friends.

Cecil remained attentive, writing her regular letters inquiring about her health. Mercedes was very much up and down. In December 1961 she wrote:

> I see so many people round me ageing and so many people ill. It makes me feel it would be wise to die at the age of 45 and I wish that I had. Only Anita Loos still seems spry and Gloria Swanson—they seem to be the eternal young ones!![2]

In the early months of 1963 Mercedes was ill, and the following year she underwent a painful leg operation, followed by fever. In a letter to William McCarthy, she clarified her thoughts about the papers lodged at the Rosenbach. The Garbo letters were a gift, and even McCarthy was not allowed to read them. She worried about Dietrich's letters: "Marlene is becoming such a world-wide figure . . ."[3] She explained that she felt bad letting these letters out of her hands but confessed she had not the heart or courage to burn them. She continued:

> So it seemed a god-sent moment when you took them. I only hope, as the years go on, and you are no longer there, that they will be *respected* and *protected* from the eyes of vulgar people.[4]

One of her most loyal friends during this period was the sculptress Malvina Hoffman. The two shared the business of trying to make ends meet and helping others when they could. Mercedes also relied heavily on William McCarthy for friendship and the occasional handout:

> Certainly as we grow older life becomes increasingly sad and difficult. I never so much realized this when I was young. But now I do. I see in my own life how many things have changed during the past years. Friends, either by death or otherwise, have gone out of one's life. This is why I cherish so much your friendship and Malvina's too, who has gone through so many years with me.[5]

McCarthy committed suicide in 1965, and Malvina Hoffman died in 1966.

Ever adventurous, Mercedes had become a friend of Andy Warhol's and regularly shared Thanksgiving with him and his friends. Warhol once met Garbo at a picnic with Mercedes and presented her with a drawing of a butterfly. In due course she crumpled it up, but he rescued it and had his mother write on it, "Crumpled butterfly by Greta Garbo."[6] Through Mercedes, Andy Warhol got in touch with the English actress Isabel Jeans,* a great favorite of Cecil's. Then aged seventy, Jeans wrote to Mercedes:

> Your friend Andy Warhol has sent me some records of "The Twist." They really are *something.* It was so sweet & charming of him. They are very amusing to play & people like to hear them, but Heavens the noise. The world has gone mad.[7]

Another friend was Kieran Tunney,** an author and playwright. A long-suffering man who allowed actresses such as Dame Sybil Thorndike to phone him at any hour of the night, he was a natural friend for Mercedes. He felt sorry for her, seemingly deserted by the world she had once known and relying only on young actresses who made friends with her in the hope of meeting Garbo. Presently he had become her "walker." She rang him night and morning, and he took her out to parties. In turn she took him to visit faithful old friends or some of the

*Isabel Jeans (1891–1985), versatile actress seen often on the West End stage. She met Mercedes in Hollywood in the 1930s. Cecil dressed her as Aunt Alicia in *Gigi* (1958).

**Kieran Tunney, author of *Tallulah—Darling of the Gods, Interrupted Autobiography,* and several plays, including a long-unstaged play, *Aurora.*

young actresses—"usually torture of the most pretentious, self-consciously Bohemian kind."[8]

But in the end even the all-tolerant Tunney despaired of her. He found her demands on his friendship "excessive."[9] She claimed she was neglected; he marveled that her celebrated friendships had lasted as long as they had:

> If sleep failed her, she thought nothing of calling one at two or three in the morning to discuss the meaning of existence, sleeping and waking, or a tract on a Far Eastern religion that she believed could change all our lives. And if one was invited to Southampton or Bridgehampton for a weekend Mercedes expected one to arrange that she too was included even if the host had never met or heard of her; and if and when one succeeded in such an awkward task, it was quite on the cards she might sulk for the entire weekend if the household couldn't or wouldn't cope with whatever diet she was on at that particular time![10]

Tunney finally reduced seeing Mercedes to a strict minimum, "aiming to retain my sanity."[11]

A younger friend, Wilder Luke Burnap, remained devoted to Mercedes, and his mother visited her almost every day in the last year of her life. Burnap adored her despite her occasional lapses into nastiness. She told him many stories of her life, and one day he asked her, "Mercedes, what is your secret?" She replied, "I think there is no secret, because I'm sitting here all alone."[12]

In April 1966, Cecil telephoned Mercedes and found her "dying by slow degrees." She mumbled that she thought she was dying but "just out of cantankerousness" was fighting to live. Aware that the end was not far off, Cecil prevailed upon Garbo to send her—at the very least—a postcard. Garbo's reaction was hostile: "Why must you bring up such a subject? I've got enough to cope with. I'm in trouble enough. I can't tell you what it is.* But it's enough! I don't want any more troubles."[13]

Mercedes lingered on until May 9, 1968, dying at 315 East Sixty-

*A relative of Garbo's was ill in the hospital, and she was going to see him every day.

eighth Street "after a long illness." Described in her obituary as "poet, playwright and scenarist," it was noted that she was "a regal-looking woman of Spanish descent," "a close friend of Greta Garbo and Marlene Dietrich," and "a feminist."[14] The funeral was private. Cecil recorded his own epitaph in his diaries:

> So the tragic Mercedes has succumbed at last. Perhaps it is nearly ten years ago that she was stricken—& while near to death vowed that she would not give in. Her characteristic stubbornness has seen her through many years of pain, illness & sadness. I am only sorry that the pain—& the expense—& the fortitude has had to continue so long.
>
> I cannot be sorry at her death. I am only sorry that she should have been so unfulfilled as a character. In her youth she showed zest & originality. She was one of the most rebellious & brazen of Lesbians. She married—a nice man—a bad painter (Abram Poole) but refused to be known as Mrs. She was always M. de A. (never "Miss"). She managed not only to make a beeline for all the women who interested her, but by some fluke—or some genius gift of her own, became intimate friends. She—I'm not sure of the facts, informed Maude Adams that her house was on fire; she became part of her life subsequently, as she did of Isadora Duncan, Marie Doro, Nazimova, oh countless women.
>
> She had excellent, severe Spanish taste—in her furnishings & in her interiors using only black & white—& was never willing to accept the vulgarity of so many American standards. She was strikingly un-American in her black tricorn & buckled shoes, highwayman coat & jet black dyed hair.
>
> She was always about to write a play for Eva Le Gallienne, or deliver herself of a novel or a thesis on Indian philosophy, but her sole publication—an autobiography—was a big disappointment. She became rather idiotic, petty & petulant. Looking for grievances, she found them.
>
> She managed to make it difficult for friends, impossible for her lovers. She became ill, she became poor, but she never became old. She had a gallantry that could be recognised in her sprightly step. When I telephoned to enquire if I could come to see her in her bed of illness she said: "It would give you too much of a

shock. You see the pain has been so great behind the eye that it has entirely turned my hair white."

Several times I tried to cajole G. to relent, to send a message to the pining, still adoring Mercedes. "I have enough troubles without that!" I had the idea of sending flowers to Mercedes & pretending they came from G. Would that I had done that. It would never have been discovered. As it is, after suffering the horrors of New York hospital treatment at the hands of rude nurses & doctors alike, all Mercedes's money has gone. She became threadbare. She pined to leave the vulgarity of Hollywood & New York to visit Europe once more. But she had not the wherewithal—or the money. Now, without a kind word from the woman she loved more than any of the many women in her life, Mercedes has gone to a lonely grave. I am relieved that her long drawn out unhappiness has at last come to an end.[15]

CHAPTER 17

CECIL SELLS HIS STORY

Cecil had been publishing volumes of his diaries since 1961. *The Wandering Years,* volume one, was about his early life to 1939, and *The Years Between* took him through the war years to 1944. The dilemma of the next volume was whether to publish details of his relationship with Garbo or to omit it completely. Cecil's natural instinct was to publish everything, and in this particular case he felt it was an important part of his life, the omission of which would falsify the record. On the other hand, having been close to Garbo, he was perfectly aware what the consequences would be. The fate of Mercedes loomed large before him.

It was partly Garbo's treatment of Mercedes that persuaded Cecil to publish. "I feel angry that she never made a gesture of forgiveness towards Mercedes," he wrote in September 1968, "and I know she would not give any generous help to me if I were in need of it. Perhaps I am just manufacturing a situation wherein I would feel it possible to go ahead and be damned."[1]

Cecil had completed a typescript by the summer of 1967, and in January 1968 he signed a contract with Weidenfeld & Nicolson. In due course the proofs were corrected, and the first extracts leaked into the American press in November 1971. *McCall's* published an excerpt, and *Newsweek* picked it up. In his diary, Cecil tried to come to terms with what he had done:

> This piece is written as catharsis. Perhaps if I get some of it down on paper I will feel freer to go about everyday existence without a care. As it is I am suffering those awful qualms that send one's bowels panting for release & one's stomach positively aches. Bindie Lambton,* the angel, has telephoned from London to send her love, to say she knows I must be suffering, but that I must not explain or complain, that things will get worse before they are better. . . .
>
> Now that this bombshell has exploded, all my comfortings about a seven day wonder—& what is an article in [a] newspaper anyway? seem quite ineffectual. I am disturbed—& deeply so. I know it could have been avoided—& I am to blame, but I decided to be brave & damn all—but now the crunch has come it is difficult to know what is best to clear the matter from my mind. If I continue with my garden sculpture the figure becomes the embodiment of my troubles—if I start a painting in the studio likewise that becomes part of the general malaise.
>
> It is a feeling that used to dog me more often in early life. When I had published a photograph that I knew shouldn't be published there was an outcry & God how I suffered. Lately perhaps because I have grown more careful these crises seem further apart—mercifully—for I believe in spite of experiences with the press, I am more sensitive & easily upset than ever before. . . .
>
> The awful feelings of guilt & anxiety continued to dog me. I

*Viscountess Lambton, niece of Freda Dudley Ward, married to the Conservative politician Lord Lambton.

Garbo with Cecile de Rothschild in Paris, 1979.

had headaches & felt very rotten. I couldn't sleep without waking to think of some further detail in my Diary as published in *McCall's* that would offend Greta or a great number of friends. Then when I thought the excitement had died down I opened the *Telegraph* & saw a photograph of Greta & myself. Oh no! My stomach went to water. I rushed to the loo. . . .

Still worrying—but a bit more cheerful. Eileen* telephoned early the next day. There was some very good news in the post. A formal letter offering me a knighthood. Oh! this was almost too much to take in—I felt this poor human brain was at bursting point. The[se] last days the cup has been overfilled. Of course this was very pleasant. Secretly I had hoped for such an honour for many years. Although knights come down low in the scale it would be a great feather in an industrialist's cap to be thus rewarded. It is not as a result of having friends at court (Weidenfeld with Wilson) or being gradually upgraded in some huge organisation (Fred [Ashton] at Cov. Garden Opera house). This was a question of "Alone I done it." I was sad my mother had not known of it—or even my Aunts Cada & Jessie. But I felt suddenly a good deal more elderly & eminent. Still it is a very nice tribute—& I feel I have deserved it—not for my talent—but for character, tenacity, energy—& wide reaching efforts.

Yet now that it has happened (or will it be taken away from me because of the Garbo article?) it is strange how little the elevation occupies my thoughts. The day goes by just as usual—& just every now & then I think "How impressive" then I think of other knights, Redgrave, Rattigan, Helpmann & then I'm not quite so impressed. But I am happy about it—& must try to enjoy it as the culmination of a long span of work & I must enjoy the fact that a lot of people are going to be very happy about it too.[2]

Cecil's knighthood was announced on January 1, 1972, and in due course he went to Buckingham Palace to be dubbed by the Queen. Thereafter matters were less easy. From the moment he published his Garbo revelations, he was never quite sure when some old friend might

*Eileen Hose (1919–87), Beaton's secretary from 1953 to 1980 and then his literary executor.

turn on him or cut him dead. One of those who were displeased with him was his hostess on the yacht, Cecile de Rothschild. On a Connaissance des Arts tour of North Germany in May 1972, Garbo's friend weighed into the attack: "Let me ask you how much you made out of Garbo on the *McCall's, Times, Oggi* etc world circulation. I mean how much with *Vogue* photographs *et tout ça* during the past twenty years have you made?" Cecil tried to give a straight reply. He reckoned it to be about £4,000. The baronne rebuked him:

> "Not bad is it? I mean I wouldn't mind being given £4,000 to spend on the kitchen." She laughed that nasal choking voice. "Not bad eh? For someone who didn't need the publicity. Even Stokowski didn't sell his story to the papers."*[3]

The Happy Years was published in London in June, and at first Cecil refused to read the reviews. There was a considerable amount of attendant publicity. By and large, the reviewers got the point of what Cecil was trying to do—not so much to boast that he had had an affair with Garbo as to give a portrait of her, using all his considerable skills as an observer. Of those reviews that mattered, the important ones were by Beverley Nichols and Cyril Connolly. Beverley Nichols wrote in *The Spectator:*

> This is either a true story or it is nothing. I believe it to be true from the first line to the last. . . . Beaton has given Garbo a new dimension and greatly increased her stature in the history of our times.[4]

Cyril Connolly, a more distinguished critic, reviewed the book in *The Sunday Times:*

> I do not think he has behaved any worse than a painter who exhibits an astonishingly life-like portrait, without permission, of an *incommunicata* sitter.[5]

*According to Mercedes, he did send reports to newspapers.

But there were hostile voices too, such as E. S. Turner, writing in *The Listener:*

> To this reviewer the picture of Mr Beaton fondling the vertebrae of *La Divina* is as near-sacrilegious as that of Mr Eric Linklater bussing Botticelli's *Primavera* when he found her in her wartime hiding-place.*[6]

And old rivalries die hard, as was proved by Auberon Waugh, writing two reviews, the first for *Harper's & Queen,* the second for the *Chicago Tribune:*

> For all that it has plainly been most carefully revised and edited, and for all the fact that it seems studied and over-cautious in places, this volume is warmly recommended for its account of some dismal years of British history, most engagingly told.[7]

A year later, Waugh was more savage with the American edition of the book:

> The saddest and most bizarre part of the Beaton story comes in his description of a love affair which apparently blossomed between himself and Greta Garbo. As these two social and emotional waifs act out their chosen parts—he as the flamboyant but sensitive extrovert in the throes of an ideal passion, she as the startled fawn—we see the Beaton predicament in a hideous, cold light: first we see that beyond the affectation and the false values there is an emotional desert of sadness and loneliness; then we see that beyond the sadness and loneliness there is an object of the cruelest and most unutterable comedy.[8]

The latter review hurt Cecil when he read it during a particularly grueling publicity tour in the spring of 1973. But before that the ever-nervous photographer had worse nightmares to endure. He began

*Eric Linklater (1899–1974), novelist and playwright, worked in the Directorate of Public Relations, War Office, 1941–45.

to see Garbo look-alikes everywhere, on airplanes and in the streets. This became an obsession. In his later diaries he devoted much space to an analysis of what he called "my crime," and though he declared steadfastly that given the chance to reconsider publication he would still have gone ahead, there were periods of deep remorse.

One of his worse moments came in Venice in the late summer of 1973. He was walking with an American friend, the art dealer Sam Green, and saw Valentina Schlee approaching, wearing dark glasses:

> This was the first time I'd encountered her since the publication of the Diaries with so many allusions to the little man (her husband) in them. Would she slap my face? Would she give me the cut direct? We passed nearer and nearer. She eyed me coldly. As we passed one another I very exaggeratedly doffed my straw hat. "Oh my Darlink Cessaille. Oh my Heavens!" We kissed, laughed, made banal observations. Was she having a holiday, I asked. "Are there any holidays any more?" she asked.[9]

Sam Green commented, "Cecil really thought she was going to strike him."[10]

Garbo never commented publicly, nor did she resort to her lawyer, but Cecil lived his last years under a burden of guilt. He took some comfort from a description of Garbo sent to him by Patrick O'Higgins, an Upper East Side neighbor. He described Garbo shopping at a nearby Italian greengrocer's in April 1973:

> She had two bags in which she put the vegetables she was buying. She wore dark glasses but was full of smiles and everyone very solicitous of her though respectful of her wish for anonymity.[11]

This image, a little reminiscent of Katharine Hepburn in the opening scenes of the film *The Madwoman of Chaillot,* was almost Cecil's last of the woman who had so long preoccupied him. But there was to be one final meeting.

For some years Cecil had been suffering blinding headaches. In July 1974 he suffered a severe stroke that prevented the use of his right hand, impaired his memory for names, and caused him to lose his former elegant poise. He fought to overcome his difficulties and gradually learned to write and draw with his left hand and take photographs.

In October 1975, Garbo went to England with Sam Green, who was at this time her most faithful companion. Sam often traveled with Cecil too and was determined to cheer him up by taking Garbo to visit him. "I figured it would do him good," he said. "And she wouldn't suffer from the experience either."[12] The pair reached Salisbury station, whereupon Garbo panicked and began to speculate on the danger that Cecil might have arranged to have a photographer up a tree: "But he'll use it in some way."[13] Sam announced that he was certainly going to Broadchalke. She had no choice but to go along.

Cecil was delighted to see her, and Garbo snuggled up to him, sitting on his knee, her gray hair tied back with a bootlace. But as Cecil made his slow progress to the dining room, Garbo turned to his secretary, Eileen, and commented, "Well, I couldn't have married him, could I? Him being like this!"[14]

The next day, as Garbo prepared to leave for London, Cecil made as if to hug her, saying, "Greta, the love of my life!" Deeply embarrassed, Garbo spotted the visitors book. She shunned the embrace and broke the rule of a lifetime, signing her name in full. She made sure she never saw Cecil again.

When Cecil went to New York in February 1978, he tried many times to reach Garbo on the telephone, but there was never an answer. This saddened him greatly. On January 18, 1980, a few days after his seventy-sixth birthday, he died at Broadchalke. Garbo sent no flowers to bid him farewell.

CHAPTER 18

GARBO: "I MUST BE HOME BEFORE SEVEN."

Valentina and Garbo lived in the same building on East Fifty-second Street, a few floors apart, for twenty-five years after Georges Schlee died. The Schlee apartment and the Garbo one were striking in their similarity, with paneled walls and copies of Louis XV and Louis XVI furniture and candelabra. Certain artists were represented in both places. Garbo had a few gouaches by Dimitri Bouchène, the Russian stage designer, who lived in Paris and was one of the last survivors of the World of Art group. Valentina had over thirty of his oils, pastels, and gouaches. Both women possessed works by Sergei Soudeikine, Edward Molyneux, Adolphe Monticelli (Garbo's only "in the manner of"); their libraries, consisting mainly of designer-installed leather-bound books that had little hope of being read, contained the same Atlantic edition of H. G. Wells's works

(New York, 1924–27). Georges Schlee would have felt perfectly at home in either apartment. Indeed, he had felt perfectly at home in either apartment.

An understanding had been established among the building's porters that if one madame buzzed to come down, the other madame must wait. Garbo liked to go out by day, Madame Schlee by night. Indeed, Garbo used to say, "I must be home before seven, before Madame Schlee goes out."[1] The theory was that they would never meet, but of course from time to time they did. Sam Green recalled walking home with Garbo one evening, a little after seven, and seeing Valentina walking toward them, looking defiant. Garbo turned away. It was an uncomfortable encounter.

Valentina retained certain friends, such as Gloria Vanderbilt, but her old age was rather lonely. She lived in New York all winter and, maintaining the habit of a lifetime, spent her summers in Venice in a large suite at the Cipriani. The line there was that people "scattered when they saw her coming." Her intensity, her eccentricity, her exaggerated Russian manner and way of talking of religion and spooky, superstitious things held little general appeal. At times she was bad-tempered and quite unfriendly.

In the spring of 1970, Cecil had made the pilgrimage to see Valentina in the big fourteenth-floor apartment with its views uptown and downtown and across the East River. Her drawing room was grand and spacious, with about eight large windows facing the Pepsi-Cola sign that takes up such a prominent place on the river landscape. Leather-bound books lined one wall, some of which were turned face-out to display the motif on the front. Nothing in the apartment had changed since Schlee's death. His pens still lay next to the blotter in his study, and a profusion of photographs was on display: snapshots of Valentina with Noël Coward and the Duchess of Windsor, as well as with Rex Harrison, who lived on the floor immediately above.

Cecil left a detailed account of his visit:

> Went to Valentina's apartment in order to get from her one of her theatrical dresses for my museum collection [at the Victoria and Albert]. I have not been to the apartment for 20 years, partly because of the Schlee situation & Garbo—& only because Valen-

tina is one of the worst cracking [?] egocentric maniacs. Nowadays in retirement few people put up with her—so she was ready to give me all.

At first I was staggered to see how like Garbo's apartment this is. Maybe it's the same shape (it's in the same building) but the flush of overdecoration is the same—the bad ormolu mixed with grand Louis XV. The eczema of flower paintings (bad on walls) & it's really kitsch. However the shock was Valentina herself. Her teeth have been replaced by others, her nose looks fatter—her eyes smaller—she is colourless now—whereas she had once created a great effect of beauty. "Darrlink, do you like my hair?" (She can't speak English yet.) "I wash it myself. I cut it—You feel it." . . . She . . . talks with over-emphasis of the hands—about the Windsors—& all the least interesting subjects. She eulogised an English-French style chair—she put the lights on for her Monticellis—then she showed me a huge hibiscus tree. It had been given to her when small by Maggie Teyte in exchange for a dress for *Pelleas & Melisande.* She had nurtured it with vitamins—new earth—washing—every sort of care—& she said that each time she returned from abroad it put out flowers to welcome her. It had put one out for me today.

It is remarkable how she manages to preserve her Russian way of life in this very difficult period. Somehow she still has a couple of maids to look after her—but otherwise she is very much alone—& she treats every small event as a great milestone. I liked very much the fuss that she made in supplying me with a drink of tonic water. The amount of ice to be carefully judged—& to the maid "Now please go & cut a nice slice of lemon." Nothing offhand—great service taken over everything. In her own way there is no denying she is an artist.

Then she brought out a grey chiffon wisp of a dress she had made for Tammy Grimes in *High Spirits.** It was a masterpiece of cut & of mathematics. "It's Chinese," she said as she fingered the seams. I realised that she believes completely in her talent being god-given & that it must be kept sacrosanct—& not

*Tammy Grimes starred in *High Spirits,* a musical version of *Blithe Spirit,* in New York in 1964.

> abused—some manager had recently rung her for 5 costumes to be made in 4 days. She gave him the most appalling rebuke. When, having denuded herself of all but a pair of black knickers & a bra—she displayed the beauty of the dress in its manifold excellencies, she then proceeded to pack it up for me. She was at once a marvel—the old but delicate hands treated the silk folds with such exquisite care & gestures. It was a work of art to see her wrapping the wisp in some rather crumpled pieces of silk paper. "They are not new but they are clean." This folded that way, that folded this way—up & over—she was leaning forward for a considerable time in an agonisingly painful position (she has lumbago) but she noticed nothing except what she was doing—preparing a work of art for posterity. As she maneuvered the final gesture with the baby-like sleeves folded into a little roll, she leant down & kissed it. "Good-bye," she said. It was really very touching—because absolutely genuine.[2]

Ten years later, Valentina met Diana Vreeland at Gloria Vanderbilt's and invited her to dinner. Mrs. Vreeland duly went, and recalled that it was all very formal. There were lots of toasts and grinnings, raisings of glasses at one another, but not much conversation. Mrs. Vreeland's conclusion was harsh: "It was kind of hard to see how the twenty-four hours went round," she said.[3] But by this time Valentina was well into her eighties and was declining into illness and confusion. In the summer of 1984, she was found wandering in Venice and only just escaped being taken to a hospital. Her Venice days over, she remained in New York thereafter, enduring various spells in hospitals but always coming home to East Fifty-second Street. A victim of Parkinson's disease, she was attended by a series of nurses. In extreme old age she used to go down and sit in the lobby, observing the few comings and goings in the building. She died on September 14, 1989, said to be aged ninety. Her funeral was held on the morning of September 18, by some strange irony Garbo's eighty-fourth birthday.

Valentina was a largely forgotten figure, but she was given a good send-off in *The New York Times.* Bill Blass was one who paid tribute to her: "She made wonderful clothes but nobody looked as well in them as she did."[4]

Shortly after Valentina's death, the elevator attendant had seen Garbo leaving her apartment. He broke the news to her that Madame Schlee was dead. Garbo burst into tears.

She was already a lame, if defiant, old lady. In the months that followed, the contents of Valentina's apartment were sold at Christie's East, and increasingly grim photographs were taken of Garbo on her occasional excursions out for medical treatment. Seven months after Valentina's death, on April 15, 1990, Garbo died in New York Hospital.

SOURCES

Principal Published Sources

Acosta, Mercedes de. *Here Lies the Heart.* New York: Reynal and Company, 1960.

Bainbridge, John. *Garbo.* Garden City, N.Y.: Doubleday, 1955.

Beaton, Cecil. *The Wandering Years: Diaries, 1922–1939.* Boston: Little, Brown, 1961.

———. *The Years Between: Diaries, 1939–1944.* London: Weidenfeld & Nicolson, 1965.

———. *Cecil Beaton: Memoirs of the 40's.* New York: McGraw-Hill, 1972.

———. *The Strenuous Years: Diaries, 1948–1955.* London: Weidenfeld & Nicolson, 1973.

———. *The Restless Years: Diaries, 1955–1963.* London: Weidenfeld & Nicolson, 1976.

———. *The Parting Years: Diaries, 1963–1974.* London: Weidenfeld & Nicolson, 1978.

Buckle, Richard, ed. *Self-Portrait with Friends: The Selected Diaries of Cecil Beaton, 1922–1974.* New York: Times Books, 1979.

Riva, Maria. *Marlene Dietrich.* New York: Knopf, 1992.

Vickers, Hugo. *Cecil Beaton: A Biography.* Boston: Little, Brown, 1986.

Viertel, Salka. *The Kindness of Strangers.* New York: Holt, Rinehart and Winston, 1969.

Unpublished Sources

Sir Cecil Beaton: The papers of Sir Cecil Beaton are housed in the library of his old college, St. John's College, Cambridge. These comprise the 145 volumes of manuscript diaries, the letters from his family and friends, and certain office papers. A few diaries and letters are sealed at the discretion of his literary executors.

Mercedes de Acosta: The majority of the papers of Mercedes de Acosta were sold by Miss de Acosta to the Rosenbach Museum and Library, Philadelphia, Pennsylvania. These include four typescript drafts of *Here Lies the Heart.* The author has quoted from two of them.

The following papers at the Rosenbach were also consulted: the film script of *Desperate;* the letters received by Mercedes de Acosta from Cecil Beaton, Marlene Dietrich, Isadora Duncan, Pundit Ram Gopal, Gayelord Hauser, Isabel Jeans, Poppy Kirk, Eva Le Gallienne, and Ona Munson; the letters of Mercedes de Acosta to Richard Buckle and William McCarthy; various press cuttings relating to Mercedes de Acosta and Greta Garbo.

In the course of general research, other correspondence was examined, including the letters of Maude Adams, Gladys Calthrop, Lady Diana Cooper, Elsie de Wolfe, Marie Doro, Arnold Genthe, Loren McIver, Elisabeth Marbury, Raymond Mortimer, Marjorie Moss, Abram Poole, Natacha Rambova, Alice B. Toklas, and Hope Williams.

The letters written by Greta Garbo to Mercedes de Acosta are sealed until the year 2000.

There is a box of the papers of Mercedes de Acosta (including her address books) in the University Library, Georgetown University, Washington, D.C.

The Countess of Avon: The letters from Cecil Beaton to the Countess of Avon and her letters to him are the property of Lady Avon.

Hugo Vickers: Many quotations in this book come from the author's own diaries (kept since 1976). He also owns the letters written by Cecil Beaton to Hal Burton.

NOTES

Chapter 1. Friends and Lovers

1. Anita Loos to Cecil Beaton, 29 September 1932.
2. Ibid.
3. Mercedes de Acosta, *Here Lies the Heart* (New York: Reynal & Company, 1960), p. 220.
4. Ibid., p. 224.
5. Mercedes de Acosta, second manuscript, p. 345.
6. Mercedes de Acosta, *Desperate* (MGM script, January 1932), p. 16.
7. Mercedes de Acosta, *Here Lies the Heart,* p. 233.
8. Cecil Beaton, *The Glass of Fashion* (London: Weidenfeld & Nicolson, 1954), p. 120.
9. Mercedes de Acosta, second manuscript, p. 70.
10. Mercedes de Acosta, *Here Lies the Heart,* p. 39.
11. Mercedes de Acosta, early manuscript, p. 130.
12. "Elsa Maxwell's Party Line," *New York Post,* 20 April 1943.
13. Mercedes de Acosta, first manuscript, p. 29.
14. Ibid., pp. 29–30.
15. Ibid., p. 30.
16. Ibid., p. 32.
17. Ibid., pp. 33–34.
18. Ibid., p. 46.

19. Mercedes de Acosta, second manuscript, p. 186.
20. Ibid.
21. Ibid., p. 221.
22. Ibid., p. 338.
23. Alice B. Toklas to Anita Loos, 8 May 1960, quoted in *Staying On Alone—The Letters of Alice B. Toklas,* edited by Edward Burns (New York: Random House, 1974), p. 319.
24. Dorothy Fellowes-Gordon to author, 5 March 1991.
25. John Richardson to author, 12 February 1991.
26. Mercedes de Acosta, first manuscript, p. 64.
27. Isadora Duncan to Mercedes, 1927.
28. Mercedes de Acosta, *Here Lies the Heart,* pp. 131–32.
29. Ibid., p. 74.
30. Mercedes de Acosta, second manuscript, p. 123.
31. Dorothy Fellowes-Gordon to author, 7 August 1991.
32. Mercedes de Acosta, *Here Lies the Heart,* p. 142.
33. Ibid., p. 143.
34. Mercedes de Acosta, first manuscript, p. 207.
35. *New York Herald* [undated cutting, but April 1923].
36. Mercedes de Acosta, first manuscript, p. 175.
37. *New York Telegraph,* 21 June 1925.
38. Ibid.
39. Noël Coward, *Present Indicative* (London: Heinemann, 1937), pp. 254–55.
40. Dorothy Fellowes-Gordon to author, 5 March 1991.
41. Mercedes de Acosta, *Here Lies the Heart,* p. 165.
42. Mercedes de Acosta, first manuscript, p. 181.
43. Mercedes de Acosta, *Here Lies the Heart,* p. 162.
44. *Brooklyn Eagle,* quoted in Frederick Sands and Sven Broman, *The Divine Garbo* (New York: Grosset & Dunlap, 1979), p. 77.
45. Tallulah Bankhead, *Tallulah* (New York: Harper & Bros., 1952), p. 198.
46. David Parsons (nephew of Iris Tree) to Cecil Beaton, 18 March 1972.
47. Kenneth Tynan, *Curtains* (New York: Atheneum, 1961), p. 347.
48. Ibid., p. 350.
49. *New York Times,* 5 September 1965, Section VI, p. 26. Quoted in article by Hollis Alpert.
50. Mercedes de Acosta, *Here Lies the Heart,* p. 209.

51. Ibid., p. 213.
52. Ibid., pp. 213–14.
53. Ibid., p. 214.
54. Mercedes de Acosta, second manuscript, p. 351.
55. Ibid., p. 353.
56. Ibid., p. 357.
57. Mercedes de Acosta, *Here Lies the Heart,* p. 225.
58. Mercedes de Acosta, first manuscript, p. 361.
59. Ibid., pp. 364–65.
60. Ibid., pp. 373–74.
61. Mercedes de Acosta, *Here Lies the Heart,* p. 319.
62. Cecil Beaton, *The Wandering Years: Diaries, 1922–1939* (Boston: Little, Brown, 1961), p. 256.
63. Ibid.
64. Cecil Beaton, unpublished diary, March 1932; Hugo Vickers, *Cecil Beaton: A Biography* (Boston: Little, Brown, 1985), p. 159.
65. Cecil Beaton, *The Wandering Years,* p. 260.
66. Ibid., p. 259.
67. Ibid., p. 260.
68. Mercedes de Acosta to Cecil Beaton, winter 1933.

Chapter 2. Cecil

1. *St. Cyprian's Chronicle,* Christmas Term, 1916 (review by D.G.F.).
2. Ibid., Christmas Term, 1917 (review by J.H.T.E.).
3. Cecil Beaton, unpublished diary, 13 December 1928.
4. Ibid., 15 December 1928.
5. Ibid., 16 November 1928.
6. Mercedes de Acosta, *Here Lies the Heart,* p. 132; and Mercedes de Acosta, second manuscript, p. 228.
7. *Here Lies the Heart,* p. 132.
8. *Evening Telegraph,* 13 November 1929.
9. Cecil Beaton, unpublished diary, 6 January 1930.
10. Ibid.
11. Ibid.
12. Ibid., 2 February 1930.

13. Ibid.
14. Cecil Beaton, *The Book of Beauty* (London: Duckworth, 1930), pp. 46–48.
15. Cecil Beaton, unpublished diary, 9 October 1923.
16. Ibid., December 1966.
17. Ibid., 1 February 1930.
18. Ibid., 23 February 1930.
19. Dorothy Tennov, *Love and Limerence* (New York: Stein and Day, 1979), p. 91 (quoting Stendhal, *Love*).
20. Sir Peter Quennell to author, 21 October 1981.
21. Quoted in Vickers, *Cecil Beaton,* p. 162.
22. Sir John Gielgud to author, 13 November 1982.
23. Coral Browne to author, 24 February 1985.
24. *Sketch,* 25 July 1934.
25. Cecil Beaton, *Cecil Beaton's Scrapbook* (London: Batsford, 1937), pp. 53–55.

Chapter 3. Dietrich: "She has sex, but no particular gender."

1. Associated Press report (New York), 15 October 1932.
2. *Screen Book,* August 1933.
3. Mercedes de Acosta, *Here Lies the Heart,* p. 240.
4. *Daily Telegraph,* 7 May 1992.
5. Gaylyn Studlar, *In the Realm of Pleasure* (Urbana and Chicago: University of Illinois Press, 1988), p. 5.
6. David Shipman, *Movie Talk* (New York: St. Martin's Press, 1989), p. 58.
7. Kenneth Tynan, *The Sound of Two Hands Clapping* (New York: Holt, Rinehart and Winston, 1975), p. 84.
8. Mercedes de Acosta, *Here Lies the Heart,* pp. 241–42.
9. Mercedes de Acosta, second manuscript, p. 389.
10. Mercedes de Acosta, *Here Lies the Heart,* p. 242.
11. Mercedes de Acosta, second manuscript, p. 391.
12. Derived from Dietrich to Mercedes [unsigned], 15 September 1932.
13. Derived from Dietrich to Mercedes [undated, but September 1932].

14. Derived from Dietrich to Mercedes, 19 September 1932.
15. Mercedes to Dietrich [original in French], 8 October [or possibly November] 1932.
16. Derived from Dietrich to Mercedes, 4 October 1932.
17. Derived from Dietrich to Mercedes [undated, but 1932].
18. Mercedes de Acosta, *Here Lies the Heart,* p. 243.
19. Mercedes de Acosta, note in her address book (de Acosta papers, Georgetown University, Washington, D.C.).
20. Francis Wyndham to author, 17 December 1991.
21. Maddy Vegtel, "Blonde Venus and Swedish Sphinx," *Vanity Fair,* June 1934.
22. Derived from Dietrich to Mercedes, 14 May 1933.
23. Dietrich to Mercedes cable from *Europa,* 9:09 A.M., 17 May 1933.
24. Mercedes to Dietrich, ca. 1932, quoted in Maria Riva, *Marlene Dietrich* (New York: Knopf, 1992), p. 168.
25. Ibid., p. 180.
26. Salka Viertel, *The Kindness of Strangers* (New York: Holt, Rinehart and Winston, 1969), p. 142.
27. Ibid.
28. Ibid.
29. Ibid.
30. Ibid., p. 143.
31. Ibid., p. 152.
32. Mercedes de Acosta, *Here Lies the Heart,* p. 251.
33. Dietrich to Mercedes, cable from Versailles, 10 July 1933.
34. Mercedes de Acosta, second manuscript, p. 406.
35. Ibid., p. 415.
36. Salka Viertel, *The Kindness of Strangers,* p. 197.
37. Mercedes de Acosta, second manuscript, p. 390.
38. Ibid., reverse of p. 392.
39. Mercedes de Acosta, *Here Lies the Heart,* p. 261.
40. Mercedes de Acosta, second manuscript, p. 419.
41. Mercedes de Acosta, second manuscript, p. 421.
42. Mercedes de Acosta, *Here Lies the Heart,* p. 270; Mercedes de Acosta, second manuscript, p. 433.
43. Mercedes de Acosta, *Here Lies the Heart,* p. 272.
44. Gavin Lambert, *On Cukor* (New York: G. P. Putnam's Sons, 1972), p. 111.

45. George Cukor [said] to Cecil Beaton, 15 April 1963 (in Cecil Beaton, unpublished diary).
46. *New York Post,* 18 April 1960.
47. Mercedes de Acosta, *Here Lies the Heart,* p. 20.
48. Dietrich to Mercedes, ca. 1959.

Chapter 4. Stokowski, Ona Munson, Georges Schlee, and Valentina

1. Cecil Beaton, unpublished diary, 6 January 1934.
2. Irene Selznick to author, 26 May 1981.
3. Quoted in *New York Post,* 11 August 1954.
4. Ina Claire to author, 21 June 1983.
5. 1932 Hollywood clipping in Ona Munson's album, Billy Rose Theatre Collection, New York.
6. *Detroit Free Press,* 12 January 1925.
7. Mercedes de Acosta, *Here Lies the Heart,* p. 240.
8. Mercedes de Acosta, second manuscript, p. 487.
9. Ona Munson to Mercedes, 11 March 1940.
10. Ona Munson to Mercedes, 20 March 1940.
11. Mercedes de Acosta, *Here Lies the Heart,* p. 306.
12. "Elsa Maxwell's Party Line," *New York Post,* 20 April 1943.
13. Ibid.
14. Salka Viertel, *The Kindness of Strangers,* p. 300.
15. Gayelord Hauser to Mercedes, Beverly Hills, 9 November 1939 (de Acosta papers, Rosenbach Library).
16. *Time* magazine, 15 October 1964.
17. Salka Viertel, *The Kindness of Strangers,* p. 299.
18. Diana Vreeland to author, 10 February 1984.
19. Truman Capote to author, 28 June 1983.
20. Cleveland Amory with Earl Blackwell, *Celebrity Register* (New York: Harper & Row, 1963), p. 627.
21. Valentina Schlee to author, 11 February 1984.
22. Valentina Schlee to author, 17 August 1983.
23. Neil Letson, introduction to sale catalogue: "Property from the Estate of Valentina Schlee, New York," Christie's East, 30 January 1990.
24. Caroline Reynolds Milbank, *Couture—The Great Fashion Designers* (London: Thames & Hudson, 1985), p. 174.

25. Mercedes de Acosta, second manuscript, p. 303.
26. Neil Letson, Christie's sale catalogue.
27. Caroline Reynolds Milbank, *Couture,* p. 174.
28. Valentina Schlee to author, 17 August 1983.
29. Caroline Reynolds Milbank, *Couture,* p. 177.
30. Valentina Schlee to author, 11 February 1984.

Chapter 5. Garbo and Cecil: "My bed is very small and chaste."

1. Cecil Beaton, *Cecil Beaton: Memoirs of the 40's* (New York: McGraw-Hill, 1972), p. 105.
2. Cecil Beaton, unpublished diary, March 1946.
3. Cecil Beaton, *Memoirs of the 40's,* p. 105.
4. Cecil Beaton, unpublished diary, 1946.
5. Ibid., March 1946.
6. Cecil Beaton, *Memoirs of the 40's,* p. 121.
7. Cecil Beaton, miscellaneous lecture notes.
8. Cecil Beaton, *Memoirs of the 40's,* p. 121.
9. Paraphrased from a letter written by Garbo to Cecil, undated but certainly June 1946, and before 27 June. (The original letter was removed from Cecil's house in 1977 and sold in New York on 7 November 1990 for $1,700.)
10. Based on a cablegram from Garbo to Cecil, 28 June 1946. (Removed from his house in 1977 and put to auction in New York in November 1990.)
11. Based on a letter from Garbo to Cecil, 27 June 1946 (removed from his house in 1977 and put to auction in New York in November 1990).
12. Cecil Beaton, *Memoirs of the 40's,* p. 141.
13. *New York Times,* 7 July 1946.
14. Ibid., 18 July 1946.
15. Ibid., 4 September 1946.
16. *Picture Post,* 26 October 1946.
17. Cecil Beaton, unpublished diary, August 1946. A slightly rewritten version appears in *Memoirs of the 40's,* pp. 140–41.
18. Cecil Beaton, unpublished diary, August 1946.

19. Cecil Beaton to Clarissa Churchill, Hotel Mark Hopkins, San Francisco, 1 September 1946 (Countess of Avon papers).
20. Cecil Beaton, unpublished diary, September 1946.
21. Cecil Beaton to Clarissa Churchill, 16 September 1946 (Countess of Avon papers).
22. Cecil Beaton, unpublished diary, October 1946.
23. Cecil Beaton to Clarissa Churchill, 14 November 1946 (Countess of Avon papers).
24. Cecil Beaton, unpublished diary, November 1946.
25. Cecil to Garbo, 9 March 1947.
26. Ibid.
27. Cecil to Garbo, between 24 March and 9 April 1947.
28. Margaret Case to Cecil Beaton, one Tuesday in May 1947.
29. Cecil to Garbo, 15 May 1947.
30. Cecil to Garbo, 7 August 1947.
31. Cecil to Garbo, 12 August 1947.
32. Cecil to Garbo, 27 August 1947.
33. Ibid.
34. Duncan Fallowell, "David Herbert—Not Your Ordinary Tangerine" (*Quest* magazine, November 1990).
35. *The Noël Coward Diaries,* edited by Graham Payn and Sheridan Morley (Boston: Little, Brown, 1982), [9 September 1947], p. 91.
36. Cecil to Garbo, 29 September 1947.
37. Cecil to Garbo, 5 October 1947.

Chapter 6. Garbo and Cecil: The Affair

1. Truman Capote to author, 28 June 1983.
2. Cecil Beaton, unpublished diary, March 1944.
3. Ibid., 23 October 1947.
4. Ibid., 23 [28?] October 1947.
5. Ibid.
6. Ibid.
7. Ibid., 3 November 1947.
8. Ibid.
9. Ibid., 4 November 1947.

10. Ibid.
11. Ibid., ca. 19 November 1947.
12. Ibid.
13. Ibid., 1 December 1947.
14. Ibid.
15. Ibid., December 1947.
16. Ibid.
17. Ibid., 3 December 1947.
18. Ibid., 4 December 1947.
19. Ibid., 8 December 1947.
20. Ibid., 11 December 1947.
21. Ibid.
22. Ibid., 12 December 1947.
23. Ibid.
24. Ibid., 20 December 1947.
25. Ibid.
26. Cecil to Clarissa Churchill, 23 December 1947 (Countess of Avon papers).
27. Cecil Beaton, unpublished diary, 23 December 1947.
28. Ibid., 24 December 1947.
29. Ibid., 25 December 1947.
30. Ibid., 26 December 1947.
31. Ibid., December 1947.
32. Ibid., 31 December 1947.
33. Garbo to Cecil, hotel telephone message, 2 January 1948.
34. Cecil Beaton, unpublished diary, 3 January 1948.
35. Ibid.
36. Ibid.
37. Ibid., 4 January 1948.
38. Ibid., January 1948.
39. Ibid., 13 January 1948.
40. Ibid.
41. Ibid., February 1948.
42. Ibid.
43. Ibid.
44. Ibid., 6 February 1948.
45. Ibid.
46. Ibid.

47. Ibid., 21 February 1948.
48. Ibid., 23 February 1948.
49. Ibid.
50. Cecil to Garbo, 28 February 1948.
51. Garbo to Cecil, 28 February 1948.
52. Cecil Beaton, unpublished diary, 3 March 1948.
53. Ibid., 4 March 1948.
54. Ibid.
55. Ibid.
56. Ibid.
57. Ibid.
58. Ibid.
59. Ibid.
60. Ibid.
61. Ibid., 8 March 1948.
62. Ibid., 12 March 1948.
63. Ibid., 13 March 1948.
64. Ibid., March 1948.
65. Ibid.
66. Ibid.
67. Ibid.
68. Ibid., 15 March 1948.
69. Ibid.
70. Cecil to Garbo, 21 March 1948.

Chapter 7. The Broadchalke Letters

1. Kenneth Tynan, *Curtains* (London: Longmans, 1961), p. 349.
2. Unsigned telegram [but Garbo to Cecil], 31 March 1948.
3. Cecil to Garbo, 3 April 1948.
4. Cecil to Garbo, 4 April 1948.
5. Ibid.
6. Cecil to Garbo, between 4 and 18 April 1948.
7. Cecil to Garbo, 18 April 1948.
8. Cecil to Garbo, 28 April 1948.
9. Cecil to Garbo, 4 May 1948.

10. Cecil to Garbo [undated, but May–June 1948].
11. Cecil to Garbo [undated, but June 1948].
12. Ibid.
13. Ibid.
14. Ibid.
15. Cecil to Garbo [undated, but June 1948].
16. Cecil to Garbo, 6 or 13 June 1948.
17. Paraphrased from a letter from Garbo to Cecil [envelope dated 25 June 1948] (removed from Cecil's house in 1977 and sold at auction for $1,550 in New York in November 1990).
18. Cecil to Garbo, 20 June 1948.
19. Cecil to Garbo, 18 July 1948.
20. Ibid.
21. Alice B. Toklas to Samuel Steward, 22 July 1948, quoted in *Staying On Alone,* p. 130.
22. Cecil to Garbo, 15 August 1948 (1st letter).
23. Cecil to Garbo, 15 August 1948 (2nd letter).
24. Cecil to Garbo, 17 August 1948.
25. Cecil to Garbo, 24 August 1948.
26. Ibid.
27. Ibid.
28. *New York Times,* 10 September 1948.
29. Cecil Beaton, unpublished diary, winter 1948–49.
30. Cecil to Garbo, 21 November 1948.
31. Cecil to Garbo, 5 December 1948.
32. Ibid.
33. Cecil Beaton, unpublished diary, winter 1948–49.
34. Ibid.
35. Ibid.
36. Ibid.
37. Ibid.
38. Cecil to Garbo, 21 February 1949.
39. Ibid.
40. Ibid.
41. Cecil to Garbo, 6 March 1949.
42. Ibid.
43. Cecil to Garbo, April 1949.
44. Cecil to Garbo, 11 April 1949.

45. Ibid.
46. Cecil to Garbo, between 6 and 27 June 1949.

Chapter 8. Mercedes and Poppy Kirk

1. Sybille Bedford to author, 16 September 1992.
2. Ibid.
3. Poppy Kirk to Mercedes, 9 March 1949.
4. Mercedes de Acosta, *Here Lies the Heart,* p. 339.
5. Sybille Bedford to author, 16 September 1992.
6. Ibid.

Chapter 9. Darling Sir: "I wish you would let me save you."

1. Cecil to Garbo, 27 June 1949.
2. Ibid.
3. Paraphrased from a letter from Garbo to Cecil [undated, but June 1949].
4. Cecil to Garbo, June 1949.
5. Ibid.
6. Ibid., 10 July 1949.
7. Unidentified press report, 1 August 1949.
8. *Elle* magazine, 29 August 1949.
9. Ibid.
10. Cecil to Garbo, 29 July 1949.
11. Paraphrased from a letter from Garbo to Cecil, 15 August 1949.
12. Cecil to Garbo, 22 August 1949.
13. Cecil to Garbo, 24 August 1949.
14. Cecil Beaton, unpublished diary, 28 September 1949.
15. Ibid.
16. Ibid.
17. Ibid.
18. Ibid., 2 October 1949.
19. Ibid.

20. Ibid.
21. Ibid.
22. Poppy to Mercedes, 14 September 1949.
23. Mercedes de Acosta, *Here Lies the Heart,* p. 350.
24. Cecil to Garbo, 29 November 1949.
25. Paraphrased from a letter from Garbo to Cecil, 4 December 1949.
26. Cecil to Garbo, 2 April 1950.
27. Ibid.
28. Paraphrased from a letter from Garbo to Cecil [undated, but first week of April 1950].
29. Cecil to Garbo, 17 April 1950.
30. Cecil to Garbo, 30 April 1950.
31. "Love from the Wild Man," Cecil to Garbo, 20 June 1950.
32. Cecil to Garbo, 10 July 1950.
33. Cecil to Garbo, 16 July 1950.
34. Paraphrased from a letter from Garbo to Cecil [undated, but July–7 August 1950].
35. Cecil to Garbo, 12 August 1950.
36. Cecil to Garbo, September 1950.
37. Ibid.
38. Cecil to Garbo, 19 September 1950.
39. Cecil to Garbo, 29 October 1950.
40. Cecil to Garbo, postscript to letter, 30 October 1950.
41. Cecil to Garbo, 8 November 1950.
42. Ibid.
43. Paraphrased from a letter from Garbo to Cecil [undated, but November 1950].
44. Cecil's unpublished diary, November 1950.
45. Cecil to Garbo, 11 November 1950.
46. Cecil Beaton, unpublished diary, December 1950.
47. Ibid., winter 1950–51.

Chapter 10. "Shall I hang up my hat with Mr. Beaton?"

1. Cecil to Garbo, 16 April 1951.
2. Cecil to Garbo, 1 May 1951.

3. Paraphrased from a letter from Garbo to Cecil [undated, but April 1951].
4. Cecil to Garbo, 1 May 1951.
5. Ibid.
6. Cecil to Garbo, 8 May 1951.
7. Paraphrased from a letter from Garbo to Cecil, 11 June 1951.
8. Paraphrased from a letter from Garbo to Cecil [undated, but July 1951].
9. Cecil to Garbo, 22 July 1951.
10. Cecil to Garbo, 31 July 1951.
11. Paraphrased from a letter from Garbo to Cecil, 12 September 1951.
12. Paraphrased from a letter from Garbo to Cecil (from Hampshire House, New York City), 17 September 1951.
13. Cecil to Garbo, 21 September 1951 (1st letter).
14. Cecil to Garbo, 21 September 1951 (2nd letter).
15. Cecil Beaton, unpublished diary, early 1952.
16. Hal Burton to author, 19 July 1982.
17. Alastair Forbes to author, October 1980.
18. Philip Hoare, *Serious Pleasures* (New York: Viking Penguin, 1991), p. 313.
19. Cecil Beaton, unpublished diary, June 1952.
20. Daphne Fielding to author, 24 November 1981.
21. Augustus John to Cecil [undated, but 1951–52].
22. Lady Hartwell to author, 14 May 1980.
23. James Pope-Hennessy to Nolwen de Janzé, 2 December 1951, quoted in *A Lonely Business,* edited by Peter Quennell (London: Weidenfeld & Nicolson, 1981), p. 78.
24. Cecil Beaton, unpublished diary, early 1952.
25. Ibid.
26. Alice B. Toklas to Carl Van Vechten, 27 November 1951, quoted in *Staying On Alone,* p. 247.
27. Ibid.
28. Ram Gopal to Mercedes, 19 January 1955.
29. *France-Soir,* 16–17 December 1951.
30. Cecil to Garbo, 12 December 1951.
31. Ibid.
32. Cecil Beaton, unpublished diary, early 1952.
33. Cecil to Lady Diana Cooper, 4 April 1952.

34. Paraphrased from a letter from Garbo to Cecil [undated, but December 1951].
35. Cecil Beaton, unpublished diary, January 1952.
36. Ibid., early 1952.
37. Paraphrased from a letter from Garbo to Cecil, January 1952.
38. Cecil Beaton, unpublished diary, January 1952.
39. Cecil to Lady Juliet Duff, 7 February 1952.
40. Cecil to Hal Burton, 10 February 1952.
41. Cecil to Hal Burton, 16 March 1952.
42. Cecil Beaton, unpublished diary, April 1952.
43. Ibid.
44. Paraphrased from a letter from Garbo to Cecil [undated, but April 1952].

Chapter 11. "The goddess has gone."

1. Paraphrased from a letter from Garbo to Cecil, from Cannes, postmarked 29 July 1952.
2. Cecil to Garbo, 10 August 1952.
3. Paraphrased from a letter from Garbo to Cecil, August 1952.
4. Cecil to Garbo, 8 October 1952.
5. Truman Capote to Cecil, from Rome, 8 November 1952.
6. Cecil to Hal Burton, 17 November 1952.
7. Cecil to Mercedes, 19 November 1952.
8. Cecil Beaton, unpublished diary, November 1952.
9. Ibid.
10. Ibid., 19 December 1952.
11. Ibid., January 1953.
12. Ibid.
13. Ibid., 4 March 1953.
14. Cecil to Garbo, 14 March 1953.
15. Cecil to Mercedes, [6] April 1953.
16. Rex Harrison, *Rex: An Autobiography* (Boston: G. K. Hall, 1975), p. 129.
17. Lilli Palmer, *Change Lobsters and Dance* (New York: Warner, 1976), pp. 208–9.

18. Ibid., p. 209.
19. Ibid.
20. Ibid., p. 212.
21. *New York Times,* 16 August 1953.
22. *Daily American,* 13 August 1953—article entitled "It Happened in Italy," by Bill Pepper.
23. Mercedes to Cecil, 5 October 1953.
24. Cecil to Mercedes, 11 October 1953.
25. Paraphrased from a letter from Garbo to Cecil [undated, but December 1953].
26. Cecil Beaton, unpublished diary, 22 January 1954.
27. Cecil to Hal Burton, 12 February 1954.
28. Cecil Beaton, unpublished diary, April 1954.
29. Cecil to Garbo, 12 April 1954.
30. Ibid.
31. Cecil to Mercedes, 21 April 1954.
32. Paraphrased from a letter from Garbo to Cecil [undated, but July 1954].
33. Cecil to Garbo, 30 [July] 1954.
34. *Time* magazine, 9 August 1954.
35. Cecil to Mercedes, 6 December 1954.
36. Cecil Beaton, unpublished diary, 5 December 1954.
37. Cecil to Garbo, 11 January 1955.
38. Cecil to Mercedes, 23 March 1955.
39. Truman Capote to Cecil, 7 February 1955.
40. *The Noël Coward Diaries,* [May 1955], p. 265.

Chapter 12. "She leaves—she doesn't leave."

1. *New York Times,* 24 March 1955.
2. Cecil to Mercedes, 17 May 1955.
3. Amory and Blackwell, *Celebrity Register,* article on Garbo, p. 230.
4. Cecil to Mercedes, 27 July 1955.
5. Ram Gopal to Mercedes, 17 March 1955.
6. Ram Gopal to Mercedes, 16 May 1955.
7. *The Noël Coward Diaries,* [30 October 1955], p. 289.

8. Cecil to Hal Burton, 15 January 1956.
9. Cecil to Garbo, [4] May 1956.
10. Paraphrased from a letter from Garbo to Cecil [undated, but May 1956].
11. Cecil to Garbo, [29] May 1956.
12. Ram Gopal to Mercedes, 14 September 1956.
13. Paraphrased from a letter from Garbo to Cecil [undated, but late summer 1956].
14. Cecil Beaton, unpublished diary, October 1956.
15. Ibid.
16. Ibid.
17. Ibid.
18. Cecil to Mercedes, 23 October 1956.
19. Cecil Beaton, unpublished diary, October 1956.
20. Ibid.
21. Ibid.
22. Ibid.
23. Ibid.
24. Ibid.
25. Ibid.
26. Ibid.
27. Cecil to Garbo, 11 November 1956.
28. Paraphrased from a letter from Garbo to Cecil [undated, but late November 1956].

Chapter 13. Drugs and Diet Doctors

1. Cecil to Mercedes, 15 March 1957.
2. Ram Gopal to Mercedes, 22 May 1957.
3. *The Noël Coward Diaries,* [7 July 1957], p. 359.
4. Cecil Beaton, unpublished diary, winter 1958.
5. Wilder Luke Burnap to author, 30 September 1992.
6. Ram Gopal to Mercedes, 23 December 1957.
7. Cecil to Garbo, 3 November 1957.
8. Cecil Beaton, unpublished diary, winter 1958.
9. Cecil to Garbo, 25 May [1958].

10. *New York Times*, 23 August 1958.
11. Cecil to Mercedes, 16 November 1958.
12. Cecil Beaton, unpublished diary, winter 1959.
13. Ibid., 31 January 1959.
14. Mercedes to Cecil, 18 December 1959.

Chapter 14. Resentment and Regrets

1. Cecil Beaton, unpublished diary, end of November/beginning of December 1960, and winter 1961.
2. Cecil to Mercedes, 26 March 1960.
3. *Staying On Alone*, p. 380.
4. Cecil Beaton, unpublished diary, winter 1961.
5. Cecil to Mercedes, 20 July 1960.
6. Cecil Beaton, unpublished diary, end of November/beginning of December 1960.
7. Ibid.
8. Ibid.
9. Ibid.
10. Ibid., winter 1961.
11. Cecil to Mercedes, from Hotel Grande Bretagne, Athens, 2 August 1961.
12. Cecil to Mercedes, 7 [October] 1961.
13. Cecil Beaton, unpublished diary, 17–27 October 1961.
14. Mercedes to Cecil, 11 December 1961.
15. Cecil to Mercedes, 18 December 1961.
16. Cecil to Mercedes, 2 March 1962.
17. Paraphrased from a letter from Garbo to Cecil, 17 July 1962.
18. Cecil to Mercedes, 12 September 1962.
19. Cecil to Mercedes, 3 July 1963.

Chapter 15. After Schlee

1. *The Noël Coward Diaries*, [14 July 1964], p. 568.
2. Cecil Beaton, unpublished diary, September 1965.

3. *Time* file report, October 1964.
4. *Time* file report, 8 October 1964.
5. Diana Vreeland to author, 15 November 1981.
6. Garbo to Cecil, cable from New York, 23 December 1964.
7. Cecil Beaton, unpublished diary, September 1965.
8. Ibid., Sciathos, September 1965.
9. Ibid., August 1965.
10. *New York Times,* 5 September 1965.
11. Ibid.
12. Ibid., 19 September 1965.
13. Paraphrased from a typed letter from Garbo to Cecil, 17 December 1965.

Chapter 16. Mercedes: "I'm sitting here all alone."

1. Mercedes to Richard Buckle, 22 April 1961.
2. Mercedes to Cecil, 11 December 1961.
3. Mercedes to William McCarthy, 31 October 1964.
4. Ibid.
5. Mercedes to William McCarthy, October 1964.
6. Bob Colacello, *Holy Terror—Andy Warhol Close Up* (New York: HarperCollins, 1990), pp. 23–24.
7. Isabel Jeans to Mercedes, 10 January 1962.
8. Kieran Tunney, *Interrupted Autobiography* (London: Quartet Books, 1989), p. 38.
9. Ibid., p. 42.
10. Ibid.
11. Ibid., p. 43.
12. Wilder Luke Burnap to author, 30 September 1992.
13. Cecil Beaton, unpublished diary, April 1966.
14. *New York Times,* 10 May 1968.
15. Cecil Beaton, unpublished diary, May 1968.

Chapter 17. Cecil Sells His Story

1. Cecil Beaton, unpublished diary, September 1968.
2. Ibid., 21 November 1971.
3. Ibid., 21 May 1972.
4. *Spectator*, 27 May 1972.
5. *Sunday Times*, 28 May 1972.
6. *The Listener*, 1 June 1972.
7. *Harper's & Queen*, April 1972.
8. *Chicago Tribune*, 8 April 1973.
9. Cecil Beaton, unpublished diary, August 1973.
10. Samuel Adams Green to author, 21 July 1992.
11. Cecil Beaton, unpublished diary, April 1973.
12. Samuel Adams Green to author, 12 June 1981.
13. Ibid.
14. Eileen Hose to author, 7 April 1980.

Chapter 18. Garbo: "I must be home before seven."

1. Diana Vreeland to author, 15 November 1981.
2. Cecil Beaton, unpublished diary [undated but April 1970].
3. Diana Vreeland to author, 20 November 1981.
4. *New York Times*, 15 September 1989.

INDEX

ABOUT THE AUTHOR

HUGO VICKERS is Cecil Beaton's literary executor and official biographer. He was given complete access to all of Beaton's papers. In addition to his bestselling *Cecil Beaton: A Biography,* he is the author of *Gladys, Duchess of Marlborough* and *Vivien Leigh.* He is also a frequent television commentator. He lives in Hampshire and London.

ABOUT THE TYPE

This book was set in Galliard, a typeface designed by Matthew Carter for the Mergenthaler Linotype Company in 1978. Galliard is based on the sixteenth-century typefaces of Robert Granjon, which give it classic lines yet interject a contemporary look.